Abraham Lincoln

A DOCUMENTARY PORTRAIT THROUGH HIS
SPEECHES AND WRITINGS

Abraham Lincoln

A DOCUMENTARY PORTRAIT THROUGH HIS
SPEECHES AND WRITINGS

Edited and with an Introduction by
DON E. FEHRENBACHER

Stanford University Press
STANFORD, CALIFORNIA

Stanford University Press
Stanford, California
© 1964 by the Board of Trustees of the
Leland Stanford Junior University
First published in 1964 by the
New American Library of World Literature, Inc.
Reissued in 1977 by Stanford University Press
Printed in the United States of America
Cloth ISBN 0-8047-0942-4
Paper ISBN 0-8047-0946-7

Original printing 1964
Last figure below indicates year of this printing:
04   03   02   01   00   99   98   97   96   95

This book is printed on acid-free paper.

Stanford University Press publications are distributed exclusively by Stanford University Press within
the United States, Canada, and Mexico; they are
distributed exclusively by Cambridge University
Press throughout the rest of the world.

Preface

These letters, speeches, and public papers of Abraham Lincoln constitute less than one-tenth of all his published works. Most of the truly notable items are included, however, and the selection as a whole offers the reader an authentic and fairly coherent account of Lincoln's career, from village obscurity to national leadership and martyrdom. Approximately four-fifths of the documents are complete. The others, plainly designated, are abridgments and excerpts—chiefly from political speeches and presidential messages. The Letter to Erastus Corning and Others (No. 77) is taken from the New York *Tribune,* June 15, 1863. For all other documents, I have followed the text in *The Collected Works of Abraham Lincoln* (8 vols. plus Index; New Brunswick, N. J., 1953–1955), edited by Roy P. Basler, with the assistance of Marion Dolores Pratt and Lloyd A. Dunlap, and published by the Rutgers University Press. With a few minor exceptions, I have allowed Lincoln's erratic spelling and punctuation to stand unchanged. I thank the Institute of American History at Stanford University for financial assistance; Jane Buddeke for her services as a typist, Edward L. Burlingame for his advice and encouragement; and my wife, Virginia Fehrenbacher, for proofreading and much other help.

D. E. F.

Contents

Introduction

It would be possible to read a different book about Abraham Lincoln in every week of a long lifetime. Yet all the vast accumulation of reminiscence, tribute, and scholarship leaves us with a figure still partly lost in the silences of the past and obscured by the mists of an extravagant legend. The very familiarness, the routine ubiquity of his name and face, tend to veil the man from our understanding. We can never meet him, so to speak, for the first time.

Although his image is sharply etched on the public consciousness, Lincoln actually disclosed less of himself than many famous Americans who seem indistinct and remote in comparison with him. He left no diary or other storehouse of his private thoughts. He did not live to write his memoirs. His family letters are scarce and seldom revealing. He never sustained a long and intimate correspondence with one person. Even in his closest everyday relationships there was something withheld. The men who knew him best generally agreed that he was habitually reticent and undemonstrative to the verge of coldness. During neither his frequent attacks of melancholy nor his moments of gaiety, when he became a delightful companion, did he expose the secret recesses of his mind. For liquor, which often loosens a reluctant tongue, he had no taste whatever. The man's public record is well documented, to be sure, and the external details of his private life have been assembled in great array. We know his height and weight, the shape of his foot and the span of his forehead, what he wore, what he earned and spent, how he amused himself, where he traveled, and much of what he said. But at the core of all such information there is an enigma that baffled his contemporaries and has resisted the probing of later investigators. William H. Herndon, who claimed first rank among his interpreters, admitted in the end that "Lincoln is unknown and possibly always will be."

The greatest mystery, however, is not what Lincoln was in life but what he has become since his death. His biographers have a difficult, yet finite task. They must sift the testimony of countless witnesses and follow traces that sometimes disappear, in search of the lawyer-politician who actually lived at the corner of Eighth and Jackson streets in Springfield, who rode the court circuit, debated with Stephen A. Douglas, and for a little more than four years served as the sixteenth President of the United States. The study of Lincoln's reputation, on the other hand, is a task of illimitable proportions for the cultural historian. In addition to the plain facts of his career, it embraces everything believed about him, every feeling that he has evoked. Its range is as wide as the experience of a whole people and as high as their highest aspirations. Indeed, if we could fully understand what Lincoln has meant to succeeding generations of Americans, we would have a clearer perception of that elusive thing called the "American character."

But the problem of explaining Lincoln's reputation transcends our own national boundaries; for the ultimate mystery, perhaps, is the amplitude of his fame and the reverence in which he is held among the people of every continent. Lincoln, after all, was not a world leader in the manner of Woodrow Wilson and Franklin D. Roosevelt. He participated in no international wars, attended no summit conferences, administered no bounty of foreign aid, made no decisions that were immediately felt in remote corners of the earth. His life was provincial and his achievement distinctively domestic. Yet Leo Tolstoi tells of a tribal chieftain in the wild isolation of the Caucasus who begged him for information about Abraham Lincoln, "the greatest general and greatest ruler of the world." The story is unique in its setting and characters, but as an example it could be multiplied indefinitely.

Of course his universal appeal springs partly from the Emancipation Proclamation and the somewhat erroneous impression that with this one flourish of a pen he swept away the institution of Negro slavery in the United States. At the same time, by saving the Union from distintegration, he vindicated the cause of popular government and so earned the gratitude of its advocates around the world. Beyond his specific deeds, however, he is honored for his qualities as a leader and for the ideals that he seemed to embody. Other nations have, in effect, accepted America's nomination of Lincoln as its representative man. More precisely, they have made him a symbol of whatever greatness and goodness they attribute to the United States and its people—the absolute antithesis of the "ugly American." Thus, on foreign soil especially, the image of Lincoln tends to merge with the image of his country.

When James Russell Lowell called Lincoln the "first American," he meant that this man, unlike earlier seaboard leaders, was cut entirely from native material. Nature, the poet wrote, had thrown aside her old-world molds and shaped a new hero from "sweet clay . . . of the unexhausted West." But the phrase came to have additional meaning, for Lincoln has long since replaced Washington as "first in the hearts of his countrymen." Such a judgment is supported by overwhelming evidence, whether it be taken from polls of public opinion or the quantity of scholarship or the yearly ritual of birthday editorials or the platform eloquence of politicians—among whom, as David Donald observes, Lincoln is now "everybody's grandfather." No one ever asks: "What would Washington do if he were here today?" It is Lincoln who "walks at midnight," brooding over the sorrows of the modern world, who lends his strength in times of trouble and "leads us onward from the dead." The nomenclature of their shrines in the nation's capital has become curiously appropriate. For Washington there is a "monument"; for Lincoln, "a memorial."

Anyone who ventures an explanation of Lincoln's prime rank among national heroes soon finds himself trying to weigh imponderables. In what degree, for example, has the man's popularity accrued directly from the magnitude of the Civil War and from the American public's perennial fascination with the conflict? Is there a significant connection between the durability of his fame and the persistence of the Negro problem in the twentieth century?

Did martyrdom greatly increase his stature, and if so, why does James A. Garfield remain a dim and commonplace figure? Lincoln, it has been said, is larger than his context, but how much larger and for what reasons?

The essential difference between Lincoln and every other American hero may lie in the structure of his career, which is dramatically perfect, or in its unique style or its poetic intensity. From obscure origins and through long years of ordinary apprenticeship, he rose to the plateau of national affairs, then swiftly to the summit. There he stood for a brief but critical interval, simultaneously performing two memorable feats of statesmanship, only to plummet from view at the moment of supreme triumph. For him there was no gentle slope toward old age, no tapering anticlimax, but instead, apotheosis. His life thus had classic simplicity and unity. Yet its emotional range extends all the way from low comedy to exalted tragedy. Lincoln, even the real Lincoln of history, was a rare mixture of earthiness and sublimity, of laughter and sadness, of cold intellect and fertile intuition. He therefore appeals to many moods and seems relevant to almost every category of human experience.

In time, of course, Lincoln became much more than he had been. The manufacture of a legend was stimulated by the drama of his death, but it actually began somewhat earlier—perhaps with the campaign biographies. He himself had a hand in the work, enough so to inspire Richard Hofstadter's title, "Abraham Lincoln and the Self-Made Myth," and to elicit from Edmund Wilson the statement that "he created himself as a poetic figure." One simple illustration is his quaint decision, at the age of fifty-one, to recast his public image by growing a beard. The change, which helped make him "Father Abraham," visually separated the presidential years from all that preceded them, and it probably encouraged the development of a conspicuous duality in the Lincoln legend.

That there is such a legend or myth, and one of astonishing proportions, can scarcely be open to argument, but its interpreters are not always talking about exactly the same thing. In the first place, much of what has been written and believed about Lincoln is demonstrably untrue or at least unverifiable. He was not the illegitimate son of John C. Calhoun; the story of his love for Ann Rutledge rests upon very flimsy evidence; so does his alleged remark about hitting "that thing hard" when he viewed a New Orleans slave market; and he did not leave Mary Todd waiting for him in vain on their first appointed wedding day. But these and all other pieces of fancy or dubious history are only a minor part of the whole matter. The legendary Lincoln is not primarily a work of fiction. He is more essentially a figure created by the amplification of real virtues, deeds, and events to such a degree that they acquired symbolic and universal meaning.

Lincoln, for instance, is the very embodiment of political martyrdom. The shock produced by his death has probably never been equaled in the United States. It came at a time of jubilation and released tension, like one last thunderbolt from a clearing sky. Furthermore, it was the first such calamity in American history—a new kind of national ordeal. But if there were no precedents close at hand, some mourners easily discovered a loftier parallel. Born in a log cabin as crude as any stable, counselor of malice toward none and charity for all, murdered on Good Friday, Lincoln had sacrificed himself to save his country and redeem a race from bondage. Thus, redeemer, savior, and martyr, he became the object of a veneration that sometimes approached worship. In the work of poets, especially, he acquired aspects of divinity:

> That homely visage, as at first it turned
> Full-featured on a half believing throng,
> Became transfigured until they who gazed
> Visioned a nimbus seeming to surround
> The dark dishevelled hair.

Much of the so-called "deification" of Lincoln is obviously metaphor, but it is also myth, blending national and religious feeling in one majestic figure who may be admired as a hero or invoked as a god.

In contrast with this tendency to elevate Lincoln above mortal men, there were determined efforts to humanize him. Here, the emphasis was upon his frontier origins, upon his roughhewn appearance and physical strength, his rollicking humor, native wisdom, and homely virtues, upon the boy reading eagerly beside a flickering fire and the youth splitting fence rails in a western forest. Out of such material came a folk hero in the colorful tradition of Davy Crockett and Paul Bunyan. Partly imagined, partly conventionalized from history, this Lincoln too is legendary, although cast in a humbler mold than the national demigod. The two heroes, one earthy and the other sublime, are not easily reconciled, and their incongruity has no doubt fostered the notion of some historians that Lincoln was transformed by his experience in the Presidency.

Folk heroes and demigods belong at the dawn of a nation's history, where race memory fuses with imagination. But for the United States, as David M. Potter has noted, there was only a foreshortened past and a "Golden Age . . . telescoped into the Industrial Revolution." This meant that Americans must fashion their national hero out of familiar and relatively contemporary materials. He would have to be a real person, recorded literally by camera and pen, yet somehow "able to transcend these disenchanting testimonies." In one sense, however, Lincoln does belong to a dawn era: that of the modern industrial world. The technology of transportation and communication, for example, separates him sharply from Washington's generation, and yet he lived just at the beginning of a marvelous revolution. He traveled by steamboat and railroad, but not by automobile or airplane. He used the telegraph, but not the telephone. Most important of all, he was photographed about one hundred times, but there were no unposed snapshots, no moving pictures, and the sound of his voice is lost forever. We see him always, Richard Current reminds us, sitting "absolutely still, with his head against the photographer's rack, while the tedious seconds ticked by." Our visual record is therefore without the intimacy that might have been "disenchanting." The inscrutable face of the photographs even heightens the sense of mystery. For Lincoln, technology may have struck just the right balance, making him real enough to be completely believable, and yet remote enough to become mythological.

Lincoln the national hero is both splendidly timeless and firmly rooted in his own age, but this may be something other than paradox. Americans are still drawing heavily upon the nineteenth century, their century of promise when the present was lighted up by the glow of the future. Idealized now as a vanished era of supreme individualism, it makes an altogether appropriate setting for transcendent heroism. To say that Lincoln is one of the nineteenth century's representative figures therefore actually supplements any explanation of why he is the representative American for all times. Imperialism, industrialization, social reform, popular government, and nationalism—these are the major themes of nineteenth-century history. In the United States, the equivalent of imperialism was continental expansion; industrialization, although sometimes encouraged by the state, was largely the achievement of private, competitive capitalism; the most revolutionary social reform was the abolition of slavery; and both popular government and nationalism were put to a supreme test in the Civil War. With all of these themes, in one way or another, Lincoln has been closely identified.

Of course the historical Lincoln cannot be readily assimilated to the popular enthusiasm and public policies that swept the nation westward to the Pacific. He was cool toward the annexation of Texas and severely critical of the war against Mexico. He spoke contemptuously of "Young America" and its imperialistic designs. As for manifest destiny, he believed that the American mission was to exemplify democratic principles, not to enlarge the territorial domain by force. It is true that as President he signed the Homestead and Pacific Railroad bills, which accelerated the physical conquest of the West, but his role in both cases was one of acquiescence rather than leadership.

Instead, Lincoln was associated with continental expansion as an actual participant in the westward movement and as the finest product of the frontier environment. This was Lowell's "first American," whose family exchanged a cabin in Kentucky for one in Indiana and later pushed on to Illinois, who cleared trees, tilled the soil, and even played brief parts as Mississippi riverman and Indian fighter. Lincoln the Westerner, it has been noted, became a major folk hero. More than that, however, he became one of the prime exhibits offered by Frederick Jackson

Turner and the "frontier school" of American historians. According to Turner, the long experience of conquering the wilderness had differentiated America from Europe and thereby shaped virtually all the ideals, institutions, and traits that were peculiarly American. The frontier had given the nation its distinctive character, and Lincoln was the "greatest of frontiersmen." Thus scholarship combined with folklore to make Lincoln's pioneer origins the paramount factor in his selection as the representative American.

Now if the irony were only intentional, this portrayal of Lincoln would be a masterpiece instead of a misrepresentation. One must stretch the meaning of the word to make a typical "frontiersman" out of a youth who cared little for hunting, trapping, fishing, or roaming the forest, and who never lived in a Western territory or in a region still menaced by Indians. Lincoln's boyhood experience might be best described as postfrontier pioneering, appropriately symbolized by the ax rather than the rifle. And whereas a frontiersman presumably turns his back on civilization to confront the wilderness, Lincoln, at the first opportunity, did exactly the opposite. His participation in the westward movement ended as soon as he became his own master, and nothing on the far horizon, not even a territorial governorship, ever induced him to rejoin the procession. Without a trace of the frontiersman's chronic restlessness, he settled down promptly and permanently in Sangamon County, first as a villager, then as a townsman. Before entering the practice of law, he tried various other pursuits but never considered returning to agriculture. He had no feeling for the soil, no hunger for land, and in Springfield did not even keep a good garden. "As to your farm matter, I have no sympathy with you," he told a friend in 1842. "*I* have no farm, nor ever expect to have; and, consequently, have not studied the subject enough to be much interested with it." His whole adult life was centered in the town, and for refreshment he preferred an evening at the theater to a stroll through the countryside. Of Nature he had apparently seen enough in his youth.

It would be a serious mistake, of course, to underestimate the influence of a man's early environment upon his character and outlook. Yet Lincoln's role in history was largely an achievement of will—a will directed along lines far different from those of his youth. He belongs primarily to the urban movement, rather than the westward movement, and to the postfrontier stage of American development. With the passing of the frontier in any locality, there was often a liberation of creative energies previously submerged in the physical struggle for existence. The channels of self-expression were still relatively scarce, however, and men of unusual capacity tended to cluster in a few professions, and especially in politics. Out of other postfrontier communities arose national leaders like Andrew Jackson, Henry Clay, and William Jennings Bryan—each of them becoming, as Lincoln did, the spokesman of a new political order. In the careers of such men, the dynamic qualities of the second-generation West were converted to the service of the whole nation. The frontier image of Lincoln, although not without some foundation in fact, is historically more false than true because it virtually ignores thirty years of transition between the backwoods and the Presidency.

Less stereotyped than the frontier theme is the interpretation of Lincoln's connection with the economic forces of his time. Here, modern controversy has fashioned a variety of distorted images. Every interest group, every band on the spectrum of opinion, wants Lincoln's help and manages somehow to call him as a witness. He is offered as a perfect specimen of the self-made man and hailed as a consistent friend of the business community. He can be quoted in favor of leaving "each man free to acquire property as fast as he can," and against any law "to prevent a man from getting rich." He acknowledged the "rights" of capital, said that labor was "like any other commodity in the market," and rejected the idea of class struggle. In his Whig days, he even denounced deficit spending by the Federal government. On the other hand, he wanted the "humblest man" to have "an equal chance to get rich"; he asserted that labor was the "superior" of capital and deserved "much the higher consideration"; he endorsed labor's right to strike; and, in a passage that Franklin D. Roosevelt liked to cite, he declared: "The legitimate object of government is to do for the people what needs to be done, but which they can not, by in-

dividual effort, do at all, or do so well, for themselves."
These and other authentic quotations are supplemented
by a large number of spurious ones, each fabricated to
bolster an argument. Thus Lincoln is all too often lifted
out of his own economic setting and made to pass judgment upon some aspect of a world that he never knew.

Now Lincoln, in fact, does not adequately embody the
economic spirit of nineteenth-century America, and to
the complex economy of the twentieth century he is almost totally irrelevant. Unlike so many of his contemporaries, he showed little personal interest in railroad
promotion, land speculation, or the other shortcuts to
affluence. He had no important stake in the expanding
capitalism of his day. Furthermore, Lincoln's economic
thought, as historians like Richard Hofstadter and T.
Harry Williams have explained, was shaped by his own
experience in a preindustrial society. The typical American, in his eyes, was a self-employed artisan, shopkeeper,
or farmer, who combined the roles of worker and small
capitalist. As for the hiring of labor by larger agglomera-
tions of capital, it amounted to only a minor aspect of
the whole economy. In any case, there were no permanent
classes in the country. The hired laborer would, in the
normal course of events, join the ranks of the self-employed majority and perhaps even become an employer
of others. Advancement was "the order of things in a
society of equals."

This simple faith in free competition as the matrix of
universal opportunity was characteristic of Lincoln's generation and not at that time widely separated from reality.
But his ideas came from consulting the past rather than
anticipating the future. More or less oblivious to the
economic revolution already under way, he had no inkling
that problems associated with the emergence of "big business" would soon replace slavery at the center of public
controversy. Above all, he certainly did not realize that
his own presidential administration would one day be
used to mark the transition from preindustrial to modern
America. He signed tariff, banking, and railroad bills
without much interest or reflection, and he was far too
absorbed in the pressing business at hand to ponder the
economic implications of the Civil War. In short, Lin-

coln's economic philosophy was unoriginal, superficial, fragmentary, and only casually related to his main lines of thought. It contributes little to our understanding of his major achievements and nothing to the solution of our own major problems.

One more item must be added to our list of negatives. Lincoln, the author of the greatest single reform in American history, was not himself a reformer by nature. From the social ferment and humanitarian zeal of his era he remained comparatively aloof. The various movements for better care of physically handicapped persons, better treatment of the insane, improvement of prison conditions, universal peace, temperance, and women's rights received, at the most, his passive sympathy. He never dedicated himself to any of them. A lawyer and politician, he displayed no interest in legal reform, no yearning to revise the political system. Crusades just did not suit his temperament. He was by no means a cynic, but he tended to accept the world as he found it.

Not even by his stand on the slavery issue does Lincoln qualify as a true reformer. Although he never concealed his belief that the institution was morally wrong, he did not approve of abolitionism or challenge the constitutional rights of the southern states. Neither did he deny that one of those rights was an effective fugitive-slave law. Until 1854, Lincoln seems to have been content with the hope that time would erase the evil. Then the Kansas-Nebraska Act aroused him to action, and the Dred Scott decision confirmed his belief that freedom was on the defensive against an aggressive slave power. He spoke now of "ultimate extinction," but proposed nothing more than the exclusion of slavery from the Federal territories—something that had been largely achieved before the repeal of the Missouri Compromise. When the Civil War began, President Lincoln insisted that the slavery question must be subordinated to the task of saving the Union. At the same time, he tried unsuccessfully to inaugurate a program of voluntary, compensated, gradual emancipation. He issued his great proclamation under heavy pressure from the militant antislavery elements and with certain personal misgivings, justifying it entirely in military terms. Privately, Lincoln regarded the dissolution of slavery with deep satisfaction, but he thought of himself as presiding over a revolution rather than instigating it. "I claim not to have controlled events," he wrote in 1864, "but confess plainly that events have controlled me."

Lincoln's intellectual energy was actually confined, even during the presidential years, to a narrow range of interests. This concentration, which accounts for much of his personal force, left him more or less insulated from a large part of nineteenth-century history. His connection with westward expansion, with the rise of industrial capitalism, and with the spirit of social reform is tenuous at best. In many respects, he was not a representative American at all. But when we turn to the themes of democracy and nationalism, we are suddenly at the heart of the matter. Lincoln, who saved and rededicated a nation, is appropriately linked with contemporary nation-builders like Cavour, Mazzini, and Bismarck. History lends strong support to the analogy, as it does to the assertion of Lord Charnwood that Lincoln's name stands first "among those associated with the cause of popular government."

Although Lincoln regularly paid scrupulous respect to the rights of the states, his deeper feelings were always attached to the nation. "The Union with him in sentiment rose to the sublimity of a religious mysticism," said the perceptive Alexander H. Stephens. Frequently quoted, this remark is, by itself, somewhat misleading. For Lincoln's nationalism was born of reason as well as faith, and we cannot be sure that it was his ultimate commitment. The United States, he believed, held a unique place in history because of its origin in the Declaration of Independence. It had been dedicated to a set of principles that affirmed the original equality of all men everywhere and proclaimed their right to secure the blessings of liberty through self-government. Thus the Union was like a precious vessel filled with precious contents, and to destroy it would be a double disaster, not only for Americans but for the rest of the world. One may argue, of course, that in rejecting compromise during the great crisis of 1860-1861, Lincoln sacrificed the national interest to the antislavery cause, and that by refusing to countenance secession, he denied Southerners the right of self-determination. But in his eyes, the Civil War was the supreme test of whether a

nation "so conceived and so dedicated" could "long endure." If a dissatisfied minority were permitted either to
dictate public policy by threatening dissolution or to carry
out that threat with impunity, then the whole principle of
democratic government would be lost—and with it, "the
last best hope of earth."

In some of the most moving prose ever written, Lincoln
rededicated the American nation to the advancement of
human liberty and thus gave universal meaning to a domestic conflict. This was his great literary achievement. But
what, exactly, is his place in the history of the Civil War
itself? Did Lincoln make a difference in the course of
events, and if so, how much of a difference? In *The Hero
in History,* Sidney Hook draws a distinction between the
"eventful man" and the "event-making man." Both appear
at the "forking points of history" and decisively influence
the choices of direction. The eventful man, however, is
a rather ordinary person who just happens to be the one
upon whom the choice devolves. His pathway to fame has
been cleared by circumstances for which he bears little
or no responsibility. The event-making man, on the other
hand, has helped create the fork at which he stands, and
in pursuing his chosen course, he displays extraordinary
qualities of leadership that leave "the positive imprint of
his personality upon history." Now while Lincoln was
alive, not many Americans would have placed him securely
in this latter category, and he himself specifically dis-
avowed the role of event-maker. Perhaps an examination
of several "forking points" will reveal why these judgments have been reversed.

To the creation of the "forking point" at which he stood
in 1861, Lincoln had contributed more than is generally
realized. The secession crisis resulted directly from the
rise of the Republican party in the North. Illinois was a
pivotal state in the sectionalized struggle for political
power, and there, Lincoln played a leading role in the
fusion of heterogeneous antislavery elements. As much as
any man in the country, he was a founder of the Republican party. But more than that, his own success in 1860
had a counterpart—the failure of Stephen A. Douglas—
for which Lincoln was in no small degree responsible.
Douglas, by bitterly opposing the Lecompton Constitution

for Kansas in 1858, had alienated much of the South, while at the same time increasing his popularity among moderate antislavery men in the free states. It was this latter trend that might have prevented the Republicans from capturing the Presidency, and it was Lincoln who saw the danger most clearly. He worked harder than any other party leader to destroy the impression that Douglas had suddenly become a champion of the antislavery cause. He fortified the wavering resolution of many Republicans at a critical moment and thus cleared the way for victory in 1860.

The Republican National Convention of 1860 nominated Lincoln for the Presidency instead of the highly favored William H. Seward. This was not a complete surprise, however. Lincoln had been campaigning actively for the nomination during much of the preceding year, and by convention time he was Seward's strongest rival. It is therefore utterly inaccurate to label him a "dark horse." If Seward had won the nomination (and probably no one but Lincoln could have prevented it), then the Republicans might not have carried the election; for Seward, because of his reputation as a radical and his outspoken opposition to nativism, was weaker than Lincoln in the most critical states of the North. The election of Lincoln, in turn, set off the secession movement, although here the Republican choice of a candidate made little difference. Southerners were motivated by their fear and hatred of the triumphant party, not by the lineaments of its new leader. In determining the Northern response to secession, on the other hand, Lincoln, as President-elect and as President, played a decisive role. More firmly than Seward, the putative "radical," he resisted compromise while refusing to countenance disunion. This does not mean that he deliberately chose war, but he did choose the risk of war rather than the alternatives laid before him by the secessionists and compromisers. Clearly, Lincoln was, in more than one respect, an event-making man during the years 1860–1861.

The next major question is whether Lincoln's leadership was a decisive factor in the war itself. Historians have tended to agree that the Confederacy, despite superior generalship (in the earlier stages of the conflict, at least) and despite the strategic advantage of its defensive position, was doomed by the overwhelming preponderance of the North in manpower and economic strength. Yet this Northern superiority was relatively inert and could be brought to bear effectively only by skillful and patient direction. Lincoln's great accomplishment was to articulate the national purpose so convincingly and mobilize the national will so thoroughly that the Union could not be shaken by military defeats or internal discord. Of his performance as commander-in-chief, there are evaluations that range from "ineptitude" to "genius." Measured, however, against Jefferson Davis and most of the generals on both sides, rather than against some standard of perfection, Lincoln seems to have had a stronger "instinct for victory," a clearer knowledge of what must be done to achieve it, and a better understanding of the connections between war and statecraft. Indeed, David Potter has suggested that the South might have won its independence "if the Union and the Confederacy had exchanged presidents with one another."

The war was virtually over when Lincoln died. He had presided over the abolition of slavery and the preservation of the Union, but the work of reconstruction had just begun. Was his assassination another important "forking point" in American history, and if so, how did it change the course of events? The conventional answer runs something like this: Lincoln had developed a sensible and generous plan for restoration of the Union. His successor, Andrew Johnson, tried to follow the plan, but with such obstinacy and ineptness that he was overridden by the Radical Republicans, who imposed their own vindictive system of military reconstruction upon the South. The result was a heritage of sectional bitterness that could have been avoided if Lincoln had served out his second term. This interpretation has certain flaws, however. For one thing, there is reason to doubt that Lincoln's program would have proved satisfactory in the long run. It probably laid too much emphasis upon the swift rehabilitation of Southern states and too little upon the needs of four million freed slaves. Without the Fourteenth and Fifteenth Amendments (both the work of the Radicals), today's Negro would be severely handicapped in his struggle for equal rights. Furthermore, it is probably a mistake to assume that Lincoln, like Johnson, would have fought stubbornly against all odds for the presidential plan, and that he, *unlike* Johnson, could have triumphed completely over the Radicals. Instead, if he had survived, the battle that Johnson lost might never have been fought. Wiser, more flexible, and possessing greater political strength, Lincoln was capable of arranging a compromise that combined the better features of the Radical program with his own magnanimity and humane understanding. This may well be the historical alternative that was erased at Ford's Theater on the night of April 14, 1865.

One final problem is that of appraising Lincoln's influence on the Presidency itself. Some scholars consider him a weak executive; others, a strong executive; and there is abundant evidence to support both judgments. As far as the ordinary affairs of state were concerned, he seemed willing to let the government run itself without much direction from the White House. He exerted little control over Congress and allowed his cabinet officers a surprising amount of independence. This passivity may be attributed to his preoccupation with the war. According to David Donald, however, it also reflected his adherence to the Whig view of the Presidency, which had been formulated during the struggle against the "dictatorship" of Andrew Jackson. Yet, in his role as commander-in-chief, Lincoln exercised powers never before claimed by any President. With doubtful authority, he suspended the writ of habeas corpus, proclaimed slavery abolished throughout most of the Confederacy, instituted a system of military conscription, and erected reconstruction governments in several Southern states. Each of these actions amounted to a bold expansion, if not an outright violation, of the Constitution. Thus a curious ambiguity runs through Lincoln's conception of the Presidency, owing primarily to his distinction between ordinary and extraordinary executive powers. The latter, he believed, came into existence only during a national crisis, and their limits were determined as much by the proportions of that crisis as by the restraints of the Constitution. It was this theory of emergency powers, dangerous to apply but sometimes indispensable, that governed Lincoln's major decisions and stamped his influence so indelibly upon the institution of the Presidency.

In the letters, speeches, and public papers of Abraham Lincoln, one finds the real man, but not the whole man. Much of what we know about him comes from other sources, and much of what he was remains unknown or indistinct. The rollicking storyteller is little in evidence, for example, since he belongs largely to an oral tradition preserved only in fragments and by second hand. Also, the intimacy of the writings tends to decline with the statesman's rise to prominence, as even private letters become increasingly a part of his public behavior. Yet the contours of Lincoln's character and career are plainly visible in his prose, and we can recapture the quality, if not the whole substance, of his thought. Most of that prose is strictly functional; to read it is to see him in action, pursuing practical results, rather than ultimate truth. Only at rare moments, such as the dedication of Gettysburg Cemetery, did the occasion demand the utmost from his literary power. Then leadership blended with poetry in the display of magnificent strength and intense feeling under perfect artistic control.

DON E. FEHRENBACHER

Stanford University
Stanford, California

1. Entering Politics:

IN 1831, upon his return from a flatboat trip to New Orleans,
Lincoln took a job as storekeeper in the little village of New
Salem, Illinois. There he found it easier to make friends than
to sell merchandise, and early the next year, at the age of twenty-
three, he became a candidate for the state legislature. His public
statement to the voters of the county, published in a Springfield
newspaper, is the earliest extant writing of any significance from
Lincoln's hand. In it, he discussed a number of specific issues
before proceeding to the conclusion, which is here reproduced.
Service in the Black Hawk War from April to July 1832 interrupted his campaign but enhanced his local popularity. Though
defeated in the election, he managed to finish eighth in a field of
thirteen and received almost the unanimous vote of the New
Salem precinct.

. . . . Considering the great degree of modesty which should
always attend youth, it is probable I have already been
more presuming than becomes me. However, upon the subjects of which I have treated, I have spoken as I thought.
I may be wrong in regard to any or all of them; but holding it a sound maxim, that it is better to be only sometimes
right, than at all times wrong, so soon as I discover my
opinions to be erroneous, I shall be ready to renounce
them.

Every man is said to have his peculiar ambition.
Whether it be true or not, I can say for one that I have
no other so great as that of being truly esteemed of my
fellow men, by rendering myself worthy of their esteem.
How far I shall succeed in gratifying this ambition, is yet
to be developed. I am young and unknown to many of you.
I was born and have ever remained in the most humble

walks of life. I have no wealthy or popular relations to recommend me. My case is thrown exclusively upon the independent voters of this county, and if elected they will have conferred a favor upon me, for which I shall be unremitting in my labors to compensate. But if the good people in their wisdom shall see fit to keep me in the background, I have been too familiar with disappointments to be very much chagrined. Your friend and fellow-citizen,

A. Lincoln.

2. Running for Reelection:

LETTER TO THE EDITOR OF THE SANGAMO JOURNAL, JUNE 13, 1836

LINCOLN tried again in 1834 and this time was elected to the first of four straight terms in the legislature. Two years later, with the breezy confidence of an old hand at politics, he announced his candidacy for reelection and ran first among seventeen candidates in the ensuing election.

New Salem, June 13, 1836.

To the Editor of the Journal:

In your paper of last Saturday, I see a communication over the signature of "Many Voters," in which the candidates who are announced in the Journal, are called upon to "show their hands." Agreed. Here's mine!

I go for all sharing the privileges of the government, who assist in bearing its burthens. Consequently I go for admitting all whites to the right of suffrage, who pay taxes or bear arms, (by no means excluding females.)

If elected, I shall consider the whole people of Sangamon my constituents, as well those that oppose, as those that support me.

While acting as their representative, I shall be governed by their will, on all subjects upon which I have the means of knowing what their will is; and upon all others, I shall do what my own judgment teaches me will best advance their interests. Whether elected or not, I go for distributing the proceeds of the sales of the public lands to the several states, to enable our state, in common with others, to dig canals and construct rail roads, without borrowing money and paying interest on it.

If alive on the first Monday in November, I shall vote for Hugh L. White for President. Very respectfully,

A. Lincoln.

3. The Slavery Problem:

PROTEST PRESENTED IN THE ILLINOIS LEG- ISLATURE, MARCH 3, 1837

DURING the legislative session of 1836–1837, Lincoln played an important part in securing the transfer of the state capital from Vandalia to Springfield. Soon afterward, he himself moved from New Salem into Springfield to practice law in partnership with John T. Stuart. Meanwhile, the legislature had passed a set of resolutions deploring the rise of abolition societies. Lincoln and a fellow legislator recorded their own somewhat different views in a formal protest. It is noteworthy that they made no mention of slavery in the Western territories, since that issue had presumably been settled by the Missouri Compromise.

Resolutions upon the subject of domestic slavery having passed both branches of the General Assembly at its present session, the undersigned hereby protest against the passage of the same.

They believe that the institution of slavery is founded on both injustice and bad policy; but that the promulgation of abolition doctrines tends rather to increase than to abate its evils.

They believe that the Congress of the United States has no power, under the constitution, to interfere with the institution of slavery in the different States.

They believe that the Congress of the United States has

the power, under the constitution, to abolish slavery in the District of Columbia; but that that power ought not to be exercised unless at the request of the people of said District.

The difference between these opinions and those contained in the said resolutions, is their reason for entering this protest.

Dan Stone,
A. Lincoln,
Representatives from the county of Sangamon.

4. Political Philosophy:

SPEECH TO THE YOUNG MEN'S LYCEUM OF SPRINGFIELD, JANUARY 27, 1838

HERE, in Lincoln's best literary effort as a young man, one finds some of the ideas and much of the logical force that distinguished his later masterpieces. The style is a mixture. Some passages yield to the fashion of decorated oratory, but in others there are signs of the lean, muscular eloquence that he eventually perfected. In his extensive discussion of mob violence, Lincoln made only one vague reference to Elijah P. Lovejoy, the abolitionist editor who had been murdered in Alton, Illinois, less than three months earlier. This curious reticence has been attributed both to political prudence and to rhetorical subtlety. When he turned his attention to the danger of dictatorship, Lincoln warned against the "towering genius" who thirsted for glory and would have it, "whether at the expense of emancipating slaves, or enslaving freemen." These words, so filled with meaning by later events, have led Edmund Wilson to the theory that Lincoln was projecting himself into the role he described. It is an arresting thought, but one that receives little support from the historical record.

As a subject for the remarks of the evening, *the perpetuation of our political institutions,* is selected.

In the great journal of things happening under the sun,

we, the American People, find our account running, under date of the nineteenth century of the Christian era. We find ourselves in the peaceful possession, of the fairest portion of the earth, as regards extent of territory, fertility of soil, and salubrity of climate. We find ourselves under the government of a system of political institutions, conducing more essentially to the ends of civil and religious liberty, than any of which the history of former times tells us. We, when mounting the stage of existence, found ourselves the legal inheritors of these fundamental blessings. We toiled not in the acquirement or establishment of them —they are a legacy bequeathed us, by a *once* hardy, brave, and patriotic, but *now* lamented and departed race of ancestors. Their's was the task (and nobly they performed it) to possess themselves, and through themselves, us, of this goodly land; and to uprear upon its hills and its valleys, a political edifice of liberty and equal rights; 'tis ours only, to transmit these, the former, unprofaned by the foot of an invader; the latter, undecayed by the lapse of time, and untorn by usurpation—to the latest generation that fate shall permit the world to know. This task of gratitude to our fathers, justice to ourselves, duty to posterity, and love for our species in general, all imperatively require us faithfully to perform.

How, then, shall we perform it? At what point shall we expect the approach of danger? By what means shall we fortify against it? Shall we expect some transatlantic military giant, to step the Ocean, and crush us at a blow? Never! All the armies of Europe, Asia and Africa combined, with all the treasure of the earth (our own excepted) in their military chest; with a Buonaparte for a commander, could not by force, take a drink from the Ohio, or make a track on the Blue Ridge, in a trial of a thousand years.

At what point then is the approach of danger to be expected? I answer, if it ever reach us, it must spring up amongst us. It cannot come from abroad. If destruction be our lot, we must ourselves be its author and finisher. As a nation of freemen, we must live through all time, or die by suicide.

I hope I am over wary; but if I am not, there is, even now, something of ill-omen amongst us. I mean the increasing disregard for law which pervades the country; the growing disposition to substitute the wild and furious passions, in lieu of the sober judgement of Courts; and the worse than savage mobs, for the executive ministers of justice. This disposition is awfully fearful in any community; and that it now exists in ours, though grating to our feelings to admit, it would be a violation of truth, and an insult to our intelligence, to deny. Accounts of outrages committed by mobs, form the every-day news of the times. They have pervaded the country, from New England to Louisiana;—they are neither peculiar to the eternal snows of the former, nor the burning suns of the latter;—they are not the creature of climate—neither are they confined to the slaveholding, or the non-slaveholding States. Alike, they spring up among the pleasure hunting masters of Southern slaves, and the order loving citizens of the land of steady habits. Whatever, then, their cause may be, it is common to the whole country.

It would be tedious, as well as useless, to recount the horrors of all of them. Those happening in the State of Mississippi, and at St. Louis, are, perhaps, the most dangerous in example, and revolting to humanity. In the Mississippi case, they first commenced by hanging the regular gamblers: a set of men, certainly not following for a livelihood, a very useful, or very honest occupation; but one which, so far from being forbidden by the laws, was actually licensed by an act of the Legislature, passed but a single year before. Next, negroes, suspected of conspiring to raise an insurrection, were caught up and hanged in all parts of the State: then, white men, supposed to be leagued with the negroes; and finally, strangers, from neighboring States, going thither on business, were, in many instances, subjected to the same fate. Thus went on this process of hanging, from gamblers to negroes, from negroes to white citizens, and from these to strangers; till, dead men were seen literally dangling from the boughs of trees upon every road side; and in numbers almost sufficient, to rival the native Spanish moss of the country, as a drapery of the forest.

Turn, then, to that horror-striking scene at St. Louis. A single victim was only sacrificed there. His story is very short; and is, perhaps, the most highly tragic, of any thing of its length, that has ever been witnessed in real life. A mulatto man, by the name of McIntosh, was seized in the street, dragged to the suburbs of the city, chained to a tree, and actually burned to death; and all within a single hour from the time he had been a freeman, attending to his own business, and at peace with the world.

Such are the effects of mob law; and such are the scenes, becoming more and more frequent in this land so lately famed for love of law and order; and the stories of which, have even now grown too familiar, to attract any thing more, than an idle remark.

But you are, perhaps, ready to ask, "What has this to do with the perpetuation of our political institutions?" I answer, it has much to do with it. Its direct consequences are, comparatively speaking, but a small evil; and much of its danger consists, in the proneness of our minds, to regard its direct, as its only consequences. Abstractly considered, the hanging of the gamblers at Vicksburg, was of but little consequences. They constitute a portion of population, that is worse than useless in any community; and their death, if no pernicious example be set by it, is never [a] matter of reasonable regret with any one. If they were annually swept, from the stage of existence, by the plague or small pox, honest men would, perhaps, be much profited, by the operation. Similar too, is the correct reasoning, in regard to the burning of the negro at St. Louis. He had forfeited his life, by the perpetration of an outrageous murder, upon one of the most worthy and respectable citizens of the city; and had he not died as he did, he must have died by the sentence of the law, in a very short time afterwards. As to him alone, it was as well the way it was, as it could otherwise have been. But the example in either case, was fearful. When men take it in their heads to day, to hang gamblers, or burn murderers, they should recollect, that, in the confusion usually attending such transactions, they will be as likely to hang or burn some one, who is neither a gambler nor a murderer as one who is; and that, acting upon the example they set, the mob of to-morrow, may, and probably will, hang or burn some of them, by the very same mistake. And not only so; the innocent, those who have ever set their faces against violations of law in every shape, alike with the guilty, fall victims to the ravages of mob law; and thus it goes on, step by step, till all the walls erected for the defence of the persons and property of individuals, are trodden down, and disregarded. But all this even, is not the full extent of the evil. By such examples, by instances of the perpetrators of such acts going unpunished, the lawless in spirit, are encouraged to become lawless in practice; and having been used to no restraint, but dread of punishment, they thus become, absolutely unrestrained. Having ever regarded Government as their deadliest bane, they make a jubilee of the suspension of its operations; and pray for nothing so much, as its total annihilation. While, on the other hand, good men, men who love tranquility, who desire to abide by the laws, and enjoy their benefits, who would gladly spill their blood in the defence of their country; seeing their property destroyed; their families insulted, and their lives endangered; their persons injured; and seeing nothing in prospect that forebodes a change for the better; become tired of, and disgusted with, a Government that offers them no protection; and are not much averse to a change in which they imagine they have nothing to lose. Thus, then, by the operation of this mobocratic spirit, which all must admit, is now abroad in the land, the strongest bulwark of any Government, and particularly of those constituted like ours, may effectually be broken down and destroyed—I mean the *attachment* of the People. Whenever this effect shall be produced among us; whenever the vicious portion of population shall be permitted to gather in bands of hundreds and thousands, and burn churches, ravage and rob provision stores, throw printing presses into rivers, shoot editors, and hang and burn obnoxious persons at pleasure, and with impunity; depend on it, this Government cannot last. By such things, the feelings of the best citizens will become more or less alienated from it; and thus it will be left without friends, or with too few, and those few too weak, to make their friendship effectual. At such a time and under such circumstances, men of sufficient talent and ambition will not be wanting to seize the opportunity, strike the blow, and overturn that fair fabric, which for the last half century, has been the fondest hope, of the lovers of freedom, throughout the world.

I know the American People are *much* attached to their Government;—I know they would suffer *much* for its sake; —I know they would endure evils long and patiently, before they would ever think of exchanging it for another. Yet, notwithstanding all this, if the laws be continually despised and disregarded, if their rights to be secure in their persons and property, are held by no better tenure than the caprice of a mob, the alienation of their affections from the Government is the natural consequence; and to that, sooner or later, it must come.

Here then, is one point at which danger may be expected.

The question recurs "how shall we fortify against it?" The answer is simple. Let every American, every lover of liberty, every well wisher to his posterity, swear by the blood of the Revolution, never to violate in the least particular, the laws of the country; and never to tolerate their violation by others. As the patriots of seventy-six did to the support of the Declaration of Independence, so to the support of the Constitution and Laws, let every American pledge his life, his property, and his sacred honor;—let every man remember that to violate the law, is to trample on the blood of his father, and to tear the character of his own, and of his children's liberty. Let reverence for the laws, be breathed by every American mother, to the lisping babe, that prattles on her lap—let it be taught in schools, in seminaries, and in colleges;—let it be written in Primmers, spelling books, and in Almanacs;—let it be preached from the pulpit, proclaimed in legislative halls, and enforced in courts of justice. And, in short, let it become the *political religion* of the nation; and let the old and the young, the rich and the poor, the grave and the gay, of all sexes and tongues, and colors and conditions, sacrifice unceasingly upon its altars.

While ever a state of feeling, such as this, shall universally, or even, very generally prevail throughout the nation, vain will be every effort, and fruitless every attempt, to subvert our national freedom.

When I so pressingly urge a strict observance of all the laws, let me not be understood as saying there are no bad laws, nor that grievances may not arise, for the redress of which, no legal provisions have been made. I mean to say no such thing. But I do mean to say, that, although bad laws, if they exist, should be repealed as soon as possible, still while they continue in force, for the sake of example, they should be religiously observed. So also in unprovided cases. If such arise, let proper legal provisions be made for them with the least possible delay; but, till then, let them if not too intolerable, be borne with.

There is no grievance that is a fit object of redress by mob law. In any case that arises, as for instance, the promulgation of abolitionism, one of two positions is necessarily true; that is, the thing is right within itself, and therefore deserves the protection of all law and all good citizens; or, it is wrong, and therefore proper to be prohibited by legal enactments; and in neither case, is the interposition of mob law, either necessary, justifiable, or excusable.

But, it may be asked, why suppose danger to our political institutions? Have we not preserved them for more than fifty years? And why may we not for fifty times as long?

We hope there is no *sufficient* reason. We hope all dangers may be overcome; but to conclude that no danger may ever arise, would itself be extremely dangerous. There are now, and will hereafter be, many causes, dangerous in their tendency, which have not existed heretofore; and which are not too insignificant to merit atttention. That our government should have been maintained in its original form from its establishment until now, is not much to be wondered at. It had many props to support it through that period, which now are decayed, and crumbled away. Through that period, it was felt by all, to be an undecided experiment; now, it is understood to be a successful one. Then, all that sought celebrity and fame, and distinction, expected to find them in the success of that experiment. Their *all* was staked upon it:—their destiny was *inseparably* linked with it. Their ambition aspired to display before an admiring world, a practical demonstration of the truth of a proposition, which had hitherto been considered, at best no better, than problematical; namely, *the capability of a people to govern themselves*. If they succeeded, they were to be immortalized; their names were to be transferred to counties and cities, and rivers and mountains; and to be revered and sung, and toasted through all time. If they failed, they were to be called knaves and fools, and fanatics for a fleeting hour; then to sink and be forgotten. They succeeded. The experiment is successful; and thousands have won their deathless names in making it so. But the game is caught; and I believe it is true, that with the catching, end the pleasures of the chase. This field of glory is harvested, and the crop is already appropriated. But new reapers will arise, and *they,* too, will seek a field. It is to deny, what the history of the world tells us is true, to suppose that men of ambition and talents will not continue to spring up amongst us. And, when they do, they will as naturally seek the gratification of their ruling passion, as others have *so* done before them. The question then, is, can that gratification be found in supporting and maintaining an edifice that has been erected by others? Most certainly it cannot. Many great and good men sufficiently qualified for any task they should undertake, may ever be found, whose ambition would aspire to nothing beyond a seat in Congress, a gubernatorial or a presidential chair; *but such belong not to the family of the lion, or the tribe of the eagle.* What! think you these places would satisfy an Alexander, a Caesar, or a Napoleon? Never! Towering genius disdains a beaten path. It seeks regions hitherto unexplored. It sees *no distinction* in adding story to story, upon the monuments of fame, erected to the memory of others. It *denies* that it is glory enough to serve under any chief. It *scorns* to tread in the footsteps of *any* predecessor, however illustrious. It thirsts and burns for distinction; and, if possible, it will have it, whether at the expense of emancipating slaves, or enslaving freemen. Is it unreasonable then to expect, that some man possessed of the loftiest genius, coupled with ambition sufficient to push it to its utmost stretch, will at some time, spring up among us? And when such a one does, it will require the people to be united with each other, attached to the government and laws, and generally intelligent, to successfully frustrate his designs.

Distinction will be his paramount object; and although he would as willingly, perhaps more so, acquire it by doing good as harm; yet, that opportunity being past, and nothing left to be done in the way of building up, he would set boldly to the task of pulling down.

Here then, is a probable case, highly dangerous, and such a one as could not have well existed heretofore.

Another reason which *once was;* but which, to the same extent, is *now no more,* has done much in maintaining our institutions thus far. I mean the powerful influence which the interesting scenes of the revolution had upon the *passions* of the people as distinguished from their judgment. By this influence, the jealousy, envy, and avarice, incident to our nature, and so common to a state of peace, prosperity, and conscious strength, were, for the time, in a great measure smothered and rendered inactive; while the deep rooted principles of *hate,* and the powerful motive of *revenge,* instead of being turned against each other, were directed exclusively against the British nation. And thus, from the force of circumstances, the basest principles of our nature, were either made to lie dormant, or to become the active agents in the advancement of the noblest of cause[s?]—that of establishing and maintaining civil and religious liberty.

But this state of feeling *must fade, is fading, has faded,* with the circumstances that produced it.

I do not mean to say, that the scenes of the revolution *are now* or *ever will be* entirely forgotten; but that like every thing else, they must fade upon the memory of the world, and grow more and more dim by the lapse of time. In history, we hope, they will be read of, and recounted, so long as the bible shall be read;—but even granting that they will, their influence *cannot be* what it heretofore has been. Even then, they *cannot be* so universally known, nor so vividly felt, as they were by the generation just gone to rest. At the close of that struggle, nearly every adult male had been a participator in some of its scenes. The consequence was, that of those scenes, in the form of a husband, a father, a son or a brother, a *living history was* to be found in every family—a history bearing the indubitable testimonies of its own authenticity, in the limbs mangled, in the scars of wounds received, in the midst of the very scenes related—a history, too, that could be read and understood alike by all, the wise and the ignorant, the learned and the unlearned. But *those* histories are gone. They *can* be read no more forever. They *were* a fortress of strength; but, what invading foemen could *never do,* the silent artillery of time *has done;* the levelling of its walls. They are gone. They *were* a forest of giant oaks; but the all-resistless hurricane has swept over them, and left only, here and there, a lonely trunk, despoiled of its verdure, shorn of its foliage; unshading and unshaded, to murmur in a few more gentle breezes, and to combat with its mutilated limbs, a few more ruder storms, then to sink, and be no more.

They *were* the pillars of the temple of liberty; and now, that they have crumbled away, that temple must fall, unless we, their descendants, supply their places with other pillars, hewn from the solid quarry of sober reason. Passion has helped us; but can do so no more. It will in future be our enemy. Reason, cold, calculating, unimpassioned reason, must furnish all the materials for our future support and defence. Let those materials be moulded into *general intelligence, sound morality* and, in particular, *a reverence for the constitution and laws;* and, that we improved to the last; that we remained free to the last; that we revered his name to the last; that, during his long sleep, we permitted no hostile foot to pass over or desecrate his resting place; shall be that which to learn the last trump shall awaken our Washington.

Upon these let the proud fabric of freedom rest, as the rock of its basis; and as truly as has been said of the only greater institution, *"the gates of hell shall not prevail against it."*

5. *A Personal Crisis:*

LETTER TO JOHN T. STUART, JANUARY 23, 1841

IN 1840, Lincoln was busy courting and winning Mary Todd, recently arrived from Kentucky, where her family was socially prominent. But on New Year's Day, for some obscure reason, the betrothed couple broke their engagement. Lincoln, as a con-

sequence, suffered his worst and most sustained attack of
mental depression. To his law partner, John T. Stuart, now a
member of Congress, he wrote of local politics and his own
misery. Later in the year, he and Stuart dissolved their partnership, and Lincoln then formed another one with Stephen T.
Logan.

Jany. 23rd, 1841—Springfield, Ills.
Dear Stuart:
Yours of the 3rd. Inst. is recd. & I proceed to answer
it as well as I can, tho' from the deplorable state of my
mind at this time, I fear I shall give you but little satisfaction. About the matter of the congressional election, I
can only tell you, that there is a bill now before the Senate
adopting the General Ticket system; but whether the party
have fully determined on it's adoption is yet uncertain.
There is no sign of opposition to you among our friends,
and none that I can learn among our enemies; tho', of
course, there will be, if the Genl. Ticket be adopted. The
Chicago American, Peoria Register, & Sangamo Journal,
have already hoisted your flag upon their own responsibility; & the other whig papers of the District are expected to
follow immediately. On last evening there was a meeting of
our friends at Butler's; and I submitted the question
to them & found them unanamously in favour of having
you announced as a candidate. A few of us this morning,
however, concluded, that as you were already being announced in the papers, we would delay announcing you,
as by your own authority for a week or two. We thought
that to appear too keen about it might spur our opponents
on about their Genl. Ticket project. Upon the whole, I
think I may say with certainty, that your reelection is sure,
if it be in the power of the whigs to make it so.
For not giving you a general summary of news, you
must pardon me; it is not in my power to do so. I am
now the most miserable man living. If what I feel were
equally distributed to the whole human family, there would
not be one cheerful face on the earth. Whether I shall ever
be better I can not tell; I awfully forbode I shall not. To
remain as I am is impossible; I must die or be better,
it appears to me. The matter you speak of on my ac-

count, you may attend to as you say, unless you shall hear of my condition forbidding it. I say this, because I fear I shall be unable to attend to any bussiness here, and a change of scene might help me. If I could be myself, I would rather remain at home with Judge Logan. I can write no more. Your friend, as ever—

A. Lincoln

6. A Glimpse of Slavery:
LETTER TO MARY SPEED, SEPTEMBER 27, 1841

DURING the summer of 1841, Lincoln visited his friend Joshua F. Speed in Kentucky, and the two men subsequently returned to Springfield by steamboat. One sight that Lincoln never forgot is described in this paragraph from a letter he wrote to Speed's sister.

You remember there was some uneasiness about Joshua's health when we left. That little indisposition of his turned out to be nothing serious; and it was pretty nearly forgotten when we reached Springfield. We got on board the Steam Boat Lebanon, in the locks of the Canal about 12. o'clock. M. of the day we left, and reached St. Louis the next monday at 8 P.M. Nothing of interest happened during the passage, except the vexatious delays occasioned by the sand bars be thought interesting. By the way, a fine example was presented on board the boat for contemplating the effect of *condition* upon human happiness. A gentleman had purchased twelve negroes in diferent parts of Kentucky and was taking them to a farm in the South. They were chained six and six together. A small iron clevis was around the left wrist of each, and this fastened to the main chain by a shorter one at a convenient distance from, the others; so that the negroes were strung together precisely like so many fish upon a trot-line. In this condition they were being separated forever from the scenes of their childhood, their friends, their fathers and mothers, and brothers and sisters, and many of them, from their wives and children, and going into perpetual slavery where the lash of the master is proverbially more ruthless and unrelenting than any other where; and yet amid all these distressing circumstances, as we would think them, they were the most cheerful and apparently happy creatures on board. One, whose offense for which he had been sold was an over-fondness for his wife, played the fiddle almost continually; and the others danced, sung, cracked jokes, and played various games with cards from day to day. How true it is that "God tempers the wind to the shorn lamb," or in other words, that He renders the worst of human conditions tolerable, while He permits the best, to be nothing better than tolerable.

7. *The Liquor Problem:*
ADDRESS TO THE WASHINGTON TEMPERANCE SOCIETY OF SPRINGFIELD, FEBRUARY 22, 1842

HIMSELF a total abstainer, Lincoln supported the temperance movement and especially the efforts of the Washington societies, whose members were reformed drunkards organized to rescue other victims of alcoholism. The latter part of his speech to the Springfield Washingtonians is given here.

By the Washingtonians, this system of consigning the habitual drunkard to hopeless ruin, is repudiated. *They* adopt a more enlarged philanthropy. *They* go for present as well as future good. *They* labor for all *now* living, as well as all *hereafter* to live. *They* teach *hope* to all—*despair* to none. As applying to *their* cause, *they* deny the doctrine of unpardonable sin. As in Christianity it is taught, so in this *they* teach, that

> "While the lamp holds out to burn,
> The vilest sinner may return."

And, what is matter of the most profound gratulation, they, by experiment upon experiment, and example upon example, prove the maxim to be no less true in the one case than in the other. On every hand we behold those, who but yesterday, were the chief of sinners, now the chief apostles of the cause. Drunken devils are cast out by ones, by sevens, and by legions; and their unfortunate victims, like the poor possessed, who was redeemed from his long and lonely wanderings in the tombs, are publishing to the ends of the earth, how great things have been done for them.

To these *new champions,* and this *new* system of tactics, our late success is mainly owing; and to *them* we must chiefly look for the final consummation. The ball is now rolling gloriously on, and none are so able as *they* to increase its speed, and its bulk—to add to its momentum, and its magnitude. Even though unlearned in letters, for this task, none others are so well educated. To fit them for this work, they have been taught in the true school. *They* have been in *that* gulf, from which they would teach others the means of escape. *They* have passed that prison wall, which others have long declared impassable; and who that has not, shall dare to weigh opinions with *them,* as to the mode of passing.

But if it be true, as I have insisted, that those who have suffered by intemperance *personally,* and have reformed, are the most powerful and efficient instruments to push the reformation to ultimate success, it does not follow, that those who have not suffered, have no part left them to perform. Whether or not the world would be vastly benefitted by a total and final banishment from it of all intoxicating drinks, seems to me not *now* to be an open question. Three-fourths of mankind confess the affirmative with their *tongues,* and I believe, all the rest acknowledge it in their *hearts.*

Ought *any,* then to refuse their aid in doing what the good of the *whole* demands? Shall he, who cannot do *much,* be, for that reason, excused if he do *nothing?* "But," says one, "what good can I do by signing the pledge? I never drink even without signing." This question has already been asked and answered more than millions of times. Let it be answered once more. For the man to suddenly, or in any other way, to break off from the use of drams, who has indulged in them for a long course of years, and until his appetite for them has become ten or a hundred fold stronger, and more craving, than any natural appetite can be, requires a most powerful moral effort. In such an undertaking, he needs every moral support and influence, that can possibly be brought to his aid, and thrown around him. And not only so; but every moral prop, should be taken *from* whatever argument might rise in his mind to lure him to his backsliding. When he casts his eyes around him, he should be able to see, all that he respects, all that he admires, and all that [he] loves, kindly and anxiously pointing him onward; and none beckoning him back, to his former miserable "wallowing in the mire."

But it is said by some, that men will *think* and *act* for themselves; that none will disuse spirits or any thing else, merely because his neighbors do; and that *moral influence* is not that powerful engine contended for. Let us examine this. Let me ask the man who would maintain this position most stiffly, what compensation he will accept to go to church some Sunday and sit during the sermon with his wife's bonnet upon his head? Not a trifle, I'll venture. And why not? There would be nothing irreligious in it: nothing immoral, nothing uncomfortable. Then why not? Is it not because there would be something egregiously unfashionable in it? Then it is the influence of *fashion;* and what is the influence of fashion, but the influence that *other* people's actions have [on our own] actions, the strong inclination each of us feels to do as we see all our neighbors do? Nor is the influence of fashion confined to any particular thing or class of things. It is just as strong on one subject as another. Let us make it as unfashionable to withhold our names from the temperance pledge as for husbands to wear their wives bonnets to church, and instances will be just as rare in the one case as the other.

"But," say some, "we are no drunkards; and we shall not acknowledge ourselves such by joining a reformed drunkard's society, whatever our influence might be." Surely no Christian will adhere to this objection. If they believe, as they profess, that Omnipotence condescended to take on himself the form of sinful man, and, as such, to die an ignominious death for their sakes, surely they will not refuse submission to the infinitely lesser condescension, for the temporal, and perhaps eternal salvation, of a large, erring, and unfortunate class of their own fellow creatures. Nor is the condescension very great.

In my judgment, such of us as have never fallen victims, have been spared more from the absence of appetite, than from any mental or moral superiority over those who have. Indeed, I believe, if we take habitual drunkards as a class, their heads and their hearts will bear an advantageous comparison with those of any other class. There seems ever to have been a proneness in the brilliant, and the warm-blooded, to fall into this vice. The demon of intemperance ever seems to have delighted in sucking the blood of genius and of generosity. What one of us but can call to mind some dear relative, more promising in youth than all his fellows, who has fallen a sacrifice to his rapacity? He ever seems to have gone forth, like the Egyptian angel of death, commissioned to slay if not the first, the fairest born of every family. Shall he now be arrested in his desolating career? In that arrest, all can give aid that will; and who shall be excused that *can,* and will not? Far around as human breath has ever blown, he keeps our fathers, our brothers, our sons, and our friends, prostrate in the chains of moral death. To all the living every where, we cry, "come sound the moral resurrection trump, that these may rise and stand up, an exceeding great army"—"Come from the four winds, O breath! and breathe upon these slain, that they may live."

If the relative grandeur of revolutions shall be estimated by the great amount of human misery they alleviate, and the small amount they inflict, then, indeed, will this be the grandest the world shall ever have seen. Of our political revolution of '76, we all are justly proud. It has given us a degree of political freedom, far exceeding that of any other of the nations of the earth. In it the world has found a solution of that long mooted problem, as to the capability of man to govern himself. In it was the germ which has vegetated, and still is to grow and expand into the universal liberty of mankind.

But with all these glorious results, past, present, and

to come, it had its evils too. It breathed forth famine,
swam in blood and rode on fire; and long, long after, the
orphan's cry, and the widow's wail, continued to break
the sad silence that ensued. These were the price, the
inevitable price, paid for the blessings it brought.

Turn now, to the temperance revolution. In *it*, we shall
find a stronger bondage broken; a viler slavery, manu-
mitted; a greater tyrant deposed. In *it*, more of want supplied, more disease healed, more sorrow assuaged. By *it*
no orphans starving, no widows weeping. By *it*, none
wounded in feeling, none injured in interest. Even the
dram-maker, and dram seller, will have glided into other
occupations *so* gradually, as never to have felt the shock
of change; and will stand ready to join all others in the
universal song of gladness.

And what a noble ally this, to the cause of political
freedom. With such an aid, its march cannot fail to be
on and on, till every son of earth shall drink in rich
fruition, the sorrow quenching draughts of perfect liberty.
Happy day, when, all appetites controled, all passions sub-
dued, all matters subjected, *mind,* all conquering *mind,*
shall live and move the monarch of the world. Glorious
consummation! Hail fall of Fury! Reign of Reason, all
hail!

And when the victory shall be complete—when there
shall be neither a slave nor a drunkard on the earth—
how proud the title of that *Land,* which may truly claim
to be the birth-place and the cradle of both those revolutions, that shall have ended in that victory. How nobly
distinguished that People, who shall have planted, and
nurtured to maturity, both the political and moral freedom
of their species.

This is the one hundred and tenth anniversary of the
birth-day of Washington. We are met to celebrate this
day. Washington is the mightiest name of earth—*long
since* mightiest in the cause of civil liberty; *still* mightiest
in moral reformation. On that name, an eulogy is expected. It cannot be. To add brightness to the sun, or
glory to the name of Washington, is alike impossible. Let
none attempt it. In solemn awe pronounce the name, and
in its naked deathless splendor, leave it shining on.

8. *Legal Fees:*

LETTER TO JAMES S. IRWIN, NOVEMBER 2, 1842

LINCOLN and Mary Todd, having reconciled, were married on November 4, 1842. Two days earlier, thinking no doubt of his new responsibilities, he explained why the firm of Logan and Lincoln wanted to "see the money" before taking cases for out-of-town clients.

Springfield, Nov. 2, 1842.

Jas. S. Irwin Esqr.

Owing to my absence, yours of the 22nd. ult. was not received till this moment.

Judge Logan & myself are willing to attend to any business in the Supreme Court you may send us. As to fees, it is impossible to establish a rule that will apply in all, or even a great many cases. We believe we are never accused of being very unreasonable in this particular; and we would always be easily satisfied, provided we could see the money—but whatever fees we earn at a distance, if not paid *before*, we have noticed we never hear of after the work is done. We therefore, are growing a little sensitive on that point. Yours &c.

A. Lincoln

9. *Texas and Slavery:*

LETTER TO WILLIAMSON DURLEY, OCTOBER 3, 1845

LINCOLN did not run for reelection to the legislature in 1842. Recognized by then as one of the Whig leaders in Illinois, he had his eye set on a seat in Congress and meanwhile pursued his law practice. In 1844, he changed partners once more, this time entering upon his long association with William H. Herndon. That same year he campaigned strenuously for Henry Clay in the presidential election. Clay was narrowly defeated by James K. Polk, who had been more outspoken in advocating the annexation of Texas. The decisive state was New York, where the Liberty party drained off votes that would have elected Clay. A year later, Lincoln was still deploring the outcome.

Springfield, Octr. 3, 1845

Friend Durley:

When I saw you at home. it was agreed that I should write to you and your brother Madison. Until I then saw you, I was not aware of your being what is generally called an abolitionist, or, as you call yourself, a Liberty-man; though I well knew there were many such in your county. I was glad to hear you say that you intend to attempt to bring about, at the next election in Putnam, a union of the whigs proper, and such of the liberty men, as are whigs in principle on all questions save only that of slavery. So far as I can perceive, by such union, neither party need yield any thing, on *the* point in difference between them. If the whig abolitionists of New York had voted with us last fall, Mr. Clay would now be president, whig principles in the ascendent, and Texas not annexed; whereas by the division, all that either had at stake in the contest, was lost. And, indeed, it was extremely probable, beforehand, that such would be the result. As I always understood, the Liberty-men deprecated the annexation of Texas extremely; and, this being so, why they should refuse to so cast their votes as to prevent it, even to me, seemed wonderful. What was their process of reasoning, I can only judge from what a single one of them told me. It was this: "We are not to do *evil* that *good* may come." This general, proposition is doubtless correct; but did it apply? If by your votes you could have prevented the *extention,* &c. of slavery, would it not have been *good* and not *evil* so to have used your votes, even though it involved the casting of them for a slaveholder? By the *fruit* the tree is to be known. An *evil* tree can not bring forth *good* fruit. If the fruit of electing Mr. Clay would have been to prevent the extension of slavery, could the act of electing have been *evil?*

But I will not argue farther. I perhaps ought to say that individually I never was much interested in the Texas question. I never could see much good to come of annexation; inasmuch, as they were already a free republican people on our own model; on the other hand, I never could very clearly see how the annexation would augment the evil of slavery. It always seemed to me that slaves would be taken there in about equal numbers, with or without annexation. And if more *were* taken because of annexation, still there would be just so many the fewer left, where they were taken from. It is possibly true, to some extent, that with annexation, some slaves may be sent to Texas and continued in slavery, that otherwise might have been liberated. To whatever extent this may be true, I think annexation an evil. I hold it to be a paramount duty of us in the free states, due to the Union of the states, and perhaps to liberty itself (paradox though it may seem) to let the slavery of the other states alone; while, on the other hand, I hold it to be equally clear, that we should never knowingly lend ourselves directly or indirectly, to prevent that slavery from dying a natural death—to find new places for it to live in, when it can no longer exist in the old. Of course I am not now considering what would be our duty, in cases of insurrection among the slaves.

To recur to the Texas question, I understand the Liberty men to have viewed annexation as a much greater evil than I ever did; and I, would like to convince you if I could, that they could have prevented it, without violation of principle, if they had chosen.

I intend this letter for you and Madison together; and if you and he or either shall think fit to drop me a line, I shall be pleased. Yours with respect,

A. Lincoln

10. Candidate for Congress:
LETTER TO ROBERT BOAL, JANUARY 7, 1846

LINCOLN had stepped aside for John J. Hardin and Edward D. Baker in previous elections with the understanding that he would receive the Whig nomination for Congress in 1846. Hardin, however, proved unexpectedly reluctant to withdraw from the field.

Springfield, Jany. 7, 1846.

Dear Doctor:

Since I saw you last fall, I have often thought of writing you as it was then understood I would, but on reflection I have always found that I had nothing new to tell you. All has happened as I then told you I expected it would—Baker's declining, Hardin's taking the track, and so on.

If Hardin and I stood precisely equal—that is, if *neither* of us had been to congress, or if we *both* had—it would only accord with what I have always done, for the sake of peace, to give way to him; and I expect I should do it. That I *can* voluntarily postpone my pretentions, when they are no more than equal to those to which they are postponed, you have yourself seen. But to yield to Hardin under present circumstances, seems to me as nothing else than yielding to one who would gladly sacrifice me altogether. This, I would rather not submit to. That Hardin is talented, energetic, usually generous and magnanimous, I have, before this, affirmed to you, and do not now deny. You know that my only argument is that "turn about is fair play . . ." This he, practically at least, denies.

If it would not be taxing you too much, I wish you would write me, telling the aspect of things in your county, or rather your district; and also send the names of some of your whig neighbours, to whom I might, with propriety write. Unless I can get some one to do this, Hardin with his old franking list, will have the advantage of me. My reliance for a fair shake (and I want nothing more) in your county is chiefly on you, because of your position and standing, and because I am acquainted with so few others. Let this be strictly confidential, & any letter you may write me shall be the same if you desire. Let me hear from you soon. Yours truly,

A. Lincoln

11. Religion and Politics:

HANDBILL ADDRESSED TO THE VOTERS OF THE SEVENTH CONGRESSIONAL DISTRICT, JULY 31, 1846

HARDIN eventually withdrew from the congressional race, and Lincoln won the nomination without opposition. The Democrats, habitually underdogs in the Seventh District, nominated Peter Cartwright, a well-known Methodist preacher. Reports that Cartwright was accusing him of infidelity prompted Lincoln to reply in a handbill.

Fellow Citizens:

A charge having got into circulation in some of the neighborhoods of this District, in substance that I am an open scoffer at Christianity, I have by the advice of some friends concluded to notice the subject in this form. That I am not a member of any Christian Church, is true; but I have never denied the truth of the Scriptures; and I have never spoken with intentional disrespect of religion in general, or of any denomination of Christians in particular. It is true that in early life I was inclined to believe in what I understand is called the "Doctrine of Necessity"—that is, that the human mind is impelled to action, or held in rest by some power, over which the mind itself has no control; and I have sometimes (with one, two or three, but never publicly) tried to maintain this opinion in argument. The habit of arguing thus however, I have, entirely left off for more than five years. And I add here, I have always understood this same opinion to be held by several of the Christian denominations. The foregoing, is the whole truth, briefly stated, in relation to myself, upon this subject.

I do not think I could myself, be brought to support a man for office, whom I knew to be an open enemy of, and scoffer at, religion. Leaving the higher matter of eternal consequences, between him and his Maker, I still do not think any man has the right thus to insult the feelings, and injure the morals, of the community in which he may live. If, then, I was guilty of such conduct, I should blame no man who should condemn me for it; but I do blame those, whoever they may be, who falsely put such a charge in circulation against me.

July 31, 1846.   A. Lincoln.

12. *The Mexican War:*

LINCOLN'S "SPOT RESOLUTIONS" IN THE HOUSE OF REPRESENTATIVES, DECEMBER 22, 1847.

LINCOLN was elected to Congress in August 1846, but his term did not begin until December of the following year. By that time, the war against Mexico was nearing its victorious conclusion. Lincoln took the orthodox Whig position of supporting prosecution of the war while insisting that it had been "unnecessarily and unconstitutionally commenced by the President." The crux of the matter was that Texas, in entering the Union, had brought with it a dubious claim to the territory stretching southward and westward to the Rio Grande. Hostilities had begun when President Polk endorsed the claim and sent General Zachary Taylor with troops into the disputed region. Lincoln's "Spot Resolutions" were designed to expose the weakness of Polk's argument that Mexico had been the aggressor. The House gave them no consideration beyond the first reading.

Whereas the President of the United States, in his message of May 11th, 1846, has declared that "The Mexican Government not only refused to receive him" (the envoy of the U.S.) "or listen to his propositions, but, after a long continued series of menaces, have at last invaded *our territory,* and shed the blood of our fellow *citizens on our own soil"*

And again, in his message of December 8, 1846 that "We had ample cause of war against Mexico, long before the breaking out of hostilities. But even then we forbore to take redress into our own hands, until Mexico herself became the aggressor by invading *our soil* in hostile array, and shedding the blood of our *citizens"*

And yet again, in his message of December 7, 1847, that "The Mexican Government refused even to hear the terms of adjustment which he" (our minister of peace) "was authorized to propose; and finally, under wholly unjustifiable pretexts, involved the two countries in war, by invading the teritory of the State of Texas, striking the first blow, and shedding the blood of our *citizens* on *our own soil"*

And whereas this House desires to obtain a full knowledge of all the facts which go to establish whether the particular spot of soil on which the blood of our *citizens* was so shed, was, or was not, *our own soil,* at that time; therefore

Resolved by the House of Representatives, that the President of the United States be respectfully requested to inform this House—

First: Whether the spot of soil on which the blood of our *citizens* was shed, as in his messages declared, was, or was not, within the teritories of Spain, at least from the treaty of 1819 until the Mexican revolution.

Second: Whether that spot is, or is not, within the teritory which was wrested from Spain, by the Mexican revolution.

Third: Whether that spot is, or is not, within a settlement of people, which settlement had existed ever since long before the Texas revolution, until it's inhabitants fled from the approach of the U. S. Army.

Fourth: Whether that settlement is, or is not, isolated from any and all other settlements, by the Gulf of Mexico,

and the Rio Grande, on the South and West, and by wide
uninhabited regions on the North and East.

Fifth: Whether the *People* of that settlement, or a *majority* of them, or *any* of them, had ever, previous to the
bloodshed, mentioned in his messages, submitted themselves to the government or laws of Texas, or of the United
States, by *consent,* or by *compulsion,* either by accepting
office, or voting at elections, or paying taxes, or serving
on juries, or having process served upon them, or in *any
other way.*

Sixth: Whether the People of that settlement, did, or
did not, flee from the approach of the United States Army,
leaving unprotected their homes and their growing crops,
before the blood was shed, as in his messages stated; and
whether the first blood so shed, was, or was not shed,
within the *inclosure* of the People, or some of them, who
had thus fled from it.

Seventh: Whether our *citizens,* whose blood was shed,
as in his messages declared, were, or were not, at that time,
armed officers, and *soldiers,* sent into that settlement, by
the military order of the President through the Secretary
of War—and

Eighth: Whether the military force of the United States,
including those *citizens,* was, or was not, so sent into that
settlement, after Genl. Taylor had, more than once, intimated to the War Department that, in his opinion, no
such movement was necessary to the defence or protection
of Texas.

13. Presidential Power:

*LETTER TO WILLIAM H. HERNDON, FEBRUARY
15, 1848*

PURSUING the theme of his "Spot Resolutions" in a speech to
the House of Representatives on January 12, 1848, Lincoln at-
tacked the Administration's Mexican policy and described Polk
as a "bewildered, confounded, and miserably perplexed man."

Such views were not popular at home, however, and they displeased even his law partner. In one of his defensive letters to Herndon, Lincoln discussed the danger of conceding extraordinary power to the President.

Washington, Feb. 15, 1848

Dear William:

Your letter of the 29th. Jany. was received last night. Being exclusively a constitutional argument, I wish to submit some reflections upon it in the same spirit of kindness that I know actuates you. Let me first state what I understand to be your position. It is, that if it shall become *necessary, to repel invasion,* the President may, without violation of the Constitution, cross the line, and *invade* the teritory of another country; and that whether such *necessity* exists in any given case, the President is to be the *sole* judge.

Before going further, consider well whether this is, or is not your position. If it is, it is a position that neither the President himself, nor any friend of his, so far as I know, has ever taken. Their only positions are first, that the soil was *ours* where hostilities commenced, and second, that whether it was rightfully *ours* or not, *Congress had annexed it,* and the President, for that reason was bound to defend it, both of which are as clearly proved to be false in fact, as you can prove that your house is not mine. That soil was not ours; and Congress did not annex or attempt to annex it. But to return to your position: Allow the President to invade a neighboring nation, whenever *he* shall deem it necessary to repel an invasion, and you allow him to do so, *whenever he may choose to say* he deems it necessary for such purpose—and you allow him to make war at pleasure. Study to see if you can fix *any limit* to his power in this respect, after you have given him so much as you propose. If, to-day, he should choose to say he thinks it necessary to invade Canada, to prevent the British from invading us, how could you stop him? You may say to him, "I see no probability of the British invading us" but he will say to you "be silent; I see it, if you dont."

The provision of the Constitution giving the war-making power to Congress, was dictated, as I understand it, by the following reasons. Kings had always been involving and impoverishing their people in wars, pretending generally, if not always, that the good of the people was the object. This, our Convention understood to be the most oppressive of all Kingly oppressions; and they resolved to so frame the Constitution that *no one man* should hold the power of bringing this oppression upon us. But your view destroys the whole matter, and places our President where kings have always stood. Write soon again. Yours truly,

A. Lincoln

14. Family Affairs:
LETTER TO MARY LINCOLN, APRIL 16, 1848

LINCOLN was accompanied to Washington by his wife and their two sons, four-year-old Robert and Edward, a toddler in his second year. But after a few months of boarding-house life, Mary took the boys off to Lexington, Kentucky, for an extended visit with her family. Lincoln's letters to her reveal a marriage that was sometimes troubled but always filled with mutual affection.

Washington, April 16, 1848—

Dear Mary:

In this troublesome world, we are never quite satisfied. When you were here, I thought you hindered me some in attending to business; but now, having nothing but business—no variety—it has grown exceedingly tasteless to me. I hate to sit down and direct documents, and I hate to stay in this old room by myself. You know I told you in last sunday's letter, I was going to make a little speech during the week; but the week has passed away without my gétting a chance to do so; and now my interest in the subject has passed awáy too. Your second and third letters have been received since I wrote before. Dear Eddy thinks father is *"gone tapila."* Has any further discovery been made as to the breaking into your grand-mother's house? If I were she, I would not remain there alone. You mention that your uncle John Parker is likely to be at Lexington. Dont forget to present him my very kindest regards.

I went yesterday to hunt the little plaid stockings, as you wished; but found that McKnight has quit business, and Allen had not a single pair of the description you give, and only one plaid pair of any sort that I thought would fit "Eddy's dear little feet." I have a notion to make another trial to-morrow morning. If I could get them, I have an excellent chance of sending them. Mr. Warrick Tunstall, of St. Louis is here. He is to leave early this week, and to go by Lexington. He says he knows you, and will call to see you; and he voluntarily asked, if I had not some package to send to you.

I wish you to enjoy yourself in every possible way; but is there no danger of wounding the feelings of your good father, by being so openly intimate with the Wickliffe family?

Mrs. Broome has not removed yet; but she thinks of doing so to-morrow. All the house—or rather, all with whom you were on decided good terms—send their love to you. The others say nothing.

Very soon after you went away, I got what I think a very pretty set of shirt-bosom studs—modest little ones, jet, set in gold, only costing 50 cents a piece, or $1.50 for the whole.

Suppose you do not prefix the "Hon" to the address on your letters to me any more. I like the letters very much, but I would rather they should not have that upon them. It is not necessary, as I suppose you have thought, to have them to come free.

And you are entirely free from head-ache? That is good—good—considering it is the first spring you have been free from it since we were acquainted. I am afraid you will get so well, and fat, and young, as to be wanting to marry again. Tell Louisa I want her to watch you a little for me. Get weighed, and write me how much you weigh.

I did not get rid of the impression of that foolish dream

about dear Bobby till I got your letter written the same day. What did he and Eddy think of the little letters father sent them? Dont let the blessed fellows forget father.

A day or two ago Mr. Strong, here in Congress, said to me that Matilda would visit here within two or three weeks. Suppose you write her a letter, and enclose it in one of mine; and if she comes I will deliver it to her, and if she does not, I will send it to her. Most affectionately,

A. Lincoln

15. Presidential Politics:

LETTER TO WILLIAM H. HERNDON, JUNE 12, 1848

IN 1848, Congressman Lincoln abandoned his hero, Henry Clay, and worked for the presidential nomination of General Zachary Taylor, whose war record made him a more formidable candidate. Lincoln attended the Whig National Convention at Philadelphia in June, saw "Old Rough and Ready" nominated, and returned to Washington exulting over the discomfiture of the "locofocos"—that is, the Democrats.

Washington, June 12, 1848—

Dear William:

On my return from Philadelphia, where I had been attending the nomination of "Old Rough"—I found your letter in a mass of others, which had accumulated in my absence. By many, and often, it had been said they would not abide the nomination of Taylor; but since the deed has been done, they are fast falling in, and in my opinion we shall have a most overwhelming, glorious, triumph. One unmistakable sign is, that all the odds and ends are with us—Barnburners, Native Americans, Tyler men, disappointed office seeking locofocos, and the Lord knows what. This is important, if in nothing else, in showing which way the wind blows. Some of the sanguine men here, set down all the states as certain for Taylor, but

Illinois, and it as doubtful. Can not something be done, even in Illinois? Taylor's nomination takes the locos on the blind side. It turns the war thunder against them. The war is now to them, the gallows of Haman, which they built for us, and on which they are doomed to be hanged themselves.

Excuse this short letter. I have so many to write, that I can not devote much time to any one. Yours as ever,

A. Lincoln

16. A Patronage Battle:
LETTER TO WILLIAM B. PRESTON, MAY 16, 1849

LINCOLN did not seek reelection to Congress in 1848, but having campaigned strenuously for the victorious Taylor, he expected some consideration when the patronage was distributed. The highest appointment allocated to Illinois was Commissioner of the General Land Office. Lincoln first sought the post for another man, then became a candidate himself in an effort to block the selection of Justin Butterfield, a Chicago attorney. This letter to Secretary of the Navy William B. Preston was one of many he wrote pleading his case—to no avail, however, for Butterfield received the appointment. A few months later, Lincoln was offered first the secretaryship and then the governorship of Oregon Territory, but he declined.

Springfield, Ills.
May 16, 1849

Hon: W. B. Preston:
Dear Sir:

It is a delicate matter to oppose the wishes of a friend; and consequently I address you on the subject I now do, with no little hesitation. Last night I received letters from different persons at Washington assuring me it was not improbable that Justin Butterfield, of Chicago, Ills, would be appointed Commissioner of the Genl. Land-Office. It was to avert this very thing, that I called on you at your rooms one sunday evening shortly after you were installed, and besought you that, so far as in your power, no man from Illinois should be appointed to any high office, without my being at least heard on the question. You were kind enough to say you thought my request a reasonable one. Mr. Butterfield is my friend, is well qualified, and, I suppose, would be faithful in the office. So far, good. But now for the objections. In 1840 we fought a fierce and laborious battle in Illinois, many of us spending almost the entire year in the contest. The general victory came, and with it, the appointment of a set of drones, including this same Butterfield, who had never spent a dollar or lifted a finger in the fight. The place he got was that of District Attorney. The defection of Tyler came, and then B. played off and on, and kept the office till after Polk's election. Again, winter and spring before the last, when you and I were almost sweating blood to have Genl. Taylor nominated, this same man was ridiculing the idea, and going for Mr. Clay; and when Gen: T. was nominated, if he went out of the city of Chicago to aid in his election, it is more than I ever heard, or believe. Yet, when the election is secured, by other men's labor, and even against his effort, why, he is the first man on hand for the best office that our state lays any claim to. Shall this thing be? Our whigs will throw down their arms, and fight no more, if the fruit of their labor is thus disposed of. If there is one man in this state who desires B's appointment to any thing, I declare I have not heard of him. What influence operates for him, I can not conceive. Your position makes it a matter of peculiar interest to you, that the administration shall be successful; and be assured, nothing can more endanger it, than making appointments through old-hawker foreign influences, which offend, rather than gratify, the people immediately interested in the offices.

Can you not find time to write me, even half as long a letter as this? I shall be much gratified if you will. Your Obt. Servt.

A. Lincoln

17. Death in the Family:

LETTER TO JOHN D. JOHNSTON, JANUARY 12, 1851

THE LINCOLNS suffered a cruel blow when little Eddie died in February 1850. Near the end of that year, a third son, William, was born. At about the same time, Lincoln learned that his father was near death in Coles County, less than a hundred miles from Springfield. The ties between father and son had never been very strong, and Lincoln was obviously needed at home. Yet he scarcely appears at his best in this letter to his stepbrother, John D. Johnston. Thomas Lincoln died five days after it was written.

Springfield, Jany. 12, 1851—

Dear Brother:

On the day before yesterday I received a letter from Harriett, written at Greenup. She says she has just returned from your house; and that Father is very low, and will hardly recover. She also says you have written me two letters; and that although you do not expect me to come now, you wonder that I do not write. I received both your letters, and although I have not answered them, it is not because I have forgotten them, or been uninterested about them—but because it appeared to me I could write nothing which could do any good. You already know I desire that neither Father or Mother shall be in want of any comfort either in health or sickness while they live; and I feel sure you have not failed to use my name, if necessary, to procure a doctor, or any thing else for Father in his present sickness. My business is such that I could hardly leave home now, if it were not, as it is, that my own wife is sick-abed. (It is a case of baby-sickness, and I suppose is not dangerous.) I sincerely hope Father may yet recover his health; but at all events tell him to remember to call upon, and confide in, our great, and good, and merciful Maker; who will not turn away from him in any extremity. He notes the fall of a sparrow, and numbers the hairs of our heads; and He will not forget the dying man, who puts his trust in Him. Say to him that if we could meet now, it is doubtful whether it would not be more painful than pleasant; but that if it be his lot to go now, he will soon have a joyous meeting with many loved ones gone before; and where the rest of us, through the help of God, hope ere-long to join them.

Write me again when you receive this. Affectionately,

A. Lincoln

18. *Portrait of a Statesman:*
EULOGY ON HENRY CLAY, JULY 6, 1852

HENRY CLAY'S half-century of public service ended with his death in June 1852. Lincoln's eulogy, delivered at a memorial meeting in Springfield, is reproduced here only in part. Included are the section analyzing Clay's qualities of leadership, the passage treating his views on slavery, and the peroration. The portrait emerging from these words is perhaps less accurate as a representation of what Clay had been than as a description of what Lincoln himself wanted to be.

By the foregoing it is perceived that the period from the beginning of Mr. Clay's official life, in 1803, to the end of it in 1852, is but one year short of half a century; and that the sum of all the intervals in it, will not amount to ten years. But mere duration of time in office, constitutes the smallest part of Mr. Clay's history. Throughout that long period, he has constantly been the most loved, and most implicitly followed by friends, and the most dreaded by opponents, of all living American politicians. In all the great questions which have agitated the country, and particularly in those great and fearful crises, the Missouri

question—the Nullification question, and the late slavery
question, as connected with the newly acquired territory,
involving and endangering the stability of the Union, his
has been the leading and most conspicuous part. In 1824
he was first a candidate for the Presidency, and was defeated; and, although he was successively defeated for
the same office in 1832, and in 1844, there has never
been a moment since 1824 till after 1848 when a very
large portion of the American people did not cling to him
with an enthusiastic hope and purpose of still elevating
him to the Presidency. With other men, to be defeated,
was to be forgotten; but to him, defeat was but a trifling
incident, neither changing him, or the world's estimate
of him. Even those of both political parties, who have
been preferred to him for the highest office, have run far
briefer courses than he, and left him, still shining, high in
the heavens of the political world. Jackson, Van Buren,
Harrison, Polk, and Taylor, all rose *after,* and set long before him. The spell—the long enduring spell—with which
the souls of men were bound to him, is a miracle. Who can
compass it? It is probably true he owed his pre-eminence
to no one quality, but to a fortunate combination of several. He was surpassingly eloquent; but many eloquent
men fail utterly; and they are not, as a class, generally
successful. His judgment was excellent; but many men of
good judgment, live and die unnoticed. His will was indomitable; but this quality often secures to its owner nothing better than a character for useless obstinacy. These
then were Mr. Clay's leading qualities. No one of them
is very uncommon; but all taken together are rarely combined in a single individual; and this is probably the reason
why such men as Henry Clay are so rare in the world.

Mr. Clay's eloquence did not consist, as many fine
specimens of eloquence does [do], of types and figures—
of antithesis, and elegant arrangement of words and sentences; but rather of that deeply earnest and impassioned
tone, and manner, which can proceed only from great
sincerity and a thorough conviction, in the speaker of the
justice and importance of his cause. This it is, that truly
touches the chords of human sympathy; and those who
heard Mr. Clay, never failed to be moved by it, or ever
afterwards, forgot the impression. All his efforts were

made for practical effect. He never spoke merely to be heard. He never delivered a Fourth of July Oration, or an eulogy on an occasion like this. As a politician or statesman, no one was so habitually careful to avoid all sectional ground. Whatever he did, he did for the whole country. In the construction of his measures he ever carefully surveyed every part of the field, and duly weighed every conflicting interest. Feeling, as he did, and as the truth surely is, that the world's best hope depended on the continued Union of these States, he was ever jealous of, and watchful for, whatever might have the slightest tendency to separate them.

Mr. Clay's predominant sentiment, from first to last, was a deep devotion to the cause of human liberty—a strong sympathy with the oppressed every where, and an ardent wish for their elevation. With him, this was a primary and all controlling passion. Subsidiary to this was the conduct of his whole life. He loved his country partly because it was his own country, but mostly because it was a free country; and he burned with a zeal for its advancement, prosperity and glory, because he saw in such, the advancement, prosperity and glory, of human liberty, human right and human nature. He desired the prosperity of his countrymen partly because they were his countrymen, but chiefly to show to the world that freemen could be prosperous.

* * * * *

Having been led to allude to domestic slavery so frequently already, I am unwilling to close without referring more particularly to Mr. Clay's views and conduct in regard to it. He ever was, on principle and in feeling, opposed to slavery. The very earliest, and one of the latest public efforts of his life, separated by a period of more than fifty years, were both made in favor of gradual emancipation of the slaves in Kentucky. He did not perceive, that on a question of human right, the negroes were to be excepted from the human race. And yet Mr. Clay was the owner of slaves. Cast into life where slavery was already widely spread and deeply seated, he did not perceive, as I think no wise man has perceived, how it could be at *once* eradicated, without producing a greater evil, even to the cause of human liberty itself. His feeling and his judgment, therefore, ever led him to oppose both extremes of opinion on the subject. Those who would shiver into fragments the Union of these States; tear to tatters its now venerated constitution; and even burn the last copy of the Bible, rather than slavery should continue a single hour, together with all their more halting sympathisers, have received, and are receiving their just execration; and the name, and opinions, and influence of Mr. Clay, are fully, and, as I trust, effectually and enduringly, arrayed against them. But I would also, if I could, array his name, opinions, and influence against the opposite extreme— against a few, but an increasing number of men, who, for the sake of perpetuating slavery, are beginning to assail and to ridicule the white-man's charter of freedom—the declaration that "all men are created free and equal."

· · · · ·

But Henry Clay is dead. His long and eventful life is closed. Our country is prosperous and powerful; but could it have been quite all it has been, and is, and is to be, without Henry Clay? Such a man the times have demanded, and such, in the providence of God was given us. But he is gone. Let us strive to deserve, as far as mortals may, the continued care of Divine Providence, trusting that, in future national emergencies, He will not fail to provide us the instruments of safety and security.

19. Government and Slavery:

TWO UNDATED FRAGMENTS FROM LINCOLN'S HAND

THESE two striking pieces are part of a group to which the date July 1, 1854, was assigned by Lincoln's biographers, John G. Nicolay and John Hay. Yet they may have been written at different times. The fragment on slavery, especially, seems better suited to the later 1850's.

The legitimate object of government, is to do for a community of people, whatever they need to have done, but can not do, *at all,* or can not, *so well do,* for themselves—in their separate, and individual capacities.

In all that the people can individually do as well for themselves, government ought not to interfere.

The desirable things which the individuals of a people can not do, or can not well do, for themselves, fall into two classes: those which have relation to *wrongs,* and those which have not. Each of these branch off into an infinite variety of subdivisions.

The first—that in relation to wrongs—embraces all crimes, misdemesnors, and non-performance of contracts. The other embraces all which, in its nature, and without wrong, requires combined action, as public roads and highways, public schools, charities, pauperism, orphanage, estates of the deceased, and the machinery of government itself.

From this it appears that if all men were just, there still would be *some,* though not *so much,* need of government.

If A. can prove, however conclusively, that he may, of right, enslave B.—why may not B. snatch the same argument, and prove equally, that he may enslave A?—

You say A. is white, and B. is black. It is *color,* then; the lighter, having the right to enslave the darker? Take care. By this rule, you are to be slave to the first man you meet, with a fairer skin than your own.

You do not mean *color* exactly?—You mean the whites are *intellectually* the superiors of the blacks, and, therefore have the right to enslave them? Take care again. By this rule, you are to be slave to the first man you meet, with an intellect superior to your own.

But, say you, it is a question of *interest;* and, if you can make it your *interest,* you have the right to enslave another. Very well. And if he can make it his interest, he has the right to enslave you.

20. The Kansas–Nebraska Act:
SPEECH AT PEORIA, ILLINOIS, OCTOBER 16, 1854

LINCOLN did not withdraw entirely from politics between 1849 and 1854, but the tempo of his activity slackened considerably. He tacitly acquiesced in the Compromise of 1850, although it did not forbid slavery in the territory acquired from Mexico, as he would have preferred. He campaigned a little for General Winfield Scott in the presidential election of 1852, but without much enthusiasm or hope. Preoccupied more and more with the practice of law, he was suddenly aroused in 1854 by the passage of the Kansas-Nebraska Act. This measure repealed the section of the Missouri Compromise which prohibited slavery in the greater part of the Louisiana Purchase. Its chief architect, Senator Stephen A. Douglas of Illinois, insisted that the new law was merely a corollary of the Compromise of 1850, which had replaced the principle of restriction with that of popular sovereignty, thus leaving the slavery question to the decision of actual settlers in each Federal territory. Lincoln joined in the storm of Northern protest against the Kansas-Nebraska Act with deep moral conviction. At the same time, he saw a new opportunity for himself in the political upheaval resulting from it. As summer passed into autumn, he began speaking in reply to Douglas, who had come home to defend himself. His famous speech at Peoria on October 16, the only one fully recorded, was part of this running debate with the Little Giant. Some of its most important passages are reproduced here.

Preceding the Presidential election of 1852, each of the great political parties, democrats and whigs, met in convention, and adopted resolutions endorsing the compromise of '50; as a "finality," a final settlement, so far as these parties could make it so, of all slavery agitation. Previous to this, in 1851, the Illinois Legislature had indorsed it.

During this long period of time Nebraska had remained, substantially an uninhabited country, but now emigration to, and settlement within it began to take place. It is about one third as large as the present United States, and its importance so long overlooked, begins to come into view. The restriction of slavery by the Missouri Compromise directly applies to it; in fact, was first made, and has since been maintained, expressly for it. In 1853, a bill to give it a territorial government passed the House of Representatives, and, in the hands of Judge Douglas, failed of passing the Senate only for want of time. This bill contained no repeal of the Missouri Compromise. Indeed, when it was assailed because it did not contain such repeal, Judge Douglas defended it in its existing form. On January 4th, 1854, Judge Douglas introduces a new bill to give Nebraska territorial government. He accompanies this bill with a report, in which last, he expressly recommends that the Missouri Compromise shall neither be affirmed nor repealed.

Before long the bill is so modified as to make two territories instead of one; calling the Southern one Kansas.

Also, about a month after the introduction of the bill, on the judge's own motion, it is so amended as to declare the Missouri Compromise inoperative and void; and, substantially, that the People who go and settle there may establish slavery, or exclude it, as they may see fit. In this shape the bill passed both branches of congress, and became a law.

This is the *repeal* of the Missouri Compromise. The foregoing history may not be precisely accurate in every particular; but I am sure it is sufficiently so, for all the uses I shall attempt to make of it, and in it, we have before us, the chief material enabling us to correctly judge whether the repeal of the Missouri Compromise is right or wrong.

I think, and shall try to show, that it is wrong; wrong in its direct effect, letting slavery into Kansas and Nebraska—and wrong in its prospective principle, allowing it to spread to every other part of the wide world, where men can be found inclined to take it.

This *declared* indifference, but as I must think, covert *real* zeal for the spread of slavery, I can not but hate. I hate it because of the monstrous injustice of slavery itself. I hate it because it deprives our republican example of its just influence in the world—enables the enemies of free institutions, with plausibility, to taunt us as hypocrites—causes the real friends of freedom to doubt our sincerity, and especially because it forces so many really good men amongst ourselves into an open war with the very fundamental principles of civil liberty—criticising the Declaration of Independence, and insisting that there is no right principle of action but *self-interest*.

Before proceeding, let me say I think I have no prejudice against the Southern people. They are just what we would be in their situation. If slavery did not now exist amongst them, they would not introduce it. If it did now exist amongst us, we should not instantly give it up. This I believe of the masses north and south. Doubtless there are individuals, on both sides, who would not hold slaves under any circumstances; and others who would gladly introduce slavery anew, if it were out of existence. We know that some southern men do free their slaves, go north, and become tip-top abolitionists; while some northern ones go south, and become most cruel slave-masters.

When southern people tell us they are no more responsible for the origin of slavery, than we; I acknowledge the fact. When it is said that the institution exists; and that it is very difficult to get rid of it, in any satisfactory way, I can understand and appreciate the saying. I surely will not blame them for not doing what I should not know how to do myself. If all earthly power were given me, I should not know what to do, as to the existing institution. My first impulse would be to free all the slaves, and send them to Liberia,—to their own native land. But a moment's reflection would convince me, that whatever of high hope, (as I think there is) there may be in this, in the long run, its sudden execution is impossible. If they were all landed there in a day, they would all perish in the next ten days; and there are not surplus shipping and surplus money enough in the world to carry them there in many times ten days. What then? Free them all, and keep them among us as underlings? Is it quite certain that this betters their condition? I think I would not hold one in slavery, at any rate; yet the point is not clear enough for me to denounce people upon. What next? Free them, and make them politically and socially, our equals? My own feelings will not admit of this; and if mine would, we well know that those of the great mass of white people will not. Whether this feeling accords with justice and sound judgment, is not the sole question, if indeed, it is any part of it. A universal feeling, whether well or ill-founded, can not be safely disregarded. We can not, then, make them equals. It does seem to me that systems of gradual emancipation might be adopted; but for their tardiness in this, I will not undertake to judge our brethren of the south.

When they remind us of their constitutional rights, I acknowledge them, not grudgingly, but fully, and fairly; and I would give them any legislation for the reclaiming of their fugitives, which should not, in its stringency, be more likely to carry a free man into slavery, than our ordinary criminal laws are to hang an innocent one.

But all this; to my judgment, furnishes no more excuse for permitting slavery to go into our own free territory, than it would for reviving the African slave trade by law. The law which forbids the bringing of slaves *from* Africa; and that which has so long forbid the taking them *to* Nebraska, can hardly be distinguished on any moral principle; and the repeal of the former could find quite as plausible excuses as that of the latter.

．　．　．　．　．

But one great argument in the support of the repeal of the Missouri Compromise, is still to come. That argument is "the sacred right of self government." It seems our distinguished Senator has found great difficulty in getting his antagonists, even in the Senate to meet him fairly on this argument—some poet has said
    "Fools rush in where angels fear to tread."
At the hazzard of being thought one of the fools of this quotation, I meet that argument—I rush in, I take that bull by the horns.

I trust I understand, and truly estimate the right of self-government. My faith in the proposition that each man should do precisely as he pleases with all which is exclusively his own, lies at the foundation of the sense of justice there is in me. I extend the principles to communities of men, as well as to individuals. I so extend it, because it is politically wise, as well as naturally just: politically wise, in saving us from broils about matters which do not concern us. Here, or at Washington, I would not trouble myself with the oyster laws of Virginia, or the cranberry laws of Indiana.

The doctrine of self government is right—absolutely and eternally right—but it has no just application, as here attempted. Or perhaps I should rather say that whether it has such just application depends upon whether a negro is *not* or *is* a man. If he is *not* a man, why in that case, he who *is* a man may, as a matter of self-government, do just as he pleases with him. But if the negro *is* a man, is it not to that extent, a total destruction of self-government, to say that he too shall not govern *himself?* When the white man governs himself that is self-government; but when he governs himself, and also governs *another* man, that is *more* than self-government—that is despotism. If the negro is a *man,* why then my ancient faith teaches me that "all men are created equal"; and that there can be no moral right in connection with one man's making a slave of another.

Judge Douglas frequently, with bitter irony and sarcasm, paraphrases our argument by saying "The white people of Nebraska are good enough to govern themselves, *but they are not good enough to govern a few miserable negroes!!*"

Well I doubt not that the people of Nebraska are, and will continue to be as good as the average of people elsewhere. I do not say the contrary. What I do say is, that no man is good enough to govern another man, *without that other's consent.* I say this is the leading principle—the sheet anchor of American republicanism. Our Declaration of Independence says:

"We hold these truths to be self evident: that all men are created equal; that they are endowed by their Creator with certain inalienable rights; that among these are life, liberty and the pursuit of happiness. That to secure these rights, governments are instituted among men, DERIVING THEIR JUST POWERS FROM THE CONSENT OF THE GOVERNED."

I have quoted so much at this time merely to show that

according to our ancient faith, the just powers of governments are derived from the consent of the governed. Now the relation of masters and slaves is, PRO TANTO, a total violation of this principle. The master not only governs the slave without his consent; but he governs him by a set of rules altogether different from those which he prescribes for himself. Allow ALL the governed an equal voice in the government, and that, and that only is self government.

Let it not be said I am contending for the establishment of political and social equality between the whites and blacks. I have already said the contrary. I am not now combating the argument of NECESSITY, arising from the fact that the blacks are already amongst us; but I am combating what is set up as MORAL argument for allowing them to be taken where they have never yet been—arguing against the EXTENSION of a bad thing, which where it already exists, we must of necessity, manage as we best can.

In support of his application of the doctrine of self-government, Senator Douglas has sought to bring to his aid the opinions and examples of our revolutionary fathers. I am glad he has done this. I love the sentiments of those old-time men; and shall be most happy to abide by their opinions. He shows us that when it was in contemplation for the colonies to break off from Great Britain, and set up a new government for themselves, several of the states instructed their delegates to go for the measure PROVIDED EACH STATE SHOULD BE ALLOWED TO REGULATE ITS DOMESTIC CONCERNS IN ITS OWN WAY. I do not quote; but this in substance. This was right. I see nothing objectionable in it. I also think it probable that it had some reference to the existence of slavery amongst them. I will not deny that it had. But had it, in any reference to the carrying of slavery into NEW COUNTRIES? That is the question; and we will let the fathers themselves answer it.

This same generation of men, and mostly the same individuals of the generation, who declared this principle—who declared independence—who fought the war of the revolution through—who afterwards made the constitution under which we still live—these same men passed the ordinance of '87, declaring that slavery should never go to the north-west territory. I have no doubt Judge Douglas thinks they were very inconsistent in this. It is a question of discrimination between them and him. But there is not an inch of ground left for his claiming that their opinions—their example—their authority—are on his side in this controversy.

•   •   •   •   •

Let no one be deceived. The spirit of seventy-six and the spirit of Nebraska, are utter antagonisms; and the former is being rapidly displaced by the latter.

Fellow countrymen—Americans south, as well as north, shall we make no effort to arrest this? Already the liberal party throughout the world, express the apprehension "that the one retrograde institution in America, is undermining the principles of progress, and fatally violating the noblest political system the world ever saw." This is not the taunt of enemies, but the warning of friends. Is it quite safe to disregard it—to despise it? Is there no danger to liberty itself, in discarding the earliest practice, and first precept of our ancient faith? In our greedy chase to make profit of the negro, let us beware, lest we "cancel and tear to pieces" even the white man's charter of freedom.

Our republican robe is soiled, and trailed in the dust. Let us repurify it. Let us turn and wash it white, in the spirit, if not the blood, of the Revolution. Let us turn slavery from its claims of "moral right," back upon its existing legal rights, and its arguments of "necessity." Let us return it to the position our fathers gave it; and there let it rest in peace. Let us re-adopt the Declaration of Independence, and with it, the practices, and policy, which harmonize with it. Let north and south—let all Americans —let all lovers of liberty everywhere—join in the great and good work. If we do this, we shall not only have saved the Union; but we shall have so saved it, as to make, and to keep it, forever worthy of the saving. We shall have so saved it, that the succeeding millions of free happy people, the world over, shall rise up, and call us blessed, to the latest generations.

21. *Almost a Senator:*

THE election of 1854 produced an anti-Nebraska majority in the Illinois legislature, which was scheduled to choose a United States Senator. Lincoln became a candidate and entered the contest with high hopes. On the first ballot, he led the incumbent Democrat, James Shields, and needed only a few more votes to win. But thereafter his strength dwindled, while the Democrats shifted their allegiance to Governor Joel A. Matteson and soon were on the verge of victory. Determined to prevent such a disaster, Lincoln threw his support to Lyman Trumbull, an anti-Nebraska Democrat, who was elected on the tenth ballot. He explained his defeat to the father of one of the legislators.

Springfield, Ills.
Feby. 21, 1855

Hon. W. H. Henderson:
My dear Sir:

Your letter of the 4th. covering a lot of old deeds was received only two days ago. Wilton says he has the order but can not lay his hand upon it easily, and can not take time to make a thorough search, until he shall have gone to & returned from Chicago. So I lay the papers by, and wait.

The election is over, the Session is ended, and I am *not* Senator. I have to content myself with the honor of having been the first choice of a large majority of the fifty-one members who finally made the election. My larger number of friends had to surrender to Trumbull's smaller number, in order to prevent the election of Matteson, which would have been a Douglas victory. I started with 44 votes & T. with 5. It was rather hard for the 44 to have to surrender to the 5—and a less good humored man than I, perhaps would not have consented to it—and it would not have been done without my consent. I could not, however, let the whole political result go to ruin, on a point merely personal to myself.

Your son, kindly and firmly stood by me from first to last; and for which he has my everlasting gratitude. Your friend as ever,

A. Lincoln

22. *Fusionists and Nativists:*
LETTER TO OWEN LOVEJOY, AUGUST 11, 1855

THE Whig party was disintegrating by the summer of 1855, but what kind of organization would take its place was not yet clear. Opponents of the Kansas-Nebraska Act, calling themselves by such names as "Fusionists" and "Republicans," were still little more than a loose coalition, and meanwhile the Know Nothings were trying to construct a national party on nativist principles. To Owen Lovejoy, an abolitionist like his martyred brother, Elijah, Lincoln explained why the fusion of antislavery elements should proceed slowly, and why it would be unwise to engage in open battle with the Know Nothings.

Springfield,
August 11, 1855

Hon: Owen Lovejoy:
My dear Sir:

Yours of the 7th. was received the day before yesterday. Not even *you* are more anxious to prevent the extension of slavery than I; and yet the political atmosphere is such, just now, that I fear to do any thing, lest I do wrong. Know-nothingism has not yet entirely tumbled to pieces—nay, it is even a little encouraged by the late elections in Tennessee, Kentucky & Alabama. Until we can get the elements of this organization, there is not sufficient materials to successfully combat the Nebraska democracy with. We can not get them so long as they cling to a hope of success under their own organization; and I fear an open push by us now, may offend them, and tend to prevent our ever getting them. About us here, they are mostly my old political and personal friends; and I have hoped their organization would die out without the painful necessity of my taking an open stand against them. Of their principles I think little better than I do of those of the slavery extensionists. Indeed I do not perceive how any one professing to be sensitive to the wrongs of the negroes, can join in a league to degrade a class of white men.

I have no objection to "fuse" with any body provided I can fuse on ground which I think is right; and I believe the opponents of slavery extension could now do this, if it were not for this K.N.ism. In many speeches last summer I advised those who did me the honor of a hearing to "stand with any body who stands right"—and I am still quite willing to follow my own advice. I lately saw, in the Quincy Whig, the report of a preamble and resolutions, made by Mr. Williams, as chairman of a committee, to a public meeting and adopted by the meeting. I saw them but once, and have them not now at command; but so far as I can remember them, they occupy about the ground I should be willing to "fuse" upon.

As to my personal movements this summer, and fall, I am quite busy trying to pick up my lost crumbs of last year. I shall be here till September; then to the circuit till the 20th. then to Cincinnati, awhile, after a Patent right case; and back to the circuit to the end of November. I can be seen here any time this month; and at Bloomington at any time from the 10th. to the 17th. of September. As to an extra session of the Legislature, I should know no better how to bring that about, than to lift myself over a fence by the straps of my boots. Yours truly,

A. Lincoln—

23. A Farewell to Whiggery:
LETTER TO JOSHUA F. SPEED, AUGUST 24, 1855

ABOUT two weeks after writing to Lovejoy, Lincoln discussed slavery and politics in a long letter to his friend Joshua Speed. It is not surprising to find him speaking somewhat differently to an Illinois abolitionist and a Kentucky Whig. Yet his position was unmistakably clear. He considered himself still loyal to Whig principles but expected to act in the future with opponents of the extension of slavery—even with abolitionists like Lovejoy. His letter to Speed, here slightly abridged, is actually a sad farewell to the old associations of Whiggery.

Springfield, Aug: 24, 1855

Dear Speed:

You know what a poor correspondent I am. Ever since I received your very agreeable letter of the 22nd. of May I have been intending to write you in answer to it. You suggest that in political action now, you and I would differ. I suppose we would; not quite as much, however, as you may think. You know I dislike slavery; and you fully admit the abstract wrong of it. So far there is no cause of difference. But you say that sooner than yield your legal right to the slave—especially at the bidding of those who are not themselves interested, you would see the Union dissolved. I am not aware that *any one* is bidding you to yield that right; very certainly *I* am not. I leave that matter entirely to yourself. I also acknowledge *your* rights and *my* obligations, under the constitution, in regard to your slaves. I confess I hate to see the poor creatures hunted down, and caught, and carried back to their stripes, and unrewarded toils; but I bite my lip and keep quiet. In 1841 you and I had together a tedious low-water trip, on a Steam Boat from Louisville to St. Louis. You may remember, as I well do, that from Louisville to the mouth of the Ohio there were, on board, ten or a dozen slaves, shackled together with irons. That sight was a continual torment to me; and I see something like it every time I touch the Ohio, or any other slave-border. It is hardly fair for you to assume, that I have no interest in a thing which has, and continually exercises, the power of making me miserable. You ought rather to appreciate how much the great body of the Northern people do crucify their feelings, in order to maintain their loyalty to the constitution and the Union.

I do oppose the extension of slavery, because my judgment and feelings so prompt me; and I am under no obligation to the contrary. If for this you and I must differ, differ we must. You say if you were President, you would send an army and hang the leaders of the Missouri outrages upon the Kansas elections; still, if Kansas fairly votes herself a slave state, she must be admitted, or the Union must be dissolved. But how if she votes herself a slave state *unfairly*—that is, by the very means for which you say you would hang men? Must she still be admitted, or the Union be dissolved? That will be the phase of the question when it first becomes a practical one. In your assumption that there may be a *fair* decision of the slavery question in Kansas, I plainly see you and I would differ about the Nebraska-law. I look upon that enactment not as a *law,* but as *violence* from the beginning. It was conceived in violence, passed in violence, is maintained in violence, and is being executed in violence. I say it was *conceived* in violence, because the destruction of the Missouri Compromise, under the circumstances, was nothing less than violence. It was *passed* in violence, because it could not have passed at all but for the votes of many members, in violent disregard of the known will of their constituents. It is *maintained* in violence because the elections since, clearly demand it's repeal, and this demand is openly disregarded. *You* say men ought to be hung·for the way they are executing that law; and *I* say the way it is being executed is quite as good as any of its antecedents. It is being executed in the precise way which was intended from the first . . .

In my humble sphere, I shall advocate the restoration of the Missouri Compromise, so long as Kansas remains a territory; and when, by all these foul means, it seeks to come into the Union as a Slave-state, I shall oppose it. I am very loth, in any case, to withhold my assent to the enjoyment of property *acquired,* or *located,* in good faith; but I do not admit that *good faith,* in taking a negro to Kansas, to be held in slavery, is a *possibility* with any man. Any man who has sense enough to be the controller of his own property, has too much sense to misunderstand the outrageous character of this whole Nebraska business. But I digress. In my opposition to the admission of Kansas I shall have some company; but we may be beaten. If we are, I shall not, on that account, attempt to dissolve the Union. On the contrary, if we succeed, there will be enough of us to take care of the Union. I think it probable, however, we shall be beaten. Standing as a unit among yourselves, you can, directly, and indirectly, bribe enough of our men to carry the day—as you could on an open proposition to establish monarchy. Get hold of some man in the North, whose position and ability is such, that he can make the support of your measure—whatever it may be —a *democratic party necessity,* and the thing is done. . . .

You say if Kansas fairly votes herself a free state, as a christian you will rather rejoice at it. All decent slave-holders *talk* that way; and I do not doubt their candor. But they never *vote* that way. Although in a private letter, or conversation, you will express your preference that Kansas shall be free, you would vote for no man for Congress who would say the same thing publicly. No such man could be elected from any district in any slave-state. You think Stringfellow & Co ought to be hung; and yet, at the next presidential election you will vote for the exact type and representative of Stringfellow. The slave-breeders and slave-traders, are a small, odious and detested class, among you; and yet in politics, they dictate the course of all of you, and are as completely your masters, as you are the masters of your own negroes.

You enquire where I now stand. That is a disputed point. I think I am a whig; but others say there are no whigs, and that I am an abolitionist. When I was at Washington I voted for the Wilmot Proviso as good as forty times, and I never heard of any one attempting to unwhig me for that. I now do no more than oppose the *extension* of slavery.

I am not a Know-Nothing. That is certain. How could I be? How can any one who abhors the oppression of negroes, be in favor of degrading classes of white people? Our progress in degeneracy appears to me to be pretty rapid. As a nation, we began by declaring that *"all men are created equal."* We now practically read it "all men are created equal, *except negroes."* When the Know-Nothings get control, it will read "all men are created equal, except negroes, *and foreigners, and catholics."* When it comes to this I should prefer emigrating to some country where they make no pretence of loving liberty—to Russia, for instance, where despotism can be taken pure, and without the base alloy of hypocracy.

Mary will probably pass a day or two in Louisville in October. My kindest regards to Mrs. Speed. On the leading subject of this letter, I have more of her sympathy than I have of yours.

And yet let [me] say I am   Your friend forever,
                                                    A. Lincoln—

24. *Campaigning for Frémont:*
FORM LETTER TO FILLMORE MEN, SEPTEMBER, OCTOBER, 1856

THE Republican party took definite form during the early months of 1856, and Lincoln was one of its most prominent leaders in Illinois. At the national convention in June, he received strong support for the vice-presidential nomination. The selection of John C. Frémont as the new party's first presidential candidate did not suit his own preference, but he plunged vigorously into the campaign and delivered more than fifty speeches before it was over. The contest between Frémont and the Democratic nominee, James Buchanan, was complicated by the appearance of former President Millard Fillmore as the candidate of the American party, made up of Know Nothings and the remnants of Whiggery. Lincoln expended much effort trying to persuade Illinois Americans that by voting for Fillmore they would only be helping to elect Buchanan. He mailed out lithographed copies of this letter in large number.

Springfield, Sept. 8, 1856

Dear Sir,

I understand you are a Fillmore man. Let me prove to you that every vote withheld from Fremont, and given to Fillmore, *in this state,* actually lessens Fillmore's chance of being President.

Suppose Buchanan gets *all* the slave states, and Pennsylvania, and *any other* one state besides; *then he is elected,* no matter who gets all the rest.

But suppose Fillmore gets the two slave states of Maryland and Kentucky; *then* Buchanan *is not* elected; Fillmore goes into the House of Representatives, and may be made President by a compromise.

But suppose again Fillmore's friends throw away a few thousand votes on him, in *Indiana* and *Illinois,* it will inevitably give these states to Buchanan, which will more than compensate him for the loss of Maryland and Kentucky; will elect him, and leave Fillmore no chance in the H.R. or out of it.

This is as plain as the adding up of the weights of three small hogs. As Mr. Fillmore has no possible chance to carry Illinois *for himself,* it is plainly his interest to let Fremont take it, and thus keep it out of the hands of Buchanan. Be not deceived. *Buchanan* is the hard horse to beat in this race. Let him have Illinois, and nothing can beat him; *and he will get Illinois,* if men persist in throwing away votes upon Mr. Fillmore.

Does some one persuade you that Mr. Fillmore can carry Illinois? Nonsense! There are over seventy newspapers in Illinois opposing Buchanan, only three or four of which support Mr. Fillmore, *all* the rest going for Fremont. Are not these newspapers a fair index of the proportion of the voters. If not, tell me why.

Again, of these three or four Fillmore newspapers, *two* at least, are supported, in part, by the Buchanan men, as I understand. Do not they know where the shoe pinches?

They know the Fillmore movement helps *them,* and therefore they help *it.*

Do think these things over, and then act according to
your judgment. Yours very truly,   A. Lincoln
(Confidential)

25. The Central Idea of the Republic:
SPEECH AT A REPUBLICAN BANQUET IN CHI-
CAGO, DECEMBER 10, 1856

AS Lincoln had feared, the Democrats carried Illinois with a
plurality because of the votes "thrown away" on Fillmore. The
Republicans, however, swept the election of state officers. In the
nation as a whole, Buchanan won only a minority of the popular
votes but a majority of the electoral votes. President Franklin
Pierce, although set aside by his party, hailed the Democratic
victory in his last annual message to Congress. Speaking several
days later at a Republican banquet in Chicago, Lincoln ridi-
culed Pierce, called for a united opposition, and defined the
fundamental issue underlying the slavery controversy. The latter part of his speech is reproduced here.

We have another annual Presidential Message. Like a
rejected lover, making merry at the wedding of his rival,
the President felicitates hugely over the late Presidential
election. He considers the result a signal triumph of good
principles and good men, and a very pointed rebuke of
bad ones. He says the people did it. He forgets that the
"people," as he complacently calls only those who voted
for Buchanan, are in a minority of the whole people, by
about four hundred thousand voters—one full tenth of all
the voters. Remembering this, he might perceive that the
"Rebuke" may not be quite as durable as he seems to think
—that the majority may not choose to remain permanently
rebuked by that minority.

The President thinks the great body of us Fremonters,

being ardently attached to liberty, in the abstract, were duped by a few wicked and designing men. There is a slight difference of opinion on this. We think *he,* being ardently attached to the hope of a second term, *in the concrete,* was duped by men who had liberty every way. He is in the cat's paw. By much dragging of chestnuts from the fire for others to eat, his claws are burnt off to the gristle, and he is thrown aside as unfit for further use. As the fool said to King Lear, when his daughters had turned him out of doors, "He's a shelled pea's cod."

So far as the President charges us "with a desire to change the domestic institutions of existing States;" and of "doing every thing in our power to deprive the Constitution and the laws of moral authority," for the whole party, on *belief,* and for myself, on *knowledge* I pronounce the charge an unmixed, and unmitigated falsehood.

Our government rests in public opinion. Whoever can change public opinion, can change the government, practically just so much. Public opinion, or [on?] any subject, always has a *"central idea,"* from which all its minor thoughts radiate. That "central idea" in our political public opinion, at the beginning was, and until recently has continued to be, "the equality of men." And although it was always submitted patiently to what ever of inequality there seemed to be as a matter of actual necessity, its constant working has been a steady progress towards the practical equality of all men. The late Presidential election was a struggle, by one party, to discard that central idea, and to substitute for it the opposite idea that slavery is right, in the abstract, the workings of which, as a central idea, may be the perpetuity of human slavery, and its extension to all countries and colors. Less than a year ago, the Richmond *Enquirer,* an avowed advocate of slavery, regardless of color, in order to favor his views, invented the phrase, "State equality," and now the President, in his Message, adopts the *Enquirer's* catch-phrase, telling us the people "have asserted the constitutional equality of each and all of the States of the Union as States." The President flatters himself that the new central idea is completely inaugurated; and so, indeed, it is, so far as the mere fact of a Presidential election can inaugurate it. To us it is left to know that the majority of the people have not yet declared for it, and to hope that they never will.

All of us who did not vote for Mr. Buchanan, taken together, are a majority of four hundred thousand. But, in the late contest we were divided between Fremont and Fillmore. Can we not come together, for the future. Let every one who really believes, and is resolved, that free society is not, *and shall not be,* a failure, and who can conscientiously declare that in the past contest he has done only what he thought best—let every such one have charity to believe that every other one can say as much. Thus let bygones be bygones. Let past differences, as nothing be; and with steady eye on the real issue, let us reinaugurate the good old "central ideas" of the Republic. We *can* do it. The human heart *is* with us—God is with us. We shall again be able not to declare, that "all States as States, are equal," nor yet that "all citizens as citizens are equal," but to renew the broader, better declaration, including both these and much more, that "all *men* are created equal."

26. The Dred Scott Decision:

SPEECH AT SPRINGFIELD, ILLINOIS, JUNE 26, 1857

IN the famous Dred Scott decision of March 6, 1857, Chief Justice Roger B. Taney, speaking for a majority of the United States Supreme Court, declared that Congress had no power to prohibit slavery in a Federal territory. The decision provoked an angry outcry from Republicans, whose primary objective, like the Missouri Compromise, was thus labeled unconstitutional. Douglas stoutly defended the Court in a speech at Springfield on June 12, and Lincoln answered him two weeks later. In the passages selected for reproduction here, Lincoln discussed the legal force of the decision, Taney's argument that the Declaration of Independence did not embrace Negroes, and Douglas' charge that the Republicans favored "amalgamation" of the races.

And now as to the Dred Scott decision. That decision declares two propositions—first, that a negro cannot sue in the U. S. Courts; and secondly, that Congress cannot prohibit slavery in the Territories. It was made by a divided court—dividing differently on the different points. Judge Douglas does not discuss the merits of the decision; and, in that respect, I shall follow his example, believing I could no more improve on McLean and Curtis, than he could on Taney.

He denounces all who question the correctness of that decision, as offering violent resistance to it. But who resists it? Who has, in spite of the decision, declared Dred Scott free, and resisted the authority of his master over him?

Judicial decisions have two uses—first, to absolutely determine the case decided, and secondly, to indicate to the public how other similar cases will be decided when they arise. For the latter use, they are called "precedents" and "authorities."

We believe, as much as Judge Douglas, (perhaps more) in obedience to, and respect for the judicial department of government. We think its decisions on Constitutional questions, when fully settled, should control, not only the particular cases decided, but the general policy of the country, subject to be disturbed only by amendments of the Constitution as provided in that instrument itself. More than this would be revolution. But we think the Dred Scott decision is erroneous. We know the court that made it, has often over-ruled its own decisions, and we shall do what we can to have it to over-rule this. We offer no *resistance* to it.

Judicial decisions are of greater or less authority as precedents, according to circumstances. That this should be so, accords both with common sense, and the customary understanding of the legal profession.

If this important decision had been made by the unanimous concurrence of the judges, and without any apparent partisan bias, and in accordance with legal public expec-tation, and with the steady practice of the departments throughout our history, and had been in no part, based on assumed historical facts which are not really true; or, if wanting in some of these, it had been before the court

more than once, and had there been affirmed and re-
affirmed through a course of years, it then might be, perhaps would be, factious, nay, even revolutionary, to not
acquiesce in it as a precedent.

But when, as it is true we find it wanting in all these
claims to the public confidence, it is not resistance, it is
not factious, it is not even disrespectful, to treat it as not
having yet quite established a settled doctrine for the
country.

. . . . .

Three years and a half ago, Judge Douglas brought forward his famous Nebraska bill. The country was at once
in a blaze. He scorned all opposition, and carried it through
Congress. Since then he has seen himself superseded in a
Presidential nomination, by one indorsing the general doctrine of his measure, but at the same time standing clear
of the odium of its untimely agitation, and its gross breach
of national faith; and he has seen that successful rival
Constitutionally elected, not by the strength of friends,
but by the division of adversaries, being in a popular minority of nearly four hundred thousand votes. He has seen
his chief aids in his own State, Shields and Richardson,
politically speaking, successively tried, convicted, and executed, for an offense not their own, but his. And now he
sees his own case, standing next on the docket for trial.

There is a natural disgust in the minds of nearly all
white people, to the idea of an indiscriminate amalgamation of the white and black races; and Judge Douglas evi-
dently is basing his chief hope, upon the chances of being
able to appropriate the benefit of this disgust to himself.
If he can, by much drumming and repeating, fasten the
odium of that idea upon his adversaries, he thinks he can
struggle through the storm. He therefore clings to this
hope, as a drowning man to the last plank. He makes an
occasion for lugging it in from the opposition to the Dred
Scott decision. He finds the Republicans insisting that the
Declaration of Independence includes ALL men, black
as well as white; and forthwith he boldly denies that it includes negroes at all, and proceeds to argue gravely that all
who contend it does, do so only because they want to vote,
and eat, and sleep, and marry with negroes! He will have it

that they cannot be consistent else. Now I protest against that counterfeit logic which concludes that, because I do not want a black woman for a *slave* I must necessarily want her for a *wife*. I need not have her for either, I can just leave her alone. In some respects she certainly is not my equal; but in her natural right to eat the bread she earns with her own hands without asking leave of any one else, she is my equal, and the equal of all others.

Chief Justice Taney, in his opinion in the Dred Scott case, admits that the language of the Declaration is broad enough to include the whole human family, but he and Judge Douglas argue that the authors of that instrument did not intend to include negroes, by the fact that they did not at once, actually place them on an equality with the whites. Now this grave argument comes to just nothing at all, by the other fact, that they did not at once, *or ever afterwards,* actually place all white people on an equality with one or another. And this is the staple argument of both the Chief Justice and the Senator, for doing this obvious violence to the plain unmistakable language of the Declaration. I think the authors of that notable instrument intended to include *all* men, but they did not intend to declare all men equal *in all respects*. They did not mean to say all were equal in color, size, intellect, moral developments, or social capacity. They defined with tolerable distinctness, in what respects they did consider all men created equal—equal in "certain inalienable rights, among which are life, liberty, and the pursuit of happiness." This they said, and this meant. They did not mean to assert the obvious untruth, that all were then actually enjoying that equality, nor yet, that they were about to confer it immediately upon them. In fact they had no power to confer such a boon. They meant simply to declare the *right,* so that the *enforcement* of it might follow as fast as circumstances should permit. They meant to set up a standard maxim for free society, which should be familiar to all, and revered by all; constantly looked to, constantly labored for, and even though never perfectly attained, constantly approximated, and thereby constantly spreading and deepening its influence, and augmenting the happiness and value of life to all people of all colors everywhere. The assertion that "all men are created equal" was of no practical use in effecting our separation from Great Britain; and it was placed in the Declaration, not for that, but for future use. Its authors meant it to be, thank God, it is now proving itself, a stumbling block to those who in after times might seek to turn a free people back into the hateful paths of despotism. They knew the proneness of prosperity to breed tyrants, and they meant when such should re-appear in this fair land and commence their vocation they should find left for them at least one hard nut to crack.

·   ·   ·   ·   ·

I have said that the separation of the races is the only perfect preventive of amalgamation. I have no right to say all the members of the Republican party are in favor of this, nor to say that as a party they are in favor of it. There is nothing in their platform directly on the subject. But I can say a very large proportion of its members are for it, and that the chief plank in their platform—opposition to the spread of slavery—is most favorable to that separation.

Such separation, if ever effected at all, must be effected by colonization; and no political party, as such, is now doing anything directly for colonization. Party operations at present only favor or retard colonization incidentally. The enterprise is a difficult one; but "when there is a will there is a way;" and what colonization needs most is a hearty will. Will springs from the two elements of moral sense and self-interest. Let us be brought to believe it is morally right, and, at the same time, favorable to, or, at least, not against, our interest, to transfer the African to his native clime, and we shall find a way to do it, however great the task may be. The children of Israel, to such numbers as to include four hundred thousand fighting men, went out of Egyptian bondage in a body.

How differently the respective courses of the Democratic and Republican parties incidentally bear on the question of forming a will—a public sentiment—for colonization, is easy to see. The Republicans inculcate, with whatever of ability they can, that the negro is a man; that his bondage is cruelly wrong, and that the field of his oppression ought not to be enlarged. The Democrats deny his man-

hood; deny, or dwarf to insignificance, the wrong of his
bondage; so far as possible, crush all sympathy for him,
and cultivate and excite hatred and disgust against him;
compliment themselves as Union-savers for doing so; and
call the indefinite outspreading of his bondage "a sacred
right of self-government."

The plainest print cannot be read through a gold eagle;
and it will be ever hard to find many men who will send a
slave to Liberia, and pay his passage while they can send
him to a new country, Kansas for instance, and sell him
for fifteen hundred dollars, and the rise.

27. Douglas in Revolt:
LETTER TO LYMAN TRUMBULL, DECEMBER 28, 1857

SINCE the repeal of the Missouri Compromise in 1854, Kansas
had been the main battleground of the sectional conflict. In
1857, a convention dominated by proslavery elements framed
a constitution at Lecompton, Kansas, and applied for admission
to statehood. President Buchanan endorsed the application, but
Douglas and certain other Northern Democrats joined the
Republicans in bitter opposition to it. This quarrel within the
Democratic organization delighted the Republicans, and some
of them, like Horace Greeley, the influential and impulsive
editor of the New York *Tribune*, heaped lavish praise upon
Douglas in his new role as party insurgent. To Lincoln, who
already had his eye upon the Little Giant's seat in the Senate,
Greeley's enthusiasm was especially disconcerting.

Bloomington, Dec. 28, 1857—

Hon. Lyman Trumbull.
Dear Sir: What does the New-York Tribune mean by
it's constant eulogising, and admiring, and magnifying [of]
Douglas? Does it, in this, speak the sentiments of the
republicans at Washington? Have they concluded that the
republican cause, generally, can be best promoted by sac-

raficing us here in Illinois? If so we would like to know it soon; it will save us a great deal of labor to surrender at once.

As yet I have heard of no republican here going over to Douglas; but if the Tribune continues to din his praises into the ears of it's five or ten thousand republican readers in Illinois, it is more than can be hoped that all will stand firm.

I am not complaining. I only wish a fair understanding. Please write me at Springfield. Your Obt. Servt.

A. Lincoln—

28. Senatorial Candidate:
THE HOUSE DIVIDED SPEECH, JUNE 16, 1858

THE alliance of Republicans and anti-Lecompton Democrats in Congress managed to block the admission of Kansas with its proslavery constitution. Greeley and certain other Republican spokesmen in the East proposed that Douglas be rewarded by returning him to the Senate without opposition. Illinois Republicans were outraged and bitterly denounced this interference from "outsiders." At their state convention in Springfield on June 16, 1858, party leaders unanimously approved a resolution declaring that Lincoln was their "first and only choice" for the Senate. The resolution amounted to an informal nomination, and Lincoln responded that same evening with the most provocative speech of his career. From beginning to end it was directed against Douglas. Lincoln's main lines of argument were that the Kansas-Nebraska policy had only intensified the slavery controversy; that there was no tenable middle ground between proslavery and Republican principles; that the doctrine of popular sovereignty reinforced a calculated and ominous tendency toward the nationalization of slavery; and that Douglas could not be accepted as an antislavery leader.

Mr. PRESIDENT and Gentlemen of the Convention.
If we could first know *where* we are, and *whither* we

are tending, we could then better judge *what* to do, and *how* to do it.

We are now far into the *fifth* year, since a policy was initiated, with the *avowed* object, and *confident* promise, of putting an end to slavery agitation.

Under the operation of that policy, that agitation has not only, *not ceased,* but has *constantly augmented.*

In *my* opinion, it *will* not cease, until a *crisis* shall have been reached, and passed.

"A house divided against itself cannot stand."

I believe this government cannot endure, permanently half *slave* and half *free.*

I do not expect the Union to be *dissolved*—I do not expect the house to *fall*—but I *do* expect it will cease to be divided.

It will become *all* one thing, or *all* the other.

Either the *opponents* of slavery, will arrest the further spread of it, and place it where the public mind shall rest in the belief that it is in course of ultimate extinction; or its *advocates* will push it forward, till it shall become alike lawful in *all* the States, *old* as well as *new*—*North* as well as *South.*

Have we no *tendency* to the latter condition?

Let any one who doubts, carefully contemplate that now almost complete legal combination—piece of *machinery* so to speak—compounded of the Nebraska doctrine, and the Dred Scott decision. Let him consider not only *what work* the machinery is adapted to do, and *how well* adapted; but also, let him study the *history* of its construction, and trace, if he can, or rather *fail,* if he can, to trace the evidences of design, and concert of action, among its chief bosses, from the beginning.

But, so far, *Congress* only, had acted; and an *indorsement* by the people, *real* or apparent, was indispensable, to *save* the point already gained, and give chance for more.

The new year of 1854 found slavery excluded from more than half the States by State Constitutions, and from most of the national territory by Congressional prohibition.

Four days later, commenced the struggle, which ended in repealing that Congressional prohibition.

This opened all the national territory to slavery; and was the first point gained.

This necessity had not been overlooked; but had been provided for, as well as might be, in the notable argument of *"squatter sovereignty,"* otherwise called *"sacred right of self government,"* which latter phrase, though expressive of the only rightful basis of any government, was so perverted in this attempted use of it as to amount to just this: That if any *one* man choose to enslave *another,* no *third* man shall be allowed to object.

That argument was incorporated into the Nebraska bill itself, in the language which follows: *"It being the true intent and meaning of this act not to legislate slavery into any Territory or state, not exclude it therefrom; but to leave the people thereof perfectly free to form and regulate their domestic institutions in their own way, subject only to the Constitution of the United States."*

Then opened the roar of loose declamation in favor of "Squatter Sovereignty," and "Sacred right of self government."

"But," said opposition members, "let us be more *specific*—let us *amend* the bill so as to expressly declare that the people of the territory *may* exclude slavery." "Not we," said the friends of the measure; and down they voted the amendment.

While the Nebraska bill was passing through congress, a *law case,* involving the question of a negroe's freedom, by reason of his owner having voluntarily taken him first into a free state and then a territory covered by the congressional prohibition, and held him as a slave, for a long time in each, was passing through the U. S. Circuit Court for the District of Missouri; and both Nebraska bill and law suit were brought to a decision in the same month of May, 1854. The negroe's name was "Dred Scott," which name now designates the decision finally made in the case.

Before the *then* next Presidential election, the law case came *to,* and was argued *in* the Supreme Court of the United States; but the *decision* of it was deferred until *after* the election. Still, *before* the election, Senator Trumbull, on the floor of the Senate, requests the leading advocate of the Nebraska bill to state *his opinion* whether the people of a territory can constitutionally exclude slavery from their limits; and the latter answers, "That is a question for the Supreme Court."

The election came. Mr. Buchanan was elected, and the *indorsement,* such as it was, secured. That was the *second* point gained. The indorsement, however, fell short of a clear popular majority by nearly four hundred thousand votes, and so, perhaps, was not overwhelmingly reliable and satisfactory.

The *outgoing* President, in his last annual message, as impressively as possible *echoed back* upon the people the *weight* and *authority* of the indorsement.

The Supreme Court met again; *did not* announce their decision, but ordered a re-argument.

The Presidential inauguration came, and still no decision of the court; but the *incoming* President, in his inaugural address, fervently exhorted the people to abide by the forthcoming decision, *whatever it might be.*

Then, in a few days, came the decision.

The reputed author of the Nebraska bill finds an early occasion to make a speech at this capitol indorsing the Dred Scott Decision, and vehemently denouncing all opposition to it.

The new President, too, seizes the early occasion of the Silliman letter to *indorse* and strongly *construe* that decision, and to express his *astonishment* that any different view had ever been entertained.

At length a squabble springs up between the President and the author of the Nebraska bill, on the *mere* question of *fact,* whether the Lecompton constitution was or was not, in any just sense, made by the people of Kansas; and in that squabble the latter declares that all he wants is a fair vote for the people, and that he *cares* not whether slavery be voted *down* or voted *up.* I do not understand his declaration that he cares not whether slavery be voted down or voted up, to be intended by him other than as an *apt definition* of the *policy* he would impress upon the public mind—the *principle* for which he declares he has suffered much, and is ready to suffer to the end.

And well may he cling to that principle. If he has any parental feeling, well may he cling to it. That principle, is the only *shred* left of his original Nebraska doctrine. Under the Dred Scott decision, "squatter sovereignty" squatted out of existence, tumbled down like temporary scaffolding—like the mould at the foundry served through

one blast and fell back into loose sand—helped to carry
an election, and then was kicked to the winds. His late
joint struggle with the Republicans, against the Lecompton
Constitution, involves nothing of the original Nebraska
doctrine. That struggle was made on a point, the right of
a people to make their own constitution, upon which he
and the Republicans have never differed.

The several points of the Dred Scott decision, in connection with Senator Douglas' "care not" policy, constitute the piece of machinery, in its *present* state of advancement. This was the third point gained.

The *working* points of that machinery are:

First, that no negro slave, imported as such from Africa,
and no descendant of such slave can ever be a *citizen* of
any State, in the sense of that term as used in the Constitution of the United States.

This point is made in order to deprive the negro, in
every possible event, of the benefit of this provision of the
United States Constitution, which declares that—

"The citizens of each State shall be entitled to all privileges and immunities of citizens in the several States."

Secondly, that "subject to the Constitution of the United
States," neither *Congress* nor a *Territorial Legislature* can
exclude slavery from any United States territory.

This point is made in order that individual men may
fill up the territories with slaves, without danger of losing
them as property, and thus to enhance the chances of
permanency to the institution through all the future.

Thirdly, that whether the holding a negro in actual
slavery in a free State, makes him free, as against the
holder, the United States courts will not decide, but will
leave to be decided by the courts of any slave State the
negro may be forced into by the master.

This point is made, not to be pressed *immediately;* but,
if acquiesced in for a while, and apparently *indorsed* by
the people at an election, *then* to sustain the logical conclusion that what Dred Scott's master might lawfully do
with Dred Scott, in the free State of Illinois, every other
master may lawfully do with any other *one,* or one *thousand* slaves, in Illinois, or in any other free State.

Auxiliary to all this, and working hand in hand with
it, the Nebraska doctrine, or what is left of it, is to *educate*

and *mould* public opinion, at least *Northern* public opinion, to not *care* whether slavery is voted *down* or voted *up*.

This shows exactly where we now *are;* and *partially* also, whither we are tending.

It will throw additional light on the latter, to go back, and run the mind over the string of historical facts already stated. Several things will *now* appear less *dark* and *mysterious* than they did *when* they were transpiring. The people were to be left "perfectly free" "subject only to the Constitution." What the *Constitution* had to do with it, outsiders could not *then* see. Plainly enough *now,* it was an exactly fitted *niche,* for the Dred Scott decision to afterwards come in, and declare the *perfect freedom* of the people, to be just no freedom at all.

Why was the amendment, expressly declaring the right of the people to exclude slavery, voted down? Plainly enough *now,* the adoption of it, would have spoiled the niche for the Dred Scott decision.

Why was the court decision held up? Why, even a Senator's individual opinion withheld, till *after* the Presidential election? Plainly enough *now,* the speaking out *then* would have damaged the *"perfectly free"* argument upon which the election was to be carried.

Why the *outgoing* President's felicitation on the indorsement? Why the delay of a reargument? Why the incoming President's *advance* exhortation in favor of the decision?

These things *look* like the cautious *patting* and *petting* a spirited horse, preparatory to mounting him, when it is dreaded that he may give the rider a fall.

And why the hasty after indorsements of the decision by the President and others?

We can not absolutely *know* that all these exact adaptations are the result of preconcert. But when we see a lot of framed timbers, different portions of which we know have been gotten out at different times and places and by different workmen—Stephen, Franklin, Roger and James, for instance—and when we see these timbers joined together, and see they exactly make the frame of a house or a mill, all the tenons and mortices exactly fitting, and all the lengths and proportions of the different pieces exactly adapted to their respective places, and not a piece too many or too few—not omitting even scaffolding—or, if a single piece be lacking, we can see the place in the frame exactly fitted and prepared to yet bring such piece in—in *such* a case, we find it impossible to not *believe* that Stephen and Franklin and Roger and James all understood one another from the beginning, and all worked upon a common *plan* or *draft* drawn up before the first lick was struck.

It should not be overlooked that, by the Nebraska bill, the people of a *State* as well as *Territory,* were to be left *"perfectly free"* *"subject only to the Constitution."*

Why mention a *State?* They were legislating for *territories,* and not *for* or *about* States. Certainly the people of a State *are* and *ought to be* subject to the Constitution of the United States; but why is mention of this *lugged* into this merely *territorial* law? Why are the people of a *territory* and the people of a *state* therein *lumped* together, and their relation to the Constitution therein treated as being *precisely* the same?

While the opinion of *the Court,* by Chief Justice Taney, in the Dred Scott case, and the separate opinions of all the concurring Judges, expressly declare that the Constitution of the United States neither permits Congress nor a Territorial legislature to exclude slavery from any United States territory, they all *omit* to declare whether or not the same Constitution permits a *state,* or the people of a State, to exclude it.

Possibly, this was a mere *omission;* but who can be *quite* sure, if McLean or Curtis had sought to get into the opinion a declaration of unlimited power in the people of a *state* to exclude slavery from their limits, just as Chase and Macy sought to get such declaration, in behalf of the people of a territory, into the Nebraska bill—I ask, who can be quite *sure* that it would not have been voted down, in the one case, as it had been in the other.

The nearest approach to the point of declaring the power of a State over slavery, is made by Judge Nelson. He approaches it more than once, using the precise idea, and *almost* the language too, of the Nebraska act. On one occasion his exact language is, "except in cases where the power is restrained by the Constitution of the United States, the law of the State is supreme over the subject of slavery within its jurisdiction."

In what *cases* the power of the *states is* so restrained by the U. S. Constitution, is left an *open* question, precisely as the same question, as to the restraint on the power of the *territories* was left open in the Nebraska act. Put *that* and *that* together, and we have another nice little niche, which we may, ere long, see filled with another Supreme Court decision, declaring that the Constitution of the United States does not permit a *state* to exclude slavery from its limits.

And this may especially be expected if the doctrine of "care not whether slavery be voted *down* or voted *up*," shall gain upon the public mind sufficiently to give promise that such a decision can be maintained when made.

Such a decision is all that slavery now lacks of being alike lawful in all the States.

Welcome or unwelcome, such decision *is* probably coming, and will soon be upon us, unless the power of the present political dynasty shall be met and overthrown.

We shall *lie down* pleasantly dreaming that the people of *Missouri* are on the verge of making their State *free;* and we shall *awake* to the *reality,* instead, that the *Supreme* Court has made *Illinois* a *slave* State.

To meet and overthrow the power of that dynasty, is the work now before all those who would prevent that consummation.

That is *what* we have to do.

But *how* can we best do it?

There are those who denounce us *openly* to their *own* friends, and yet whisper *us softly,* that *Senator Douglas* is the *aptest* instrument there is, with which to effect that object. *They* do *not* tell us, nor has *he* told us, that he *wishes* any such object to be effected. They wish us to *infer* all, from the facts, that he now has a little quarrel with the present head of the dynasty; and that he has regularly voted with us, on a single point, upon which, he and we, have never differed.

They remind us that *he* is a very *great man,* and that the largest of *us* are very small ones. Let this be granted. But "a *living dog* is better than a *dead lion.*" Judge Douglas, if not a *dead* lion *for this work,* is at least a *caged* and *toothless* one. How can he oppose the advances of slavery? He don't *care* anything about it. His avowed *mission is impressing* the "public heart" to *care* nothing about it.

A leading Douglas Democratic newspaper thinks Douglas' superior talent will be needed to resist the revival of the African slave trade.

Does Douglas believe an effort to revive that trade is approaching? He has not said so. Does he *really* think so? But if it is, how can he resist it? For years he has labored to prove it is a *sacred right* of white men to take negro slaves into the new territories. Can he possibly show that it is *less* a sacred right to *buy* them where they can be bought cheapest? And, unquestionably they can be bought *cheaper in Africa* than in *Virginia.*

He has done all in his power to reduce the whole question of slavery to one of a mere *right of property;* and as such, how can *he* oppose the foreign slave trade—how can he refuse that trade in that "property" shall be "perfectly free"—unless he does it as a *protection* to the home production? And as the home *producers* will probably not *ask* the protection, he will be wholly without a ground of opposition.

Senator Douglas holds, we know, that a man may rightfully be *wiser to-day* than he was *yesterday*—that he may rightfully *change* when he finds himself wrong.

But, can we for that reason, run ahead, and *infer* that he *will* make any particular change, of which he, himself, has given no intimation? Can we *safely* base *our* action upon any such *vague* inference?

Now, as ever, I wish to not *misrepresent* Judge Douglas' *position,* question his *motives,* or do ought that can be personally offensive to him.

Whenever, *if ever,* he and we can come together on *principle* so that *our great cause* may have assistance from *his great ability,* I hope to have interposed no adventitious obstacle.

But clearly, he is not *now* with us—he does not *pretend* to be—he does not *promise* to *ever* be.

Our cause, then, must be intrusted to, and conducted by its own undoubted friends—those whose hands are free, whose hearts are in the work—who *do care* for the result.

Two years ago the Republicans of the nation mustered over thirteen hundred thousand strong.

We did this under the single impulse of resistance to

a common danger, with every external circumstance against us.

Of *strange, discordant,* and even, *hostile* elements, we gathered from the four winds, and *formed* and fought the battle through, under the constant hot fire of a disciplined, proud, and pampered enemy.

Did we brave all *then,* to *falter* now?—*now*—when that same enemy is *wavering,* dissevered and belligerent?

The result is not doubtful. We shall not fail—if we stand firm, we shall not fail.

Wise councils may *accelerate* or *mistakes delay* it, but, sooner or later the victory is *sure* to come.

29. *The Negro Question:*

EXTRACTS FROM THE LINCOLN-DOUGLAS DEBATES, AUGUST TO OCTOBER, 1858

DOUGLAS, coming home to campaign for reelection, spoke at Chicago on July 9, 1858, and Lincoln was there to answer him the next evening. Later in the month, Lincoln proposed that they "divide time and address the same audiences" throughout the canvass. Douglas accepted the challenge only in part. He offered to meet Lincoln just seven times in various sections of the state. So debates were held at Ottawa, August 21; Freeport, August 27; Jonesboro, September 15; Charleston, September 18; Galesburg, October 7; Quincy, October 13; and Alton, October 15. The flavor of these memorable encounters can be recaptured most readily, perhaps, by following the arguments of both men on a single theme. In the series of excerpts presented here, the subject at issue is the legal and social status of the Negro in a nation dedicated to freedom by its white founders. Chief Justice Taney had declared that when the Constitution was adopted, Negroes "had no rights which the white man was bound to respect." Douglas agreed and accused Lincoln of advocating racial equality. Lincoln denied the charge in language that may sound harsh to the modern ear. For a politician of his place and time, however, there was boldness enough in his assertion that the rights enumerated in the Declaration of Independence belonged to men of all races.

DOUGLAS AT OTTAWA: We are told by Lincoln that he is utterly opposed to the Dred Scott decision, and will not submit to it, for the reason that he says it deprives the negro of the rights of privileges of citizenship. [Laughter and applause.] That is the first and main reason which he assigns for his warfare on the Supreme Court of the United States and its decision. I ask you, are you in favor of conferring upon the negro the rights and privileges of citizenship? ["No, no."] Do you desire to strike out of our State Constitution that clause which keeps slaves and free negroes out of the State, and allow the free negroes to flow in, ["never,"] and cover your prairies with black settlements? Do you desire to turn this beautiful State into a free negro colony, ["no, no,"] in order that when Missouri abolishes slavery she can send one hundred thousand emancipated slaves into Illinois, to become citizens and voters, on an equality with yourselves? ["Never," "no."] If you desire negro citizenship, if you desire to allow them to come into the State and settle with the white man, if you desire them to vote on an equality with yourselves, and to make them eligible to office, to serve on juries, and to adjudge your rights, then support Mr. Lincoln and the Black Republican party, who are in favor of the citizenship of the negro. ["Never, never."] For one, I am opposed to negro citizenship in any and every form. [Cheers.] I believe this government was made on the white basis. ["Good."] I believe it was made by white men, for the benefit of white men and their posterity for ever, and I am in favor of confining citizenship to white men, men of European birth and descent, instead of conferring it upon negroes, Indians and other inferior races. ["Good for you." "Douglas forever."]

Mr. Lincoln, following the example and lead of all the little Abolition orators, who go around and lecture in the basements of schools and churches, reads from the Declaration of Independence, that all men were created equal, and then asks how can you deprive a negro of that equality which God and the Declaration of Independence awards to him. He and they maintain that negro equality is guarantied by the laws of God, and that it is asserted in the Declaration of Independence. If they think so, of course they have a right to say so, and so vote. I do not question Mr. Lincoln's conscientious belief that the negro was made his equal, and hence is his brother, [laughter,] but for my own part, I do not regard the negro as my equal, and positively deny that he is my brother or any kin to me whatever.

LINCOLN AT OTTAWA: Anything that argues me into his idea of perfect social and political equality with the negro, is but a specious and fantastic arrangement of words, by which a man can prove a horse chestnut to be a chestnut horse. [Laughter.] I will say here, while upon this subject, that I have no purpose directly or indirectly to interfere with the institution of slavery in the States where it exists. I believe I have no lawful right to do so, and I have no inclination to do so. I have no purpose to introduce political and social equality between the white and the black races. There is a physical difference between the two, which in my judgment will probably forever forbid their living together upon the footing of perfect equality, and inasmuch as it becomes a necessity that there must be a difference, I, as well as Judge Douglas, am in favor of the race to which I belong, having the superior position. I have never said anything to the contrary, but I hold that notwithstanding all this, there is no reason in the world why the negro is not entitled to all the natural rights enumerated in the Declaration of Independence, the right to life, liberty and the pursuit of happiness. [Loud cheers.] I hold that he is as much entitled to these as the white man. I agree with Judge Douglas he is not my equal in many respects—certainly not in color, perhaps not in moral or intellectual endowment. But in the right to eat the bread, without leave of anybody else, which his own hand earns, *he is my equal and the equal of Judge Douglas, and the equal of every living man.* [Great applause.]

DOUGLAS AT FREEPORT: The last time I came here to make a speech, while talking from the stand to you, people of Freeport, as I am doing to-day, I saw a carriage and a magnificent one it was, drive up and take a position on the outside of the crowd; a beautiful young lady was sitting on the box seat, whilst Fred. Douglass and her mother reclined inside, and the owner of the carriage acted as driver. [Laughter, cheers, cries of right, what have you to say against it, &c.] I saw this in your own town. ["What of it."] All I have to say of it is this, that if you, Black Republicans, think that the negro ought to be on a social equality with your wives and daughters, and ride in a carriage with your wife, whilst you drive the team, you have a perfect right to do so. [Good, good, and cheers, mingled with hooting and cries of white, white.] I am told that one of Fred. Douglass' kinsmen, another rich black negro, is now traveling in this part of the State making speeches for his friend Lincoln as the champion of black men. ["White men, white men," and "what have you got to say against it." That's right, &c.] All I have to say on that subject is that those of you who believe that the negro is your equal and ought to be on an equality with you socially, politically, and legally; have a right to entertain those opinions, and of course will vote for Mr. Lincoln.

LINCOLN AT CHARLESTON: I will say then that I am not, nor ever have been in favor of bringing about in any way the social and political equality of the white and black races, [applause]—that I am not nor ever have been in favor of making voters or jurors of negroes, nor of qualifying them to hold office, nor to intermarry with white people; and I will say in addition to this that there is a physical difference between the white and black races which I believe will for ever forbid the two races living together on terms of social and political equality. And inasmuch as they cannot so live, while they do remain together there must be the position of superior and inferior, and I as much as any other man am in favor of having the superior position assigned to the white race. I say upon this occasion I do not perceive that because the white man is to have the superior position the negro should be denied everything. I do not understand that because I do not want a negro woman for a slave I must necessarily want her for a wife. [Cheers and laughter.] My understanding is that I can just let her alone. I am now in my fiftieth year, and I certainly never have had a black woman for either a slave or a wife. So it seems to me quite possible for us to get along without making either slaves or wives of negroes.

DOUGLAS AT GALESBURG: The signers of the Declaration of Independence never dreamed of the negro when they were writing that document. They referred to white men, to men of European birth and European descent, when they declared the equality of all men. I see a gentleman there in the crowd shaking his head. Let me remind him that when Thomas Jefferson wrote that document he was the owner, and so continued until his death, of a large number of slaves. Did he intend to say in that Declaration that his negro slaves, which he held and treated as property, were created his equals by Divine law, and that he was violating the law of God every day of his life by holding them as slaves? ["No, no."] It must be borne in mind that when that Declaration was put forth every one of the thirteen colonies were slaveholding colonies, and every man who signed that instrument represented a slaveholding constituency. Recollect, also, that no one of them emancipated his slaves, much less put them on an equality with himself, after he signed the Declaration. On the contrary, they all continued to hold their negroes as slaves during the revolutionary war. Now, do you believe—are you willing to have it said—that every man who signed the Declaration of Independence declared the negro his equal, and then was hypocrite enough to continue to hold him as a slave, in violation of what he believed to be the divine law? ["No, no."] And yet when you say that the Declaration of Independence includes the negro, you charge the signers of it with hypocrisy.

I say to you, frankly, that in my opinion this government was made by our fathers on the white basis. It was made by white men for the benefit of white men and their posterity forever, and was intended to be administered by white men in all time to come. [That's so, and cheers.] But while I hold that under our constitution and political system the negro is not a citizen, cannot be a citizen, and ought not to be a citizen, it does not follow by any means that he should be a slave. On the contrary it does follow that the negro, as an inferior race, ought to possess every

right, every privilege, every immunity which he can safely
exercise consistent with the safety of the society in which
he lives. [That's so, and cheers.] Humanity requires, and
Christianity commands that you shall extend to every inferior being, and every dependent being, all the privileges,
immunities and advantages which can be granted to them
consistent with the safety of society. If you ask me the
nature and extent of these privileges, I answer that that
is a question which the people of each State must decide
for themselves.

LINCOLN AT GALESBURG: The Judge has alluded to the
Declaration of Independence, and insisted that negroes are
not included in that Declaration; and that it is a slander
upon the framers of that instrument, to suppose that negroes were meant therein; and he asks you: Is it possible
to believe that Mr. Jefferson, who penned the immortal
paper, could have supposed himself applying the language
of that instrument to the negro race, and yet held a portion of that race in slavery? Would he not at once have
freed them? I only have to remark upon this part of the
Judge's speech (and that, too, very briefly, for I shall not
detain myself, or you, upon that point for any great length
of time,) that I believe the entire records of the world,
from the date of the Declaration of Independence up to
within three years ago, may be searched in vain for one
single affirmation, from one single man, that the negro
was not included in the Declaration of Independence. I
think I may defy Judge Douglas to show that he ever said
so, that Washington ever said so, that any President ever
said so, that any member of Congress ever said so, or that
any living man upon the whole earth ever said so, until the
necessities of the present policy of the Democratic party,
in regard to slavery, had to invent that affirmation. [Tre-
mendous applause.] And I will remind Judge Douglas and
this audience, that while Mr. Jefferson was the owner of
slaves, as undoubtedly he was, in speaking upon this very
subject, he used the strong language that "he trembled for
his country when he remembered that God was just;"
and I will offer the highest premium in my power to Judge
Douglas if he will show that he, in all his life, ever uttered a sentiment at all akin to that of Jefferson. . . . But

the Judge will have it that if we do not confess that there is a sort of inequality between the white and black races, which justifies us in making them slaves, we must, then, insist that there is a degree of equality that requires us to make them our wives. . . . I have all the while maintained, that in so far as it should be insisted that there was an equality between the white and black races that should produce a perfect social and political equality, it was an impossibility. This you have seen in my printed speeches, and with it I have said, that in their right to "life, liberty and the pursuit of happiness," as proclaimed in that old Declaration, the inferior races are our equals. [Long-continued cheering.] And these declarations I have constantly made in reference to the abstract moral question, to contemplate and consider when we are legislating about any new country which is not already cursed with the actual presence of the evil—slavery. I have never manifested any impatience with the necessities that spring from the actual presence of black people amongst us, and the actual existence of slavery amongst us where it does already exist; but I have insisted that, in legislating for new countries, where it does not exist, there is no just rule other than that of moral and abstract right!

DOUGLAS AT QUINCY: I quoted from his Chicago speech to prove that he held one set of principles up north among the abolitionists, and from his Charleston speech to prove that he held another set down at Charleston and in southern Illinois. In his answer to this charge, he ignores entirely his Chicago speech, and merely argues that he said the same thing which he said at Charleston at another place. If he did, it follows that he has twice, instead of once, held one creed in one part of the State and a different creed in another part. . . . Mr. Lincoln told the abolitionists of Chicago that if the Declaration of Independence did not declare that the negro was created by the Almighty the equal of the white man, that you ought to take that instrument and tear out the clause which says that all men were created equal. . . . You know that in his Charleston speech, an extract from which he has read, he declared that the negro belongs to an inferior race; is physically inferior to the white man, and should always be kept in an inferior position. . . . I do not question that he said at Ottawa what he quoted, but that only convicts him further, by proving that he has twice contradicted himself instead of once. ["Good," and applause.] Let me ask him why he cannot avow his principles the same in the North as in the South—the same in every county, if he has a conviction that they are just?

LINCOLN AT QUINCY: Judge Douglas, in reply to what I have said about having upon a previous occasion made the speech at Ottawa as the one he took an extract from, at Charleston, says it only shows that I practiced the deception twice. Now, my friends, are any of you obtuse enough to swallow that? ["No, no, we're not such fools."] Judge Douglas had said I had made a speech at Charleston that I would not make up north, and I turned around and answered him by showing I *had* made that same speech up north—had made it at Ottawa—made it in his hearing—made it in *the* Abolition District—in Lovejoy's District—in the personal presence of Lovejoy himself—in the same atmosphere exactly in which I had made my Chicago speech of which he complains so much. . . . I maintain that you may take Judge Douglas' quotations from my Chicago speech, and from my Charleston speech, and the Galesburg speech,—in his speech of to-day, and compare them over, and I am willing to trust them with you upon his proposition that they show rascality or double dealing. I deny that they do.

DOUGLAS AT ALTON: I hold that the signers of the Declaration of Independence had no reference to negroes at all when they declared all men to be created equal. They did not mean negro, nor the savage Indians, nor the Fejee Islanders, nor any other barbarous race. They were speaking of white men. . . . I hold that this government was established on the white basis. It was established by white men for the benefit of white men and their posterity forever, and should be administered by white men, and none others. But it does not follow, by any means, that merely because the negro is not a citizen, and merely because he is not our equal, that, therefore, he should be a slave. On the contrary, it does follow, that we ought to extend to the negro race, and to all other dependent races all the rights, all the privileges, and all the immunities which they can exercise consistently with the safety of society. Humanity requires that we should give them all these privileges; christianity commands that we should extend those privileges to them. The question then arises what are those privileges, and what is the nature and extent of them. My answer is that that is a question which each State must answer for itself. We in Illinois have decided it for ourselves. We tried slavery, kept it up for twelve years, and finding that it was not profitable we abolished it for that reason, and became a free State. We adopted in its stead the policy that a negro in this State shall not be a slave and shall not be a citizen. We have a right to adopt that policy. For my part I think it is a wise and sound policy for us. . . . So with Kentucky. Let Kentucky adopt a policy to suit herself. If we do not like it we will keep away from it, and if she does not like ours let her stay at home, mind her own business and let us alone. If the people of all the States will act on that great principle, and each State mind its own business, attend to its own affairs, take care of its own negroes and not meddle with its neighbors, then there will be peace between the North and the South, the East and the West, throughout the whole Union. [Cheers.]

LINCOLN AT ALTON: I assert that Judge Douglas and all his friends may search the whole records of the country, and it will be a matter of great astonishment to me if they shall be able to find that one human being three years ago had ever uttered the astounding sentiment that the term "all men" in the Declaration did not include the negro. Do not let me be misunderstood. I know that more than three years ago there were men who, finding this assertion constantly in the way of their schemes to bring about the ascendancy and perpetuation of slavery, *denied the truth of it.* I know that Mr. Calhoun and all the politicians of his school denied the truth of the Declaration. . . . But I say, with a perfect knowledge of all this hawking at the Declaration without directly attacking it, that three years ago there never had lived a man who had ventured to assail it in the sneaking way of pretending to believe it and then asserting it did not include the negro. . . . And when this new principle—this new proposition that no human being ever thought of three years ago,—is brought forward, *I combat it* as having an evil tendency, if not an evil design; I combat it as having a tendency to dehumanize the negro—to take away from him the right of ever striving to be a man. I combat it as being one of the thousand things constantly done in these days to prepare the public mind to make property, and nothing but property of the *negro in all the States of this Union.*

DOUGLAS AT ALTON: I care more for the great principle of self-government, the right of the people to rule, than I do for all the negroes in Christendom. [Cheers.] I would not endanger the perpetuity of this Union. I would not blot out the great inalienable rights of the white men for all the negroes that ever existed. [Renewed applause.] Hence, I say, let us maintain this government on the principles that our fathers made it, recognizing the right of each State to keep slavery as long as its people determine, or to abolish it when they please.

30. The Freeport Doctrine:
EXTRACTS FROM THE LINCOLN-DOUGLAS DE-BATES, AUGUST TO OCTOBER, 1858

THE central issue of the debates was slavery in the territories. Here the Dred Scott decision, besides outlawing the first principle of Republicanism, had raised serious doubts about the constitutionality of popular sovereignty. For if Congress lacked the power to prohibit slavery in the territories, how could it confer such authority upon subordinate bodies, the territorial legislatures? At Freeport, Lincoln formally posed this question. Douglas, endeavoring to reconcile his "great principle" with the Court's decision, replied that the people of a territory would always be able to exclude slavery by passing laws unfriendly to its existence. Historians have tended to exaggerate the consequences of this "Freeport doctrine." Nevertheless, it did help perpetuate a breach that had already appeared in the Democratic party as a result of the furious Lecompton controversy.

LINCOLN AT FREEPORT: Can the people of a United States Territory, in any lawful way, against the wish of any citizen of the United States, exclude slavery from its limits prior to the formation of a State Constitution?

DOUGLAS AT FREEPORT: I answer emphatically, as Mr. Lincoln has heard me answer a hundred times from every stump in Illinois, that in my opinion the people of a territory can, by lawful means, exclude slavery from their limits prior to the formation of a State Constitution. [Enthusiastic Applause.] Mr. Lincoln knew that I had answered that question over and over again. He heard me argue the Nebraska bill on that principle all over the State in 1854, in 1855 and in 1856, and he has no excuse for pretending to be in doubt as to my position on that question. It matters not what way the Supreme Court may hereafter decide as to the abstract question whether slavery may or may not go into a territory under the constitution, the people have the lawful means to introduce it or exclude it as they please, for the reason that slavery cannot exist a day or an hour anywhere, unless it is supported by local police regulations. [Right, right.] Those police regulations can only be established by the local legislature, and if the people are opposed to slavery they will elect representatives to that body who will by unfriendly legislation effectually prevent the introduction of it into their midst. If, on the contrary, they are for it, their legislation will favor its extension. Hence, no matter what the decision of the Supreme Court may be on that abstract question, still the right of the people to make a slave territory or a free territory is perfect and complete under the Nebraska bill.

LINCOLN AT JONESBORO: In the Senate of the United States, in 1856, Judge Trumbull in a speech, substantially if not directly, put the same interrogatory to Judge Douglas, as to whether the people of a Territory had the lawful power to exclude slavery prior to the formation of a constitution? Judge Douglas then answered at considerable length, and his answer will be found in the *Congressional Globe,* under date of June 9th, 1856. The Judge said that whether the people could exclude slavery prior to the formation of a constitution or not *was a question to be decided by the Supreme Court.* . . . Has not the Supreme

Court decided that question? When he now says the people *may* exclude slavery, does he not make it a question for the people? Does he not virtually shift his ground and say that it is *not* a question for the Court, but for the people? This is a very simple proposition—a very plain and naked one. It seems to me that there is no difficulty in deciding it. In a variety of ways he said that it was a question for the Supreme Court. He did not stop then to tell us that whatever the Supreme Court decides the people can by withholding necessary "police regulations" keep slavery out. He did not make any such answer. I submit to you now, whether the new state of the case has not induced the Judge to sheer away from his original ground. [Applause.] Would not this be the impression of every fair-minded man?

I hold that the proposition that slavery cannot enter a new country without police regulations is historically false. It is not true at all. I hold that the history of this country shows that the institution of slavery was originally planted upon this continent *without* these "police regulations" which the Judge now thinks necessary for the actual establishment of it. Not only so, but is there not another fact—how came this Dred Scott decision to be made? It was made upon the case of a negro being taken and actually held in slavery in Minnesota Territory, claiming his freedom because the act of Congress prohibited his being so held there. *Will the Judge pretend that Dred Scott was not held there without police regulations?* There is at least one matter of record as to his having been held in slavery in the Territory, not only without police regulations, but in the teeth of Congressional legislation supposed to be valid at the time. This shows that there is vigor enough in Slavery to plant itself in a new country even against unfriendly legislation. It takes not only law but the *enforcement* of law to keep it out. That is the history of this country upon the subject.

DOUGLAS AT JONESBORO: My doctrine is, that even taking Mr. Lincoln's view that the decision recognizes the right of a man to carry his slaves into the territories of the United States, if he pleases, yet after he gets there he needs affirmative law to make that right of any value. The same doctrine not only applies to slave property, but all other kinds of property. Chief Justice Taney places it upon the ground that slave property is on an equal footing with other property. Suppose one of your merchants should move to Kansas and open a liquor store; he has a right to take groceries and liquors there, but the mode of selling them, and the circumstances under which they shall be sold, and all the remedies must be prescribed by local legislation, and if that is unfriendly it will drive him out just as effectually as if there was a constitutional provision against the sale of liquor. So the absence of local legislation to encourage and support slave property in a territory excludes it practically just as effectually as if there was a positive constitutional provision against it. Hence, I assert that under the Dred Scott decision you cannot maintain slavery a day in a territory where there is an unwilling people and unfriendly legislation.

LINCOLN AT QUINCY: We will say you are a member of the Territorial Legislature, and like Judge Douglas, you believe that the right to take and hold slaves there is a constitutional right. The first thing you do is to *swear you will support the Constitution* and all rights guaranteed therein; that you will, whenever your neighbor needs your legislation to support his constitutional rights, not withhold that legislation. If you withhold that necessary legislation for the support of the Constitution and constitutional rights, do you not commit perjury? [Cries of "Yes."] I ask every sensible man, if that is not so? ["Yes, yes"—"That's a fact."] That is undoubtedly just so, say what you please. Now that is precisely what Judge Douglas says, that this is a constitutional right. Does the Judge mean to say that the Territorial Legislature in legislating may by withholding necessary laws, or by passing unfriendly laws, *nullify that constitutional right*? Does he mean to say that? Does he mean to ignore the proposition so long known and well established in the law, that what you cannot do directly, you cannot do indirectly? Does he mean that? The truth about the matter is this: Judge Douglas has sung paeans to his "Popular Sovereignty" doctrine until his Supreme Court co-operating with him has *squatted* his Squatter Sovereignty out. [Uproarious laughter and applause.] But he will keep up this species of humbuggery about Squatter

Sovereignty. He has at last invented this sort of *do nothing Sovereignty*—[renewed laughter]—that the people may exclude slavery by a sort of "Sovereignty" that is exercised by doing nothing at all. [Continued laughter.] Is not that running his Popular Sovereignty down awfully? [Laughter.] Has it not got down as thin as the homoeopathic soup that was made by boiling the shadow of a pigeon that had starved to death? [Roars of laughter and cheering.]

DOUGLAS AT ALTON: I answer specifically if you want a further answer, and say that while under the decision of the Supreme Court, as recorded in the opinion of Chief Justice Taney, slaves are property like all other property and can be carried into territory of the United States the same as any other description of property, yet when you get them there they are subject to the local law of the territory just like all other property. You will find in a recent speech delivered by that able and eloquent statesman, Hon. Jefferson Davis, at Bangor, Maine, that he took the same view of this subject that I did in my Freeport speech.... You will also find that the distinguished Speaker of the present House of Representatives, Hon. Jas. L. Orr, construed the Kansas and Nebraska bill in this same way in 1856, and also that great intellect of the South, Alex. H. Stephens, put the same construction upon it in Congress that I did in my Freeport speech. The whole South are rallying to the support of the doctrine that if the people of a Territory want slavery they have a right to have it, and if they do not want it that no power on earth can force it upon them. I hold that there is no principle on earth more sacred to all the friends of freedom than that which says that no institution, no law, no constitution, should be forced on an unwilling people contrary to their wishes; and I assert that the Kansas and Nebraska bill contains that principle.

LINCOLN AT ALTON: Let me take the gentleman who looks me in the face before me, and let us suppose that he is a member of the Territorial Legislature. The first thing he will do will be to swear that he will support the Constitution of the United States. His neighbor by his side in the Territory has slaves and needs Territorial legislation to enable him to enjoy that constitutional right. Can he withhold the legislation which his neighbor needs for the enjoyment of a right which is fixed in his favor in the Constitution of the United States which he has sworn to support? Can he withhold it without violating his oath? And more especially, can he pass unfriendly legislation to violate his oath? Why this is a *monstrous* sort of talk about the Constitution of the United States! [Great applause.] *There has never been as outlandish or lawless a doctrine from the mouth of any respectable man on earth.* . . . I say if that Dred Scott decision is correct then the right to hold slaves in a Territory is equally a constitutional right with the right of a slaveholder to have his runaway returned. No one can show the distinction between them. The one is express, so that we cannot deny it. The other is construed to be in the constitution, so that he who believes the decision to be correct believes in the right. And the man who argues that by unfriendly legislation, in spite of that constitutional right, slavery may be driven from the Territories, cannot avoid furnishing an argument by which Abolitionists may deny the obligation to return fugitives, and claim the power to pass laws unfriendly to the right of the slaveholder to reclaim his fugitive. I do not know how such an argument may strike a popular assembly like this, but I defy anybody to go before a body of men whose minds are educated to estimating evidence and reasoning, and show that there is an iota of difference between the constitutional right to reclaim a fugitive, and the constitutional right to hold a slave, in a Territory, provided this Dred Scott decision is correct. [Cheers.] I defy any man to make an argument that will justify unfriendly legislation to deprive a slaveholder of his right to hold his slave in a Territory, that will not equally, in all its length, breadth and thickness furnish an argument for nullifying the fugitive slave law. Why there is not such an Abolitionist in the nation as Douglas, after all.

31. Illegal Voters:
LETTER TO NORMAN B. JUDD, OCTOBER 20, 1858

THE senatorial race was actually a contest for control of the state legislature, and the outcome depended primarily upon the returns in a belt of doubtful counties across the middle of Illinois. Republican leaders feared that the Democrats would import large numbers of illegal voters, especially Irish railroad workers, into the critical districts and thus carry the election by fraud. Lincoln discussed the problem in this letter to Norman B. Judd, the Republican state chairman.

Rushville, Oct. 20, 1858

Hon. N. B. Judd

My dear Sir: I now have a high degree of confidence that we shall succeed, if we are not over-run with fraudulent votes to a greater extent than usual. On alighting from the cars and walking three squares at Naples on Monday, I met about fifteen Celtic gentlemen, with black carpetsacks in their hands.

I learned that they had crossed over from the Rail-road in Brown county, but where they were going no one could tell. They dropped in about the doggeries, and were still hanging about when I left. At Brown County yesterday I was told that about four hundred of the same sort were to be brought into Schuyler, before the election, to work on some new Railroad; but on reaching here I find Bagby thinks that is not so.

What I most dread is that they will introduce into the doubtful districts numbers of men who are legal voters in all respects except *residence* and who will swear to residence and thus put it beyond our power to exclude them. They can & I fear will swear falsely on that point, because they know it is next to impossible to convict them of Perjury upon it.

Now the great remaining part of the campaign, is finding a way to head this thing off. Can it be done at all?

I have a bare suggestion. When there is a known body of these voters, could not a true man, of the *"detective"* class, be introduced among them in disguise, who could, at the nick of time, control their votes? Think this over. It would be a great thing, when this trick is attempted upon us, to have the saddle come up on the other horse.

I have talked, more fully than I can write, to Mr. Scripps, and he will talk to you.

If we can head off the fraudulent votes we shall carry the day.

Yours as ever,

A. Lincoln

32. *The Principles of Jefferson:*
LETTER TO HENRY L. PIERCE AND OTHERS,
APRIL 6, 1859

DOUGLAS won reelection by a narrow margin. Yet the campaign had raised Lincoln to national prominence. He found himself increasingly in demand as a speaker and even mentioned as a presidential possibility. This letter to several Boston Republicans was published in a number of party newspapers.

Springfield, Ills.
April 6, 1859

Messrs. Henry L. Pierce, & others.
Gentlemen:

Your kind note inviting me to attend a Festival in Boston, on the 13th. Inst. in honor of the birth-day of Thomas Jefferson, was duly received. My engagements are such that I can not attend.

Bearing in mind that about seventy years ago, two great political parties were first formed in this country, that Thomas Jefferson was the head of one of them, and Boston the head-quarters of the other, it is both curious and interesting that those supposed to descend politically from the party opposed to Jefferson, should now be celebrating his birth-day in their own original seat of empire, while those claiming political descent from him have nearly ceased to breathe his name everywhere.

Remembering too, that the Jefferson party were formed upon their supposed superior devotion to the *personal* rights of men, holding the rights of *property* to be secondary only, and greatly inferior, and then assuming that the so-called democracy of to-day, are the Jefferson, and their opponents, the anti-Jefferson parties, it will be equally interesting to note how completely the two have changed hands as to the principle upon which they were originally supposed to be divided.

The democracy of to-day hold the *liberty* of one man to be absolutely nothing, when in conflict with another man's right of *property*. Republicans, on the contrary, are for both the *man* and the *dollar;* but in cases of conflict, the man *before* the dollar.

I remember once being much amused at seeing two partially intoxicated men engage in a fight with their great-coats on, which fight, after a long, and rather harmless contest, ended in each having fought himself *out* of his own coat, and *into* that of the other. If the two leading parties of this day are really identical with the two in the days of Jefferson and Adams, they have performed about the same feat as the two drunken men.

But soberly, it is now no child's play to save the principles of Jefferson from total overthrow in this nation.

One would start with great confidence that he could convince any sane child that the simpler propositions of Euclid are true; but, nevertheless, he would fail, utterly, with one who should deny the definitions and axioms. The principles of Jefferson are the definitions and axioms of free society. And yet they are denied, and evaded, with no small show of success. One dashingly calls them "glittering generalities"; another bluntly calls them "self evident lies"; and still others insidiously argue that they apply only to "superior races."

These expressions, differing in form, are identical in object and effect—the supplanting the principles of free government, and restoring those of classification, caste, and legitimacy. They would delight a convocation of crowned heads, plotting against the people. They are the van-guard—the miners, and sappers—of returning despotism. We must repulse them, or they will subjugate us.

This is a world of compensations; and he who would *be* no slave, must consent to *have* no slave. Those who deny freedom to others, deserve it not for themselves; and, under a just God, can not long retain it.

All honor to Jefferson—to the man who, in the concrete pressure of a struggle for national independence by a single people, had the coolness, forecast, and capacity to introduce into a merely revolutionary document, an abstract truth, applicable to all men and all times, and so to embalm it there, that to-day, and in all coming days, it shall be a rebuke and a stumbling-block to the very harbingers of re-appearing tyrany and oppression. Your obedient Servant,

A. Lincoln—

33. *Insidious Popular Sovereignty:*
SPEECH AT COLUMBUS, OHIO, SEPTEMBER 16, 1859

DURING the latter part of 1859, Lincoln spoke at political meetings in Illinois, Iowa, Ohio, Indiana, Wisconsin, and Kansas. His most important expedition was into Ohio, where Republican leaders summoned him to answer a series of speeches by Douglas. Stopping first at Columbus in this afterpiece to the great debates, Lincoln resumed his assault upon the doctrine of popular sovereignty. Two extensive passages from the speech are reproduced here.

The Giant himself has been here recently. [Laughter.] I have seen a brief report of his speech. If it were otherwise unpleasant to me to introduce the subject of the negro as a topic for discussion, I might be somewhat relieved by the fact that he dealt exclusively in that subject while he was here. I shall, therefore, without much hesitation or diffidence, enter upon this subject.

The American people, on the first day of January, 1854, found the African slave trade prohibited by a law of Congress. In a majority of the States of this Union, they found African slavery, or any other sort of slavery, prohibited by State constitutions. They also found a law existing, supposed to be valid, by which slavery was excluded from almost all the territory the United States then owned. This was the condition of the country, with reference to the institution of slavery, on the 1st of January, 1854. A few days after that, a bill was introduced into Congress, which ran through its regular course in the two branches of the National Legislature, and finally passed into a law in the month of May, by which the act of Congress prohibiting slavery from going into the territories of the United States was repealed. In connection with the law itself, and, in fact, in the terms of the law, the then existing prohibition was not only repealed, but there was a declaration of a purpose on the part of Congress never thereafter to exercise any power that they might have, real or supposed, to prohibit the extension or spread of slavery. This was a very great change; for the law thus repealed was of more than thirty years' standing. Following rapidly upon the heels of this action of Congress, a decision of the Supreme Court is made, by which it is declared that Congress, if it desires to prohibit the spread of slavery into the territories, has no constitutional power to do so. Not only so, but that decision lays down principles, which, if pushed to their logical conclusion—I say pushed to their logical conclusion—would decide that the constitutions of the Free States, forbidding slavery, are themselves unconstitutional. Mark me, I do not say the judge[s?] said this, and let no man say that I affirm the judge[s?] used these words; but I only say it is my opinion that what they did say, if pressed to its logical conclusion, will inevitably result thus. [Cries of "Good! good!"]

Looking at these things, the Republican party, as I understand its principles and policy, believe that there is great danger of the institution of slavery being spread out and extended, until it is ultimately made alike lawful in all the States of this Union; so believing, to prevent that incidental and ultimate consummation, is the original and chief purpose of the Republican organization. I say "chief purpose" of the Republican organization; for it is certainly true that if the national House shall fall into the hands of the Republicans, they will have to attend to all the other matters of national house-keeping, as well as this. This chief and real purpose of the Republican party is eminently conservative. It proposes nothing save and except to restore this government to its original tone in regard to this element of slavery, and there to maintain it, looking for no further change, in reference to it, than that which the original framers of the government themselves expected and looked forward to.

The chief danger to this purpose of the Republican party is not just now the revival of the African slave trade, or the passage of a Congressional slave code, or the declaring of a second Dred Scott decision, making slavery lawful in all the States. These are not pressing us just now. They are not quite ready yet. The authors of these measures know that we are too strong for them; but they will be upon us in due time, and we will be grappling with them hand to hand, if they are not now headed off. They are not now the chief danger to the purpose of the Republican organization; but the most imminent danger that now threatens that purpose is that insidious Douglas Popular Sovereignty. This is the miner and sapper. While it does not propose to revive the African slave trade, nor to pass a slave code, nor to make a second Dred Scott decision, it is preparing us for the onslaught and charge of these ultimate enemies when they shall be ready to come on and the word of command for them to advance shall be given. I say this Douglas Popular Sovereignty—for there is a broad distinction, as I now understand it, between that article and a genuine popular sovereignty.

I believe there is a genuine popular sovereignty. I think a definition of genuine popular sovereignty, in the abstract, would be about this: That each man shall do precisely as he pleases with himself, and with all those things which exclusively concern him. Applied to government, this principle would be, that a general government shall do all those things which pertain to it, and all the local governments shall do precisely as they please in respect to those matters which exclusively concern them. I understand that this government of the United States, under which we live, is based upon this principle; and I am misunderstood if it is supposed that I have any war to make upon that principle.

Now, what is Judge Douglas' Popular Sovereignty? It is, as a principle, no other than that, if one man chooses to make a slave of another man, neither that other man nor anybody else has a right to object. [Cheers and laughter.] Applied in government, as he seeks to apply it, it is this: If, in a new territory into which a few people are beginning to enter for the purpose of making their homes, they choose to either exclude slavery from their limits, or to establish it there, however one or the other may affect the persons to be enslaved, or the infinitely greater number of persons who are afterward to inhabit that territory, or the other members of the families of communities, of which they are but an incipient member, or the general head of the family of States as parent of all—however their action may affect one or the other of these, there is no power or right to interfere. That is Douglas' popular sovereignty applied.

•　　•　　•　　•　　•

The Judge says that the people of the territories have the right, by his principle, to have slaves, if they want them. Then I say that the people of Georgia have the right to buy slaves in Africa, if they want them, and I defy any man on earth to show any distinction between the two things—to show that the one is either more wicked or more unlawful; to show, on original principles, that one is better or worse than the other; or to show by the constitution, that one differs a whit from the other. He will tell me, doubtless, that there is no constitutional provision against people taking slaves into the new territories, and I tell him that there is equally no constitutional provision against buying slaves in Africa. He will tell you that a people, in the exercise of popular sovereignty, ought to do as they please about that thing, and have slaves if they want them; and I tell you that the people of Georgia are as much entitled to popular sovereignty and to buy slaves in Africa, if they want them, as the people of the territory are to have slaves if they want them. I ask any man, dealing honestly with himself, to point out a distinction.

I have recently seen a letter of Judge Douglas', in which without stating that to be the object, he doubtless endeavors, to make a distinction between the two. He says he is unalterably opposed to the repeal of the laws against the African Slave trade. And why? He then seeks to give a reason that would not apply to his popular sovereignty in the territories. What is that reason? "The abolition of the African slave trade is a compromise of the constitution." I deny it. There is no truth in the proposition that the abolition of the African slave trade is a compromise of the constitution. No man can put his finger on anything in the constitution, or on the line of history which shows it. It is a mere barren assertion, made simply for the purpose of getting up a distinction between the revival of the African slave trade and his "great principle."

At the time the constitution of the United States was adopted it was expected that the slave trade would be abolished. I should assert, and insist upon that, if Judge Douglas denied it. But I know that it was equally expected that slavery would be excluded from the territories and I can show by history, that in regard to these two things, public opinion was exactly alike, while in regard to positive action, there was more done in the Ordinance of '87, to resist the spread of slavery than was ever done to abolish the foreign slave trade. Lest I be misunderstood, I say again that at the time of the formation of the constitution, public expectation was that the slave trade would be abolished, but no more so than the spread of slavery in the territories should be restrained. They stand alike, except that in the Ordinance of '87 there was a mark left by public opinion showing that it was more committed against the spread of slavery in the territories than against the foreign slave trade.

Compromise! What word of compromise was there about it. Why the public sense was then in favor of the abolition of the slave trade; but there was at the time a very great commercial interest involved in it and extensive capital in that branch of trade. There were doubtless the incipient stages of improvement in the South in the way of farming, dependent on the slave trade, and they made a proposition to the Congress to abolish the trade after allowing it twenty years, a sufficient time for the capital and commerce engaged in it to be transferred to other channels. They made no provision that it should be abolished [in?] twenty years; I do not doubt that they expected it would be; but they made no bargain about it. The public sentiment left no doubt in the minds of any that it would be done away. I repeat there is nothing in the history of those times, in favor of that matter being a *compromise* of the Constitution. It was the public expectation at the time, manifested in a thousand ways, that the spread of slavery should also be restricted.

Then I say if this principle is established, that there is no wrong in slavery, and whoever wants it has a right to have it, is a matter of dollars and cents, a sort of question as to how they shall deal with brutes, that between us and the negro here there is no sort of question, but that at the South the question is between the negro and the crocodile. That is all. It is a mere matter of policy; there is a perfect right according to interest to do just as you please—when this is done, where this doctrine prevails, the miners and sappers will have formed public opinion for the slave trade. They will be ready for Jeff. Davis and Stephens and other leaders of that company, to sound the bugle for the revival of the slave trade, for the second Dred Scott decision, for the flood of slavery to be poured over the free States, while we shall be here tied down and helpless and run over like sheep.

It is to be a part and parcel of this same idea, to say to men who want to adhere to the Democratic party, who have always belonged to that party, and are only looking about for some excuse to stick to it, but nevertheless hate slavery, that Douglas' Popular Sovereignty is as good a way as any to oppose slavery. They allow themselves to be persuaded easily in accordance with their previous dispositions, into this belief, that it is about as good a way of opposing slavery as any, and we can do that without straining our old party ties or breaking up old political associations. We can do so without being called negro worshippers. We can do that without being subjected to the jibes and sneers that are so readily thrown out in place of argument where no argument can be found; so let us stick to this Popular Sovereignty—this insidious Popular Sovereignty. Now let me call your attention to one thing that has really happened, which shows this gradual and steady debauching of public opinion, this course of preparation for the revival of the slave trade, for the territorial slave code, and the new Dred Scott decision that is to carry slavery into the free States. Did you ever five years ago, hear of anybody in the world saying that the negro had no share in the Declaration of National Independence; that it did not mean negroes at all; and when "all men" were spoken of negroes were not included?

I am satisfied that five years ago that proposition was not put upon paper by any living being anywhere. I have been unable at any time to find a man in an audience who would declare that he had ever known any body saying so five years ago. But last year there was not a Douglas popular sovereign in Illinois who did not say it. Is there one in Ohio but declares his firm belief that the Declaration of Independence did not mean negroes at all? I do not know how this is; I have not been here much; but I presume you are very much alike everywhere. Then I suppose that all now express the belief that the Declaration of Independence never did mean negroes. I call upon one of them to say that he said it five years ago.

If you think that now, and did not think it then, the next thing that strikes me is to remark that there has been a *change* wrought in you [laughter and applause], and a very significant change it is, being no less than changing the negro, in your estimation, from the rank of a man to that of a brute. They are taking him down, and placing him, when spoken of, among reptiles and crocodiles, as Judge Douglas himself expresses it.

Is not this change wrought in your minds a very important change? Public opinion in this country is everything. In a nation like ours this popular sovereignty and squatter sovereignty have already wrought a change in the public mind to the extent I have stated. There is no man in this crowd who can contradict it.

Now, if you are opposed to slavery honestly, as much

as anybody I ask you to note that fact, and the like of which is to follow, to be plastered on, layer after layer, until very soon you are prepared to deal with the negro everywhere as with the brute. If public sentiment has not been debauched already to this point, a new turn of the screw in that direction is all that is wanting; and this is constantly being done by the teachers of this insidious popular sovereignty. You need but one or two turns further until your minds, now ripening under these teachings will be ready for all these things, and you will receive and support, or submit to, the slave trade; revived with all its horrors; a slave code enforced in our territories, and a new Dred Scott decision to bring slavery up into the very heart of the free North. This, I must say, is but carrying out those words prophetically spoken by Mr. Clay, many, many years ago. I believe more than thirty years when he told an audience that if they would repress all tendencies to liberty and ultimate emancipation, they must go back to the era of our independence and muzzle the cannon which thundered its annual joyous return on the Fourth of July; they must blow out the moral lights around us; they must penetrate the human soul and eradicate the love of liberty; but until they did these things, and others eloquently enumerated by him, they could not repress all tendencies to ultimate emancipation.

I ask attention to the fact that in a pre-eminent degree these popular sovereigns are at this work; blowing out the moral lights around us; teaching that the negro is no longer a man but a brute; that the Declaration has nothing to do with him; that he ranks with the crocodile and the reptile; that man, with body and soul, is a matter of dollars and cents. I suggest to this portion of the Ohio Republicans, or Democrats if there be any present, the serious consideration of this fact, that there is now going on among you a steady process of debauching public opinion on this subject. With this my friends, I bid you adieu.

34. The Emerging Candidate:

LETTER TO WILLIAM E. FRAZER, NOVEMBER 1, 1859

IF he had not done so before, Lincoln began to take himself seriously as a presidential candidate in the closing months of 1859. William E. Frazer of Pennsylvania had written to propose a Republican ticket headed by Senator Simon Cameron, with Lincoln as the vice-presidential nominee. Lincoln's reply was nicely calculated to be noncommittal without giving offense.

Springfield, Ills.
Nov. 1, 1859

W. E. Frazer, Esq.
Dear Sir:
Yours of the 24th. ult. was forwarded to me from Chicago. It certainly is important to secure Pennsylvania for the Republicans, in the next Presidential contest; and not unimportant to, also, secure Illinois. As to the ticket you name, I shall be heartily for it, *after* it shall have been fairly nominated by a Republican national convention; and I can not be committed to it *before*. For my single self, I have enlisted for the permanent success of the Republican cause; and, for this object, I shall labor faithfully in the ranks, unless, as I think not probable, the judgment of the party shall assign me a different position. If the Republicans of the great State of Pennsylvania, shall present Mr. Cameron as their candidate for the Presidency, such an indorsement of his fitness for the place, could scarcely be deemed insufficient. Still, as I would not like the *public* to know, so I would not like *myself* to know I had entered a combination with any man, to the prejudice of all others whose friends respectively may consider them preferable.
Yours truly, A. Lincoln

35. Autobiography:

LETTER TO JESSE W. FELL, DECEMBER 20, 1859

LINCOLN wrote this autobiographical sketch for distribution to
interested persons by his friend, Jesse W. Fell. A Pennsylvania
editor used it in the preparation of an article which was re-
printed by various other Republican newspapers.

Springfield,
Dec. 20, 1859

J. W. Fell, Esq.
My dear Sir:

Herewith is a little sketch, as you requested. There is not
much of it, for the reason, I suppose, that there is not
much of me.

If any thing be made out of it, I wish it to be modest,
and not to go beyond the material. If it were thought necessary to incorporate any thing from any of my speeches, I
suppose there would be no objection. Of course it must
not appear to have been written by myself. Yours very
truly,   A. Lincoln

I was born Feb. 12, 1809, in Hardin County, Kentucky.
My parents were both born in Virginia, of undistinguished
families—second families, perhaps I should say. My
mother, who died in my tenth year, was of a family of the
name of Hanks, some of whom now reside in Adams, and
others in Macon counties, Illinois. My paternal grandfather, Abraham Lincoln, emigrated from Rockingham
County, Virginia, to Kentucky, about 1781 or 2, where, a
year or two later, he was killed by indians, not in battle,
but by stealth, when [where?] he was laboring to open a
farm in the forest. His ancestors, who were quakers, went
to Virginia from Berks County, Pennsylvania. An effort to
identify them with the New-England family of the same
name ended in nothing more definite, than a similarity of

Christian names in both families, such as Enoch, Levi, Mordecai, Solomon, Abraham, and the like.

My father, at the death of his father, was but six years of age; and he grew up, litterally without education. He removed from Kentucky to what is now Spencer county, Indiana, in my eighth year. We reached our new home about the time the State came into the Union. It was a wild region, with many bears and other wild animals still in the woods. There I grew up. There were some schools, so called; but no qualification was ever required of a teacher, beyond *"readin, writin, and cipherin,"* to the Rule of Three. If a straggler supposed to understand latin, happened to sojourn in the neighborhood, he was looked upon as a wizzard. There was absolutely nothing to excite ambition for education. Of course when I came of age, I did not know much. Still somehow, I could read, write, and cipher to the Rule of Three; but that was all. I have not been to school since. The little advance I now have upon this store of education, I have picked up from time to time under the pressure of necessity.

I was raised to farm work, which I continued till I was twenty two. At twenty one I came to Illinois, and passed the first year in Illinois—Macon county. Then I got to New-Salem, (at that time in Sangamon, now in Menard county, where I remained a year as a sort of Clerk in a store. Then came the Black-Hawk war; and I was elected a Captain of Volunteers—a success which gave me more pleasure than any I have had since. I went the campaign, was elated, ran for the Legislature the same year (1832) and was beaten—the only time I have been beaten by the people. The next, and three succeeding biennial elections, I was elected to the Legislature. I was not a candidate afterwards. During this Legislative period, I had studied law, and removed to Springfield to practice it. In 1846 I was once elected to the lower House of Congress. Was not a candidate for re-election. From 1849 to 1854, both inclusive, practiced law more assiduously than ever before. Always a whig in politics, and generally on the whig electoral tickets, making active canvasses. I was losing interest in politics, when the repeal of the Missouri Compromise aroused me again. What I have done since then is pretty well known.

If any personal description of me is thought desirable, it may be said, I am, in height, six feet, four inches, nearly; lean in flesh, weighing, on an average, one hundred and eighty pounds; dark complexion, with coarse black hair, and grey eyes—no other marks or brands recollected.

36. *Oratorical Climax:*

THE COOPER INSTITUTE ADDRESS, FEBRUARY 27, 1860

SIX years of campaigning against the extension of slavery, together with his bid for national recognition as a presidential candidate, reached culmination in New York City on February 27, 1860, when Lincoln addressed a distinguished Republican audience at Cooper Institute. The speech was a spectacular success, achieved on the home ground of the party's leading contender, William H. Seward. Lincoln began with a lengthy historical analysis designed to prove that the founders of the Republic had looked forward to the ultimate extinction of slavery. He then directed his remarks to the Southern people, giving special attention to John Brown's raid at Harpers Ferry, which had taken place some four months earlier. Finally, Lincoln addressed himself to his fellow Republicans. He warned them against yielding to threats from the South and against groping, like Douglas, for "some middle ground between the right and the wrong." The two latter sections are reproduced here.

And now, if they would listen—as I suppose they will not—I would address a few words to the Southern people.

I would say to them:—You consider yourselves a reasonable and a just people; and I consider that in the general qualities of reason and justice you are not inferior to any other people. Still, when you speak of us Republicans, you do so only to denounce us as reptiles, or, at the best, as no better than outlaws. You will grant a hearing to pirates or murderers, but nothing like it to "Black Re-

publicans." In all your contentions with one another, each
of you deems an unconditional condemnation of "Black
Republicanism" as the first thing to be attended to. Indeed,
such condemnation of us seems to be an indispensable
prerequisite—license, so to speak—among you to be admitted or permitted to speak at all. Now, can you, or not,
be prevailed upon to pause and to consider whether this
is quite just to us, or even to yourselves? Bring forward
your charges and specifications, and then be patient long
enough to hear us deny or justify.

You say we are sectional. We deny it. That makes an
issue; and the burden of proof is upon you. You produce
your proof; and what is it? Why, that our party has no
existence in your section—gets no votes in your section.
The fact is substantially true; but does it prove the issue?
If it does, then in case we should, without change of principle, begin to get votes in your section, we should thereby
cease to be sectional. You cannot escape this conclusion;
and yet, are you willing to abide by it? If you are, you
will probably soon find that we have ceased to be sectional,
for we shall get votes in your section this very year. You
will then begin to discover, as the truth plainly is, that your
proof does not touch the issue. The fact that we get no
votes in your section, is a fact of your making, and not
of ours. And if there be fault in that fact, that fault is
primarily yours, and remains so until you show that we
repel you by some wrong principle or practice. If we do
repel you by any wrong principle or practice, the fault is
ours; but this brings you to where you ought to have
started—to a discussion of the right or wrong of our
principle. If our principle, put in practice, would wrong
your section for the benefit of ours, or for any other object, then our principle, and we with it, are sectional, and
are justly opposed and denounced as such. Meet us, then,
on the question of whether our principle, put in practice,
would wrong your section; and so meet us as if it were
possible that something may be said on our side. Do you
accept the challenge? No! Then you really believe that
the principle which "our fathers who framed the Government under which we live" thought so clearly right as to
adopt it, and indorse it again and again, upon their of-

ficial oaths, is in fact so clearly wrong as to demand your condemnation without a moment's consideration.

Some of you delight to flaunt in our faces the warning against sectional parties given by Washington in his Farewell Address. Less than eight years before Washington gave that warning, he had, as President of the United States, approved and signed an act of Congress, enforcing the prohibition of slavery in the Northwestern Territory, which act embodied the policy of the Government upon that subject up to and at the very moment he penned that warning; and about one year after he penned it, he wrote La Fayette that he considered that prohibition a wise measure, expressing in the same connection his hope that we should at some time have a confederacy of free States.

Bearing this in mind, and seeing that sectionalism has since arisen upon this same subject, is that warning a weapon in your hands against us, or in our hands against you? Could Washington himself speak, would he cast the blame of that sectionalism upon us, who sustain his policy, or upon you who repudiate it? We respect that warning of Washington, and we commend it to you, together with his example pointing to the right application of it.

But you say you are conservative—eminently conservative—while we are revolutionary, destructive, or something of the sort. What is conservatism? Is it not adherence to the old and tried, against the new and untried? We stick to, contend for, the identical old policy on the point in controversy which was adopted by "our fathers who framed the Government under which we live;" while you with one accord reject, and scout, and spit upon that old policy, and insist upon substituting something new. True, you disagree among yourselves as to what that substitute shall be. You are divided on new propositions and plans, but you are unanimous in rejecting and denouncing the old policy of the fathers. Some of you are for reviving the foreign slave trade; some for a Congressional Slave-Code for the Territories; some for Congress forbidding the Territories to prohibit Slavery within their limits; some for maintaining Slavery in the Territories through the judiciary; some for the "gur-reat pur-rinciple" that "if one man would enslave another, no third man should object," fantastically called "Popular Sovereignty;" but never a man among you in favor of federal prohibition of slavery in federal territories, according to the practice of "our fathers who framed the Government under which we live." Not one of all your various plans can show a precedent or an advocate in the century within which our Government originated. Consider, then, whether your claim of conservatism for yourselves, and your charge of destructiveness against us, are based on the most clear and stable foundations.

Again, you say we have made the slavery question more prominent than it formerly was. We deny it. We admit that it is more prominent, but we deny that we made it so. It was not we, but you, who discarded the old policy of the fathers. We resisted, and still resist, your innovation; and thence comes the greater prominence of the question. Would you have that question reduced to its former proportions? Go back to that old policy. What has been will be again, under the same conditions. If you would have the peace of the old times, readopt the precepts and policy of the old times.

You charge that we stir up insurrections among your slaves. We deny it; and what is your proof? Harper's Ferry! John Brown!! John Brown was no Republican; and you have failed to implicate a single Republican in his Harper's Ferry enterprise. If any member of our party is guilty in that matter, you know it or you do not know it. If you do know it, you are inexcusable for not designating the man and proving the fact. If you do not know it, you are inexcusable for asserting it, and especially for persisting in the assertion after you have tried and failed to make the proof. You need not be told that persisting in a charge which one does not know to be true, is simply malicious slander.

Some of you admit that no Republican designedly aided or encouraged the Harper's Ferry affair; but still insist that our doctrines and declarations necessarily lead to such results. We do not believe it. We know we hold to no doctrine, and make no declaration, which were not held to and made by "our fathers who framed the Government under which we live." You never dealt fairly by us in relation to this affair. When it occurred, some important State elections were near at hand, and you were in evident glee with the belief that, by charging the blame upon us, you could get an advantage of us in those elections. The elections came, and your expectations were not quite fulfilled. Every Republican man knew that, as to himself at least, your charge was a slander, and he was not much inclined by it to cast his vote in your favor. Republican doctrines and declarations are accompanied with a continual protest against any interference whatever with your slaves, or with you about your slaves. Surely, this does not encourage them to revolt. True, we do, in common with "our fathers, who framed the Government under which we live," declare our belief that slavery is wrong; but the slaves do not hear us declare even this. For anything we say or do, the slaves would scarcely know there is a Republican party. I believe they would not, in fact, generally know it but for your misrepresentations of us, in their hearing. In your political contests among yourselves, each faction charges the other with sympathy with Black Republicanism; and then, to give point to the charge, defines Black Republicanism to simply be insurrection, blood and thunder among the slaves.

Slave insurrections are no more common now than they were before the Republican party was organized. What induced the Southampton insurrection, twenty-eight years ago, in which, at least, three times as many lives were lost as at Harper's Ferry? You can scarcely stretch your very elastic fancy to the conclusion that Southampton was "got up by Black Republicanism." In the present state of things in the United States, I do not think a general, or even a very extensive slave insurrection, is possible. The indispensable concert of action cannot be attained. The slaves have no means of rapid communication; nor can incendiary freemen, black or white, supply it. The explosive materials are everywhere in parcels; but there neither are, nor can be supplied, the indispensable connecting trains.

Much is said by Southern people about the affection of slaves for their masters and mistresses; and a part of it, at least, is true. A plot for an uprising could scarcely be devised and communicated to twenty individuals before some one of them, to save the life of a favorite master or mistress, would divulge it. This is the rule; and the slave revolution in Hayti was not an exception to it, but a case occurring under peculiar circumstances. The gunpowder plot of British history, though not connected with slaves, was more in point. In that case, only about twenty were admitted to the secret; and yet one of them, in his anxiety to save a friend, betrayed the plot to that friend, and, by consequence, averted the calamity. Occasional poisonings from the kitchen, and open or stealthy assassinations in the field, and local revolts extending to a score or so, will continue to occur as the natural results of slavery; but no general insurrection of slaves, as I think, can happen in this country for a long time. Whoever much fears, or much hopes for such an event, will be alike disappointed.

In the language of Mr. Jefferson, uttered many years ago, "It is still in our power to direct the process of emancipation, and deportation, peacably, and in such slow degrees, as that the evil will wear off insensibly; and their places be, *pari passu,* filled up by free white laborers. If, on the contrary, it is left to force itself on, human nature must shudder at the prospect held up."

Mr. Jefferson did not mean to say, nor do I, that the power of emancipation is in the Federal Government. He spoke of Virginia; and, as to the power of emancipation, I speak of the slaveholding States only. The Federal Government, however, as we insist, has the power of restraining the extension of the institution—the power to insure that a slave insurrection shall never occur on any American soil which is now free from slavery.

John Brown's effort was peculiar. It was not a slave insurrection. It was an attempt by white men to get up a revolt among slaves, in which the slaves refused to participate. In fact, it was so absurd that the slaves, with all their ignorance, saw plainly enough it could not succeed. That affair, in its philosophy, corresponds with the many attempts, related in history, at the assassination of kings and emperors. An enthusiast broods over the oppression of a people till he fancies himself commissioned by Heaven to liberate them. He ventures the attempt, which ends in little else than his own execution. Orsini's attempt on Louis Napoleon, and John Brown's attempt at Harper's Ferry were, in their philosophy, precisely the same. The eagerness to cast blame on old England in the one case, and on New England in the other, does not disprove the sameness of the two things.

And how much would it avail you, if you could, by the use of John Brown, Helper's Book, and the like, break up the Republican organization? Human action can be modified to some extent, but human nature cannot be changed. There is a judgment and a feeling against slavery in this nation, which cast at least a million and a half of votes. You cannot destroy that judgment and feeling—that sentiment—by breaking up the political organization which rallies around it. You can scarcely scatter and disperse an army which has been formed into order in the face of your heaviest fire; but if you could, how much would you gain by forcing the sentiment which created it out of the peaceful channel of the ballot-box, into some other channel? What would that other channel probably be? Would the number of John Browns be lessened or enlarged by the operation?

But you will break up the Union rather than submit to a denial of your Constitutional rights.

That has a somewhat reckless sound; but it would be palliated, if not fully justified, were we proposing, by the mere force of numbers, to deprive you of some right, plainly written down in the Constitution. But we are proposing no such thing.

When you make these declarations, you have a specific and well-understood allusion to an assumed Constitutional right of yours, to take slaves into the federal territories, and to hold them there as property. But no such right is specifically written in the Constitution. That instrument is literally silent about any such right. We, on the contrary, deny that such a right has any existence in the Constitution, even by implication.

Your purpose, then, plainly stated, is, that you will destroy the Government, unless you be allowed to construe and enforce the Constitution as you please, on all points in dispute between you and us. You will rule or ruin in all events.

This, plainly stated, is your language. Perhaps you will say the Supreme Court has decided the disputed Constitutional question in your favor. Not quite so. But waiving the lawyer's distinction between dictum and decision, the Court have decided the question for you in a sort of way. The Court have substantially said, it is your Constitutional right to take slaves into the federal territories, and to hold them there as property. When I say the decision was made in a sort of way, I mean it was made in a divided Court, by a bare majority of the Judges, and they not quite agreeing with one another in the reasons for making it; that it is so made as that its avowed supporters disagree with one another about its meaning, and that it was mainly based upon a mistaken statement of fact—the statement in the opinion that "the right of property in a slave is distinctly and expressly affirmed in the Constitution."

An inspection of the Constitution will show that the right of property in a slave is not "*distinctly* and *expressly* affirmed" in it. Bear in mind, the Judges do not pledge their judicial opinion that such right is *impliedly* affirmed in the Constitution; but they pledge their veracity that it is "*distinctly* and *expressly*" affirmed there—"distinctly," that is, not mingled with anything else—"expressly," that is, in words meaning just that, without the aid of any inference, and susceptible of no other meaning.

If they had only pledged their judicial opinion that such right is affirmed in the instrument by implication, it would be open to others to show that neither the word "slave" nor "slavery" is to be found in the Constitution, nor the word "property" even, in any connection with language alluding to the things slave, or slavery, and that wherever in that instrument the slave is alluded to, he is called a "person;"—and wherever his master's legal right in relation to him is alluded to, it is spoken of as "service or labor which may be due,"—as a debt payable in service or labor. Also, it would be open to show, by contemporaneous history, that this mode of alluding to slaves and slavery, instead of speaking of them, was employed on purpose to exclude from the Constitution the idea that there could be property in man.

To show all this, is easy and certain.

When this obvious mistake of the Judges shall be brought to their notice, is it not reasonable to expect that they will withdraw the mistaken statement, and reconsider the conclusion based upon it?

And then it is to be remembered that "our fathers, who framed the Government under which we live"—the men who made the Constitution—decided this same Constitutional question in our favor, long ago—decided it without division among themselves, when making the decision; without division among themselves about the meaning of it after it was made, and, so far as any evidence is left, without basing it upon any mistaken statement of facts.

Under all these circumstances, do you really feel yourselves justified to break up this Government, unless such a court decision as yours is, shall be at once submitted to as a conclusive and final rule of political action? But you will not abide the election of a Republican President! In that supposed event, you say, you will destroy the Union; and then, you say, the great crime of having destroyed it will be upon us! That is cool. A highwayman holds a pistol to my ear, and mutters through his teeth, "Stand and deliver, or I shall kill you, and then you will be a murderer!"

To be sure, what the robber demanded of me—my money—was my own; and I had a clear right to keep it; but it was no more my own than my vote is my own; and the threat of death to me, to extort my money, and the threat of destruction to the Union, to extort my vote, can scarcely be distinguished in principle.

A few words now to Republicans. *It is exceedingly desirable that all parts of this great Confederacy shall be at peace, and in harmony, one with another. Let us Republicans do our part to have it so. Even though much provoked, let us do nothing through passion and ill temper. Even though the southern people will not so much as listen to us, let us calmly consider their demands, and yield to them if, in our deliberate view of our duty, we possibly can.* Judging by all they say and do, and by the subject and nature of their controversy with us, let us determine, if we can, what will satisfy them.

Will they be satisfied if the Territories be unconditionally surrendered to them? We know they will not. In all their present complaints against us, the Territories are scarcely mentioned. Invasions and insurrections are the rage now. Will it satisfy them, if, in the future, we have nothing to do with invasions and insurrections? We know it will not. We so know, because we know we never had anything to do with invasions and insurrections; and yet this total abstaining does not exempt us from the charge and the denunciation.

The question recurs, what will satisfy them? Simply this: We must not only let them alone, but we must, somehow, convince them that we do let them alone. This, we know by experience, is no easy task. We have been so trying to convince them from the very beginning of our organization, but with no success. In all our platforms and speeches we have constantly protested our purpose to let them alone; but this has had no tendency to convince them. Alike unavailing to convince them, is the fact that they have never detected a man of us in any attempt to disturb them.

These natural, and apparently adequate means all failing, what will convince them? This, and this only: cease to call slavery *wrong,* and join them in calling it *right.* And this must be done thoroughly—done in *acts* as well as in *words.* Silence will not be tolerated—we must place ourselves avowedly with them. Senator Douglas's new sedition law must be enacted and enforced, suppressing all declarations that slavery is wrong, whether made in politics, in presses, in pulpits, or in private. We must arrest and return their fugitive slaves with greedy pleasure. We must pull down our Free State constitutions. The whole atmosphere must be disinfected from all taint of opposition to slavery, before they will cease to believe that all their troubles proceed from us.

I am quite aware they do not state their case precisely in this way. Most of them would probably say to us, "Let us alone, *do* nothing to us, and *say* what you please about slavery." But we do let them alone—have never disturbed them—so that, after all, it is what we say, which dissatisfies them. They will continue to accuse us of doing, until we cease saying.

I am also aware they have not, as yet, in terms, demanded the overthrow of our Free-State Constitutions. Yet those Constitutions declare the wrong of slavery, with more solemn emphasis, than do all other sayings against it; and when all these other sayings shall have been silenced, the overthrow of these Constitutions will be demanded, and nothing be left to resist the demand. It is nothing to the contrary, that they do not demand the whole of this just now. Demanding what they do, and for the reason they do, they can voluntarily stop nowhere short of this consummation. Holding, as they do, that slavery is morally right, and socially elevating, they cannot cease to demand a full national recognition of it, as a legal right, and a social blessing.

Nor can we justifiably withhold this, on any ground save our conviction that slavery is wrong. If slavery is right, all words, acts, laws, and constitutions against it, are themselves wrong, and should be silenced, and swept away. If it is right, we cannot justly object to its nationality—its universality; if it is wrong, they cannot justly insist upon its extension—its enlargement. All they ask, we could readily grant, if we thought slavery right; all we ask, they could as readily grant, if they thought it wrong. Their thinking it right, and our thinking it wrong, is the precise fact upon which depends the whole controversy. Thinking it right, as they do, they are not to blame for desiring its full recognition, as being right; but, thinking it wrong, as we do, can we yield to them? Can we cast our votes with their view, and against our own? In view of our moral, social, and political responsibilities, can we do this?

Wrong as we think slavery is, we can yet afford to let it alone where it is, because that much is due to the necessity arising from its actual presence in the nation; but can we, while our votes will prevent it, allow it to spread into the National Territories, and to overrun us here in these Free States? If our sense of duty forbids this, then let us stand by our duty, fearlessly and effectively. Let us be diverted by none of those sophistical contrivances wherewith we are so industriously plied and belabored—contrivances such as groping for some middle ground between the right and the wrong, vain as the search for a man who should be neither a living man nor a dead man—such a policy of "don't care" on a question about which all true men do care—such as Union appeals beseeching true Union men to yield to Disunionists, reversing the divine rule, and calling, not the sinners, but the righteous to repentance—such as invocations to Washington, imploring men to unsay what Washington said, and undo what Washington did.

Neither let us be slandered from our duty by false

accusations against us, nor frightened from it by menaces of destruction to the Government nor of dungeons to ourselves. LET US HAVE FAITH THAT RIGHT MAKES MIGHT, AND IN THAT FAITH, LET US, TO THE END, DARE TO DO OUR DUTY AS WE UNDERSTAND IT.

37. Convention Strategy:
LETTER TO SAMUEL GALLOWAY, MARCH 24, 1860

FROM New York, Lincoln continued on to New England for two arduous weeks of speechmaking. He returned home in the middle of March, weary but pleased by the results of his Eastern tour. Now more or less openly a presidential candidate, he explained his strategy to a supporter in Ohio, where another party leader, Salmon P. Chase, was eyeing the nomination.

Chicago, March 24, 1860

Hon. Samuel Galloway
My dear Sir: I am here attending a trial in court. Before leaving home I received your kind letter of the 15th. Of course I am gratified to know I have friends in Ohio who are disposed to give me the highest evidence of their friendship and confidence. Mr. Parrott of the Legislature, had written me to the same effect. If I have any chance, it consists mainly in the fact that the *whole* opposition would vote for me if nominated. (I dont mean to include the pro-slavery opposition of the South, of course.) My name is new in the field; and I suppose I am not the *first* choice of a very great many. Our policy, then, is to give no offence to others—leave them in a mood to come to us, if they shall be compelled to give up their first love. This, too, is dealing justly with all, and leaving us in a mood to support heartily whoever shall be nominated. I believe I have once before told you that I especially wish to do no ungenerous thing towards Governor Chase, because he gave us his sympathy in 1858, when scarcely any other

distinguished man did. Whatever you may do for me, consistently with these suggestions, will be appreciated, and gratefully remembered.

Please write me again. Yours very truly,

A. Lincoln

38. *Presidential Nominee:*
LETTER TO GEORGE ASHMUN, MAY 23, 1860

THE Republican National Convention assembled at Chicago in the middle of May. Seward led in the first round of balloting, but then his scattered opposition began to unite behind Lincoln. The two men stood almost even at the end of the second ballot, and on the third, Lincoln was nominated. Republican delegates had rejected the most prominent candidate in favor of a more "available" one.

Springfield, Ills. May 23, 1860

Hon. George Ashmun:
President of the Republican National Convention.

Sir: I accept the nomination tendered me by the Convention over which you presided, and of which I am formally apprized in the letter of yourself and others, acting as a committee of the convention, for that purpose.

The declaration of principles and sentiments, which accompanies your letter, meets my approval; and it shall be my care not to violate, or disregard it, in any part.

Imploring the assistance of Divine Providence, and with due regard to the views and feelings of all who were represented in the convention; to the rights of all the states, and territories, and people of the nation; to the inviolability of the constitution, and the perpetual union, harmony, and prosperity of all, I am most happy to co-operate for the practical success of the principles declared by the convention. Your obliged friend, and fellow citizen,

A. Lincoln

39. On Growing a Beard:

LETTER TO GRACE BEDELL, OCTOBER 19, 1860

LINCOLN, following the custom of the time, remained quietly
at home and left the active campaigning to other Republicans.
The Democratic party, meanwhile, had been split by the slavery
issue. One part nominated Douglas, while the other rallied behind Vice-President John C. Breckinridge of Kentucky. In
addition, certain Whig and American elements had organized
the Constitutional Union party and nominated John Bell of
Tennessee. Thus there were four contestants in the race. For
Lincoln, who had no support in the South, it was necessary to
carry nearly all of the free states. Pennsylvania and Indiana,
both of which had voted for Buchanan in 1856, held their elections of state officers early in October. The Republicans were
victorious in both of these critical preliminary tests, and after
that it seemed almost certain that Lincoln would win. He was
therefore already visualizing himself in the White House when
an eleven-year-old girl in western New York offered some advice
which he thought about and eventually followed.

Private

Springfield, Ills.
Oct 19, 1860

Miss. Grace Bedell
My dear little Miss:
 Your very agreeable letter of the 15th. is received.
 I regret the necessity of saying I have no daughters.
I have three sons—one seventeen, one nine, and one seven,
years of age. They, with their mother, constitute my whole
family.
 As to the whiskers, having never worn any, do you not
think people would call it a piece of silly affection if I were
to begin it now? Your very sincere well-wisher,

A. Lincoln

40. No Compromise:

ALTHOUGH he received less than forty percent of the popular vote, Lincoln won a clear majority in the electoral college. His victory was the signal for a secession movement in South Carolina and for industrious efforts at compromise in the reconvening Congress. Determined to stand his ground, the President-elect wrote several letters like this one to Senator Lyman Trumbull.

Private, & confidential
Springfield, Ills. Dec. 10, 1860

Hon. L. Trumbull.

My dear Sir: Let there be no compromise on the question of *extending* slavery. If there be, all our labor is lost, and, ere long, must be done again. The dangerous ground —that into which some of our friends have a hankering to run—is Pop. Sov. Have none of it. Stand firm. The tug has to come, & better now, than any time hereafter. Yours as ever,

A. Lincoln

41. On Reassuring the South:

LETTER TO JOHN A. GILMER, DECEMBER 15, 1860

AS the crisis mounted, Lincoln was repeatedly urged to abate it by issuing a public statement which would quiet Southern fears. He explained his unwillingness to do so in this letter to Congressman John A. Gilmer, a North Carolina unionist. But he did go on to answer some specific questions that Gilmer had posed. Soon afterwards, he tried unsuccessfully to bring Gilmer into his cabinet.

Strictly confidential.
Springfield, Ill. Dec 15, 1860.
Hon. John A. Gilmer:

My dear Sir—Yours of the 10th is received. I am greatly disinclined to write a letter on the subject embraced in yours; and I would not do so, even privately as I do, were it not that I fear you might misconstrue my silence. Is it desired that I shall shift the ground upon which I have been elected? I can not do it. You need only to acquaint yourself with that ground, and press it on the attention of the South. It is all in print and easy of access. May I be pardoned if I ask whether even you have ever attempted to procure the reading of the Republican platform, or my speeches, by the Southern people? If not, what reason have I to expect that any additional production of mine would meet a better fate? It would make me appear as if I repented for the crime of having been elected, and was anxious to apologize and beg forgiveness. To so represent me, would be the principal use made of any letter I might now thrust upon the public. My old record cannot be so used; and that is precisely the reason that some new declaration is so much sought.

Now, my dear sir, be assured, that I am not questioning *your* candor; I am only pointing out, that, while a new letter would hurt the cause which I think a just one, you can quite as well effect every patriotic object with the old record. Carefully read pages 18, 19, 74, 75, 88, 89, & 267 of the volume of Joint Debates between Senator Douglas and myself, with the Republican Platform adopted at Chicago, and all your questions will be substantially answered. I have no thought of recommending the abolition of slavery in the District of Columbia, nor the slave trade among the slave states, even on the conditions indicated; and if I were to make such recommendation, it is quite clear Congress would not follow it.

As to employing slaves in Arsenals and Dockyards, it is a thing I never thought of in my life, to my recollection, till I saw your letter; and I may say of it, precisely as I have said of the two points above.

As to the use of patronage in the slave states, where there are few or no Republicans, I do not expect to inquire for the politics of the appointee, or whether he does or not own slaves. I intend in that matter to accommodate the people in the several localities, if they themselves will allow me to accommodate them. In one word, I never have been, am not now, and probably never shall be, in a mood of harassing the people, either North or South.

On the territorial question, I am inflexible, as you see my position in the book. On that, there is a difference between you and us; and it is the only substantial difference. You think slavery is right and ought to be extended; we think it is wrong and ought to be restricted. For this, neither has any just occasion to be angry with the other.

As to the state laws, mentioned in your sixth question, I really know very little of them. I never have read one. If any of them are in conflict with the fugitive slave clause, or any other part of the constitution, I certainly should be glad of their repeal; but I could hardly be justified, as a citizen of Illinois, or as President of the United States, to recommend the repeal of a statute of Vermont, or South Carolina.

With the assurance of my highest regards I subscribe myself Your obt. Servt.,

A. Lincoln

42. *Departure:*

FAREWELL ADDRESS AT SPRINGFIELD, FEBRUARY 11, 1861

ON the eve of his fifty-second birthday, Lincoln began the journey from Springfield to Washington. Seven states had seceded, and Jefferson Davis was already elected President of the new Confederate government. As he headed into the troubled future, Lincoln paused for a glance at the past and a brief, tender farewell to the people of his hometown. There are several versions of the little speech. This is the one published the next day in the local Republican newspaper.

Friends,

No one who has never been placed in a like position, can understand my feelings at this hour, nor the oppressive sadness I feel at this parting. For more than a quarter of a century I have lived among you, and during all that time I have received nothing but kindness at your hands. Here I have lived from my youth until now I am an old man. Here the most sacred ties of earth were assumed; here all my children were born; and here one of them lies buried. To you, dear friends, I owe all that I have, all that I am. All the strange, chequered past seems to crowd now upon my mind. To-day I leave you; I go to assume a task more difficult than that which devolved upon General Washington. Unless the great God who assisted him, shall be with and aid me, I must fail. But if the same omniscient mind, and Almighty arm that directed and protected him, shall guide and support me, I shall not fail, I shall succeed. Let us all pray that the God of our fathers may not forsake us now. To him I commend you all— permit me to ask that with equal security and faith, you all will invoke His wisdom and guidance for me. With these few words I must leave you—for how long I know not. Friends, one and all, I must now bid you an affectionate farewell.

43. En Route:

SPEECH AT CLEVELAND, OHIO, FEBRUARY 15, 1861

CROWDS greeted the new President all along his circuitous route to Washington. Lincoln responded many times with short, impromptu speeches of no great merit or utility. In general, he seemed unable to comprehend or unwilling to admit the seriousness of the secession crisis. This excerpt from a speech at Cleveland is typical of his public utterances throughout the journey.

You have assembled to testify your respect to the Union, the constitution and the laws, and here let me say that it is with you, the people, to advance the great cause of the Union and the constitution, and not with any one man. It rests with you alone. This fact is strongly impressed on my mind at present. In a community like this, whose appearance testifies to their intelligence, I am convinced that the cause of liberty and the Union can never be in danger. Frequent allusion is made to the excitement at present existing in our national politics, and it is as well that I should also allude to it here. I think that there is no occasion for any excitement. The crisis, as it is called, is altogether an artificial crisis. In all parts of the nation there are differences of opinion and politics. There are differences of opinion even here. You did not all vote for the person who now addresses you. What is happening now will not hurt those who are farther away from here. Have they not all their rights now as they ever have had? Do they not have their fugitive slaves returned now as ever? Have they not the same constitution that they have lived under for seventy odd years? Have they not a position as citizens of this common country, and have we any power to change that position? [Cries of "No."] What then is the matter with them? Why all this excitement? Why all these complaints? As I said before, this crisis is all artificial. It has no foundation in facts. It was not argued up, as the saying is, and cannot, therefore, be argued down. Let it alone and it will go down of itself [Laughter].

44. President Lincoln:
FIRST INAUGURAL ADDRESS, MARCH 4, 1861

LINCOLN's inaugural address, anxiously awaited by a divided nation, was more carefully considered and revised than any other document from his pen. While offering words of conciliation to the dissatisfied South, he also expressed his determination to maintain the Union, but with only vague indications of how he proposed to do it. The substance of the familiar closing paragraph had been suggested by Seward. The phrasing, however, was inimitably Lincoln's.

Fellow citizens of the United States:

In compliance with a custom as old as the government itself, I appear before you to address you briefly, and to take, in your presence, the oath prescribed by the Constitution of the United States, to be taken by the President "before he enters on the execution of his office."

I do not consider it necessary, at present, for me to discuss those matters of administration about which there is no special anxiety, or excitement.

Apprehension seems to exist among the people of the Southern States, that by the accession of a Republican Administration, their property, and their peace, and personal security, are to be endangered. There has never been any reasonable cause for such apprehension. Indeed, the most ample evidence to the contrary has all the while existed, and been open to their inspection. It is found in nearly all the published speeches of him who now addresses you. I do but quote from one of those speeches when I declare that "I have no purpose, directly or indirectly, to interfere with the institution of slavery in the States where it exists. I believe I have no lawful right to do so, and I have no inclination to do so." Those who nominated and elected me did so with full knowledge that I had made this, and many similar declarations, and had never recanted them. And more than this, they placed in the platform, for my acceptance, and as a law to themselves, and to me, the clear and emphatic resolution which I now read:

"*Resolved,* That the maintenance inviolate of the rights of the States, and especially the right of each State to order and control its own domestic institutions according to its own judgment exclusively, is essential to that balance of power on which the perfection and endurance of our political fabric depend; and we denounce the lawless invasion by armed force of the soil of any State or Territory, no matter under what pretext, as among the gravest of crimes."

I now reiterate these sentiments: and in doing so, I only press upon the public attention the most conclusive evidence of which the case is susceptible, that the property, peace and security of no section are to be in anywise endangered by the now incoming Administration. I add too, that all the protection which, consistently with the Constitution and the laws, can be given, will be cheerfully given to all the States when lawfully demanded, for whatever cause—as cheerfully to one section, as to another.

There is much controversy about the delivering up of fugitives from service or labor. The clause I now read is as plainly written in the Constitution as any other of its provisions:

"No person held to service or labor in one State, under the laws thereof, escaping into another, shall, in consequence of any law or regulation therein, be discharged from such service or labor, but shall be delivered up on claim of the party to whom such service or labor may be due."

It is scarcely questioned that this provision was intended by those who made it, for the reclaiming of what we call fugitive slaves; and the intention of the law-giver is the law. All members of Congress swear their support to the whole Constitution—to this provision as much as to any other. To the proposition, then, that slaves whose cases come within the terms of this clause, "shall be delivered up," their oaths are unanimous. Now, if they would make the effort in good temper, could they not, with nearly equal unanimity, frame and pass a law, by means of which to keep good that unanimous oath?

There is some difference of opinion whether this clause should be enforced by national or by state authority; but surely that difference is not a very material one. If the slave is to be surrendered, it can be of but little consequence to him, or to others, by which authority it is done. And should any one, in any case, be content that his oath shall go unkept, on a merely unsubstantial controversy as to *how* it shall be kept?

Again, in any law upon this subject, ought not all the

safeguards of liberty known in civilized and humane juris-prudence to be introduced, so that a free man be not, in any case, surrendered as a slave? And might it not be well, at the same time, to provide by law for the enforce-ment of that clause in the Constitution which guarranties that "The citizens of each State shall be entitled to all previleges and immunities of citizens in the several States?"

I take the official oath to-day, with no mental reser-vations, and with no purpose to construe the Constitution or laws, by any hypercritical rules. And while I do not choose now to specify particular acts of Congress as proper to be enforced, I do suggest, that it will be much safer for all, both in official and private stations, to conform to, and abide by, all those acts which stand unrepealed, than to violate any of them, trusting to find impunity in having them held to be unconstitutional.

It is seventy-two years since the first inauguration of a President under our national Constitution. During that period fifteen different and greatly distinguished citizens, have, in succession, administered the executive branch of the government. They have conducted it through many perils; and, generally, with great success. Yet, with all this scope for precedent, I now enter upon the same task for the brief constitutional term of four years, under great and peculiar difficulty. A disruption of the Federal Union heretofore only menaced, is now formidably attempted.

I hold, that in contemplation of universal law, and of the Constitution, the Union of these States is perpetual. Perpetuity is implied, if not expressed, in the fundamental law of all national governments. It is safe to assert that no government proper, ever had a provision in its organic law for its own termination. Continue to execute all the express provisions of our national Constitution, and the Union will endure forever—it being impossible to destroy it, except by some action not provided for in the instru-ment itself.

Again, if the United States be not a government proper, but an association of States in the nature of contract merely, can it, as a contract, be peaceably unmade, by less than all the parties who made it? One party to a con-tract may violate it—break it, so to speak; but does it not require all to lawfully rescind it?

Descending from these general principles, we find the proposition that, in legal contemplation, the Union is perpetual, confirmed by the history of the Union itself. The Union is much older than the Constitution. It was formed in fact, by the Articles of Association in 1774. It was matured and continued by the Declaration of Independence in 1776. It was further matured and the faith of all the then thirteen States expressly plighted and engaged that it should be perpetual, by the Articles of Confederation in 1778. And finally, in 1787, one of the declared objects for ordaining and establishing the Constitution, was *to form a more perfect union.*

But if destruction of the Union, by one, or by a part only, of the States, be lawfully possible, the Union is *less* perfect than before the Constitution, having lost the vital element of perpetuity.

It follows from these views that no State, upon its own mere motion, can lawfully get out of the Union,—that *resolves* and *ordinances* to that effect are legally void; and that acts of violence, within any State or States, against the authority of the United States, are insurrectionary or revolutionary, according to circumstances.

I therefore consider that, in view of the Constitution and the laws, the Union is unbroken; and, to the extent of my ability, I shall take care, as the Constitution itself expressly enjoins upon me, that the laws of the Union be faithfully executed in all the States. Doing this I deem to be only a simple duty on my part; and I shall perform it, so far as practicable, unless my rightful masters, the American people, shall withhold the requisite means, or, in some authoritative manner, direct the contrary. I trust this will not be regarded as a menace, but only as the declared purpose of the Union that it *will* constitutionally defend, and maintain itself.

In doing this there needs to be no bloodshed or violence; and there shall be none, unless it be forced upon the national authority. The power confided to me, will be used to hold, occupy, and possess the property, and places belonging to the government, and to collect the duties and imposts; but beyond what may be necessary for these objects, there will be no invasion—no using of force against, or among the people anywhere. Where hostility to the

United States, in any interior locality, shall be so great and so universal, as to prevent competent resident citizens from holding the Federal offices, there will be no attempt to force obnoxious strangers among the people for that object. While the strict legal right may exist in the government to enforce the exercise of these offices, the attempt to do so would be so irritating, and so nearly impracticable with all, that I deem it better to forego, for the time, the uses of such offices.

The mails, unless repelled, will continue to be furnished in all parts of the Union. So far as possible, the people everywhere shall have that sense of perfect security which is most favorable to calm thought and reflection. The course here indicated will be followed, unless current events, and experience, shall show a modification, or change, to be proper; and in every case and exigency, my best discretion will be exercised, according to circumstances actually existing, and with a view and a hope of a peaceful solution of the national troubles, and the restoration of fraternal sympathies and affections.

That there are persons in one section, or another who seek to destroy the Union at all events, and are glad of any pretext to do it, I will neither affirm or deny; but if there be such, I need address no word to them. To those, however, who really love the Union, may I not speak?

Before entering upon so grave a matter as the destruction of our national fabric, with all its benefits, its memories, and its hopes, would it not be wise to ascertain precisely why we do it? Will you hazard so desperate a step, while there is any possibility that any portion of the ills you fly from, have no real existence? Will you, while the certain ills you fly to, are greater than all the real ones you fly from? Will you risk the commission of so fearful a mistake?

All profess to be content in the Union, if all constitutional rights can be maintained. Is it true, then, that any right, plainly written in the Constitution, has been denied? I think not. Happily the human mind is so constituted, that no party can reach to the audacity of doing this. Think, if you can, of a single instance in which a plainly written provision of the Constitution has ever been denied. If, by the mere force of numbers, a majority should deprive a minority of any clearly written constitutional right, it might, in a moral point of view, justify revolution—certainly would, if such right were a vital one. But such is not our case. All the vital rights of minorities, and of individuals, are so plainly assured to them, by affirmations and negations, guarranties and prohibitions, in the Constitution, that controversies never arise concerning them. But no organic law can ever be framed with a provision specifically applicable to every question which may occur in practical administration. No foresight can anticipate, nor any document of reasonable length contain express provisions for all possible questions. Shall fugitives from labor be surrendered by national or by State authority? The Constitution does not expressly say. *May* Congress prohibit slavery in the territories? The Constitution does not expressly say. *Must* Congress protect slavery in the territories? The Constitution does not expressly say.

From questions of this class spring all our constitutional controversies, and we divide upon them into majorities and minorities. If the minority will not acquiesce, the majority must, or the government must cease. There is no other alternative; for continuing the government, is acquiescence on one side or the other. If a minority, in such case, will secede rather than acquiesce, they make a precedent which, in turn, will divide and ruin them; for a minority of their own will secede from them, whenever a majority refuses to be controlled by such minority. For instance, why may not any portion of a new confederacy, a year or two hence, arbitrarily secede again, precisely as portions of the present Union now claim to secede from it. All who cherish disunion sentiments, are now being educated to the exact temper of doing this. Is there such perfect identity of interests among the States to compose a new Union, as to produce harmony only, and prevent renewed secession?

Plainly, the central idea of secession, is the essence of anarchy. A majority, held in restraint by constitutional checks, and limitations, and always changing easily, with deliberate changes of popular opinions and sentiments, is the only true sovereign of a free people. Whoever rejects it, does, of necessity, fly to anarchy or to despotism. Unanimity is impossible; the rule of a minority, as a permanent arrangement, is wholly inadmissable; so that, rejecting the majority principle, anarchy, or despotism in some form, is all that is left.

I do not forget the position assumed by some, that constitutional questions are to be decided by the Supreme Court; nor do I deny that such decisions must be binding in any case, upon the parties to a suit, as to the object of that suit, while they are also entitled to very high respect and consideration, in all paralel cases, by all other departments of the government. And while it is obviously possible that such decision may be erroneous in any given case, still the evil effect following it, being limited to that particular case, with the chance that it may be over-ruled, and never become a precedent for other cases, can better be borne than could the evils of a different practice. At the same time the candid citizen must confess that if the policy of the government, upon vital questions, affecting the whole people, is to be irrevocably fixed by decisions of the Supreme Court, the instant they are made, in ordinary litigation between parties, in personal actions, the people will have ceased, to be their own rulers, having, to that extent, practically resigned their government, into the hands of that eminent tribunal. Nor is there, in this view, any assault upon the court, or the judges. It is a duty, from which they may not shrink, to decide cases properly brought before them; and it is no fault of theirs, if others seek to turn their decisions to political purposes.

One section of our country believes slavery is *right,* and ought to be extended, while the other believes it is *wrong,* and ought not to be extended. This is the only substantial dispute. The fugitive slave clause of the Constitution, and the law for the suppression of the foreign slave trade, are each as well enforced, perhaps, as any law can ever be in a community where the moral sense of the people imperfectly supports the law itself. The great body of the people abide by the dry legal obligation in both cases, and a few break over in each. This, I think, cannot be perfectly cured; and it would be worse in both cases *after* the separation of the sections, than before. The foreign slave trade, now imperfectly suppressed, would be ultimately revived without restriction, in one section; while fugitive slaves, now only partially surrendered, would not be surrendered at all, by the other.

Physically speaking, we cannot separate. We cannot remove our respective sections from each other, nor build an impassable wall between them. A husband and wife may be divorced, and go out of the presence, and beyond the reach of each other; but the different parts of our country cannot do this. They cannot but remain face to face; and intercourse, either amicable or hostile, must continue between them. Is it possible then to make that intercourse more advantageous, or more satisfactory, *after* separation than *before*? Can aliens make treaties easier than friends can make laws? Can treaties be more faithfully enforced between aliens, than laws can among friends? Suppose you go to war, you cannot fight always; and when, after much loss on both sides, and no gain on either, you cease fighting, the identical old questions, as to terms of intercourse, are again upon you.

This country, with its institutions, belongs to the people who inhabit it. Whenever they shall grow weary of the existing government, they can exercise their *constitutional* right of amending it, or their *revolutionary* right to dismember, or overthrow it. I can not be ignorant of the fact that many worthy, and patriotic citizens are desirous of having the national constitution amended. While I make no recommendation of amendments, I fully recognize the rightful authority of the people over the whole subject, to be exercised in either of the modes prescribed in the instrument itself; and I should, under existing circumstances, favor, rather than oppose, a fair oppertunity being afforded the people to act upon it.

I will venture to add that, to me, the convention mode seems preferable, in that it allows amendments to originate with the people themselves, instead of only permitting them to take, or reject, propositions, originated by others, not especially chosen for the purpose, and which might not be precisely such, as they would wish to either accept or refuse. I understand a proposed amendment to the Constitution—which amendment, however, I have not seen, has passed Congress, to the effect that the federal government, shall never interfere with the domestic institutions of the States, including that of persons held to service. To avoid misconstruction of what I have said, I depart from my purpose not to speak of particular amendments, so far as to say that, holding such a provision to now be implied constitutional law, I have no objection to its being made express, and irrevocable.

The Chief Magistrate derives all his authority from the people, and they have conferred none upon him to fix terms for the separation of the States. The people themselves can do this also if they choose; but the executive, as such, has nothing to do with it. His duty is to administer the present government, as it came to his hands, and to transmit it, unimpaired by him, to his successor.

Why should there not be a patient confidence in the ultimate justice of the people? Is there any better, or equal hope, in the world? In our present differences, is either party without faith of being in the right? If the Almighty Ruler of nations, with his eternal truth and justice, be on your side of the North, or on yours of the South, that truth, and that justice, will surely prevail, by the judgment of this great tribunal, the American people.

By the frame of the government under which we live, this same people have wisely given their public servants but little power for mischief; and have, with equal wisdom, provided for the return of that little to their own hands at very short intervals.

While the people retain their virtue, and vigilence, no administration, by any extreme of wickedness or folly, can very seriously injure the government, in the short space of four years.

My countrymen, one and all, think calmly and *well,* upon this whole subject. Nothing valuable can be lost by taking time. If there be an object to *hurry* any of you, in hot haste, to a step which you would never take *deliberately,* that object will be frustrated by taking time; but no good object can be frustrated by it. Such of you as are now dissatisfied, still have the old Constitution unimpaired, and, on the sensitive point, the laws of your own framing under it; while the new administration will have no immediate power, if it would, to change either. If it were admitted that you who are dissatisfied, hold the right side in the dispute, there still is no single good reason for precipitate action. Intelligence, patriotism, Christianity, and a firm reliance on Him, who has never yet forsaken this favored land, are still competent to adjust, in the best way, all our present difficulty.

In *your* hands, my dissatisfied fellow countrymen, and not in *mine,* is the momentous issue of civil war. The government will not assail *you.* You can have no conflict, without being yourselves the aggressors. *You* have no oath registered in Heaven to destroy the government, while *I* shall have the most solemn one to "preserve, protect and defend" it.

I am loth to close. We are not enemies, but friends. We must not be enemies. Though passion may have strained, it must not break our bonds of affection. The mystic chords of memory, streching from every battlefield, and patriot grave, to every living heart and hearthstone, all over this broad land, will yet swell the chorus of the Union, when again touched, as surely they will be, by the better angels of our nature.

45. *The War Begins:*

PRESIDENTIAL PROCLAMATION, APRIL 15, 1861

FOR more than a month after taking the oath of office, Lincoln continued the passive policy of his predecessor, James Buchanan. He made no move to coerce the seceded states, but at the same time he refused to order evacuation of the few forts in the deep South that were still held by Federal troops. One of these was Fort Sumter, at the entrance to the harbor of Charleston, South Carolina. Confederate batteries opened fire on April 12, and the garrison surrendered the next day. Lincoln responded with this proclamation calling out the state militia and convening Congress in special session. Four days later, he proclaimed a blockade of seaports from South Carolina to Texas, and on May 3 he ordered substantial increases in the Army and Navy of the United States.

April 15, 1861
By the President of the United States
A Proclamation.

Whereas the laws of the United States have been for some time past, and now are opposed, and the execution thereof obstructed, in the States of South Carolina, Georgia, Alabama, Florida, Mississippi, Louisiana and Texas, by combinations too powerful to be suppressed by the ordinary course of judicial proceedings, or by the powers vested in the Marshals by law,

Now therefore, I, Abraham Lincoln, President of the United States, in virtue of the power in me vested by the Constitution, and the laws, have thought fit to call forth, and hereby do call forth, the militia of the several States of the Union, to the aggregate number of seventy-five thousand, in order to suppress said combinations, and to cause the laws to be duly executed. The details, for this object, will be immediately communicated to the State authorities through the War Department.

I appeal to all loyal citizens to favor, facilitate and aid this effort to maintain the honor, the integrity, and the existence of our National Union, and the perpetuity of popular government; and to redress wrongs already long enough endured.

I deem it proper to say that the first service assigned to the forces hereby called forth will probably be to repossess the forts, places, and property which have been seized from the Union; and in every event, the utmost care will be observed, consistently with the objects aforesaid, to avoid any devastation, any destruction of, or interference with, property, or any disturbance of peaceful citizens in any part of the country.

And I hereby command the persons composing the combinations aforesaid to disperse, and retire peaceably to their respective abodes within twenty days from this date.

Deeming that the present condition of public affairs presents an extraordinary occasion, I do hereby, in virtue of the power in me vested by the Constitution, convene both Houses of Congress. Senators and Representatives are therefore summoned to assemble at their respective chambers, at 12 o'clock, noon, on Thursday, the fourth day of July, next, then and there to consider and determine, such measures, as, in their wisdom, the public safety, and interest may seem to demand.

In Witness Whereof I have hereunto set my hand, and caused the Seal of the United States to be affixed.

Done at the city of Washington this fifteenth day of April in the year of our Lord One thousand, Eight hundred and Sixty-one, and of the Independence of the United States the Eighty-fifth.

[Seal]

Abraham Lincoln

By the President
William H. Seward, Secretary of State.

46. A Friend Lost:

LETTER TO EPHRAIM D. AND PHOEBE ELLS-WORTH, MAY 25, 1861

ONE of the first casualties of the Civil War was Lincoln's young friend, Colonel Elmer E. Ellsworth, shot and killed while hauling down a Confederate flag in Alexandria, Virginia. So began the toll of lives that would weigh ever more oppressively upon his spirit. He wrote promptly to Ellsworth's parents in Mechanicville, New York.

Washington D. C.
May 25, 1861

To the Father and Mother of Col.
Elmer E. Ellsworth:

My dear Sir and Madam, In the untimely loss of your noble son, our affliction here, is scarcely less than your own. So much of promised usefulness to one's country, and of bright hopes for one's self and friends, have rarely been so suddenly dashed, as in his fall. In size, in years, and in youthful appearance, a boy only, his power to command men, was surpassingly great. This power, combined with a fine intellect, an indomitable energy, and a taste altogether military, constituted in him, as seemed to me, the best natural talent, in that department, I ever knew. And yet he was singularly modest and deferential in social intercourse. My acquaintance with him began less than two years ago; yet through the latter half of the intervening period, it was as intimate as the disparity of our ages, and my engrossing engagements, would permit. To me, he appeared to have no indulgences or pastimes; and I never heard him utter a profane, or an intemperate word. What was conclusive of his good heart, he never forgot his parents. The honors he labored for so laudably, and, in the sad end, so gallantly gave his life, he meant for them, no less than for himself.

In the hope that it may be no intrusion upon the sacredness of your sorrow, I have ventured to address you this tribute to the memory of my young friend, and your brave and early fallen child.

May God give you that consolation which is beyond all earthly power. Sincerely your friend in a common affliction—

A. Lincoln

47. *Mobilizing the National Will:*
MESSAGE TO CONGRESS IN SPECIAL SESSION, JULY 4, 1861

LINCOLN, in taking the first vigorous steps toward suppression of the rebellion, had quite obviously exceeded his constitutional authority. To Congress, when it assembled in special session, he offered an eloquent justification of his conduct. He also attempted to define the nature of the impending struggle. Four extensive extracts from the message are presented here.

It is thus seen that the assault upon, and reduction of, Fort Sumter, was, in no sense, a matter of self defence on the part of the assailants. They well knew that the garrison in the Fort could, by no possibility, commit aggression upon them. They knew—they were expressly notified—that the giving of bread to the few brave and hungry men of the garrison, was all which would on that occasion be attempted, unless themselves, by resisting so much, should provoke more. They knew that this Government desired to keep the garrison in the Fort, not to assail them, but merely to maintain visible possession, and thus to preserve the Union from actual, and immediate dissolution—trusting, as herein-before stated, to time, discussion, and the ballot-box, for final adjustment; and they assailed, and reduced the Fort, for precisely the reverse object—to drive out the visible authority of the Federal Union, and thus force it to immediate dissolution.

That this was their object, the Executive well understood; and having said to them in the inaugural address, "You can have no conflict without being yourselves the aggressors," he took pains, not only to keep this declaration good, but also to keep the case so free from the power of ingenious sophistry, as that the world should not be able to misunderstand it. By the affair at Fort Sumter, with its surrounding circumstances, that point was reached. Then, and thereby, the assailants of the Government, began the conflict of arms, without a gun in sight, or in expectancy, to return their fire, save only the few in the Fort, sent to that harbor, years before, for their own protection, and still ready to give that protection, in whatever was lawful. In this act, discarding all else, they have forced upon the country, the distinct issue: "Immediate dissolution, or blood."

And this issue embraces more than the fate of these United States. It presents to the whole family of man, the question, whether a constitutional republic, or a democracy—a government of the people, by the same people—can, or cannot, maintain its territorial integrity, against its own domestic foes. It presents the question, whether discontented individuals, too few in numbers to control administration, according to organic law, in any case, can always, upon the pretences made in this case, or on any other pretences, or arbitrarily, without any pretence, break up their Government, and thus practically put an end to free government upon the earth. It forces us to ask: "Is there, in all republics, this inherent, and fatal weakness?"

"Must a government, of necessity, be too *strong* for the liberties of its own people, or too *weak* to maintain its own existence?"

So viewing the issue, no choice was left but to call out the war power of the Government; and so to resist force, employed for its destruction, by force, for its preservation.

. . . . .

Soon after the first call for militia, it was considered a duty to authorize the Commanding General, in proper cases, according to his discretion, to suspend the privilege of the writ of habeas corpus; or, in other words, to arrest, and detain, without resort to the ordinary processes and forms of law, such individuals as he might deem dangerous to the public safety. This authority has purposely been exercised but very sparingly. Nevertheless, the legality and propriety of what has been done under it, are questioned; and the attention of the country has been called to the proposition that one who is sworn to "take care that the laws be faithfully executed," should not himself violate them. Of course some consideration was given to the questions of power, and propriety, before this matter was acted upon. The whole of the laws which were required to be faithfully executed, were being resisted, and failing of execution, in nearly one-third of the States. Must they be allowed to finally fail of execution, even had it been perfectly clear, that by the use of the means necessary to their execution, some single law, made in such extreme tenderness of the citizen's liberty, that practically, it relieves more of the guilty, than of the innocent, should, to a very limited extent, be violated? To state the question more directly, are all the laws, *but one,* to go unexecuted, and the government itself go to pieces, lest that one be violated? Even in such a case, would not the official oath be broken, if the government should be overthrown, when it was believed that disregarding the single law, would tend to preserve it? But it was not believed that this question was presented. It was not believed that any law was violated. The provision of the Constitution that "The privilege of the writ of habeas corpus, shall not be suspended unless when, in cases of rebellion or invasion, the public safety may require it," is equivalent to a provision—

is a provision—that such privilege may be suspended when, in cases of rebellion, or invasion, the public safety *does* require it. It was decided that we have a case of rebellion, and that the public safety does require the qualified suspension of the privilege of the writ which was authorized to be made. Now it is insisted that Congress, and not the Executive, is vested with this power. But the Constitution itself, is silent as to which, or who, is to exercise the power; and as the provision was plainly made for a dangerous emergency, it cannot be believed the framers of the instrument intended, that in every case, the danger should run its course, until Congress could be called together; the very assembling of which might be prevented, as was intended in this case, by the rebellion.

. . . . .

It might seem, at first thought, to be of little difference whether the present movement at the South be called "secession" or "rebellion." The movers, however, well understand the difference. At the beginning, they knew they could never raise their treason to any respectable magnitude, by any name which implies *violation* of law. They knew their people possessed as much of moral sense, as much of devotion to law and order, and as much pride in, and reverence for, the history, and government, of their common country, as any other civilized, and patriotic people. They knew they could make no advancement directly in the teeth of these strong and noble sentiments. Accordingly they commenced by an insidious debauching of the public mind. They invented an ingenious sophism, which, if conceded, was followed by perfectly logical steps, through all the incidents, to the complete destruction of the Union. The sophism itself is, that any state of the Union may, *consistently* with the national Constitution, and therefore *lawfully,* and *peacefully,* withdraw from the Union, without the consent of the Union, or of any other state. The little disguise that the supposed right is to be exercised only for just cause, themselves to be the sole judge of its justice, is too thin to merit any notice.

With rebellion thus sugar-coated, they have been drugging the public mind of their section for more than thirty years; and, until at length, they have brought many good men to a willingness to take up arms against the government the day *after* some assemblage of men have enacted the farcical pretence of taking their State out of the Union, who could have been brought to no such thing the day *before*.

This sophism derives much—perhaps the whole—of its currency, from the assumption, that there is some omnipotent, and sacred supremacy, pertaining to a *State*—to each State of our Federal Union. Our States have neither more, nor less power, than that reserved to them, in the Union, by the Constitution—no one of them ever having been a State *out* of the Union. The original ones passed into the Union even *before* they cast off their British colonial dependence; and the new ones each came into the Union directly from a condition of dependence, excepting Texas. And even Texas, in its temporary independence, was never designated a State. The new ones only took the designation of States, on coming into the Union, while that name was first adopted for the old ones, in, and by, the Declaration of Independence. Therein the "United Colonies" were declared to be "Free and Independent States"; but, even then, the object plainly was not to declare their independence of *one another*, or of the *Union;* but directly the contrary, as their mutual pledge, and their mutual action, before, at the time, and afterwards, abundantly show. The express plighting of faith, by each and all of the original thirteen, in the Articles of Confederation, two years later, that the Union shall be perpetual, is most conclusive. Having never been States, either in substance, or in name, *outside* of the Union, whence this magical omnipotence of "State rights," asserting a claim of power to lawfully destroy the Union itself? Much is said about the "sovereignty" of the States; but the word, even, is not in the national Constitution; nor, as is believed, in any of the State constitutions. What is a "sovereignty," in the political sense of the term? Would it be far wrong to define it "A political community, without a political superior"? Tested by this, no one of our States, except Texas, ever was a sovereignty. And even Texas gave up the character on coming into the Union; by which act, she acknowledged the Constitution of the United States, and the laws and treaties of the United States made in pursuance of the Constitution, to be, for her, the supreme law of the land. The States have their *status* IN the Union, and they have no other *legal status*. If they break from this, they can only do so against law, and by revolution. The Union, and not themselves separately, procured their independence, and their liberty. By conquest, or purchase, the Union gave each of them, whatever of independence, and liberty, it has. The Union is older than any of the States; and, in fact, it created them as States. Originally, some dependent colonies made the Union; and, in turn, the Union threw off their old dependence, for them, and made them States, such as they are. Not one of them ever had a State constitution, independent of the Union. Of course, it is not forgotten that all the new States framed their constitutions, before they entered the Union; nevertheless, dependent upon, and preparatory to, coming into the Union.

Unquestionably the States have the powers, and rights, reserved to them in, and by the National Constitution; but among these, surely, are not included all conceivable powers, however mischievous, or destructive; but, at most, such only, as were known in the world, at the time, as governmental powers; and certainly, a power to destroy the government itself, had never been known as a governmental—as a merely administrative power. This relative matter of National power, and State rights, as a principle, is no other than the principle of *generality,* and *locality.* Whatever concerns the whole, should be confided to the whole—to the general government; while, whatever concerns *only* the State, should be left exclusively, to the State. This is all there is of original principle about it. Whether the National Constitution, in defining boundaries between the two, has applied the principle with exact accuracy, is not to be questioned. We are all bound by that defining, without question.

What is now combatted, is the position that secession is *consistent* with the Constitution—is *lawful,* and *peaceful.* It is not contended that there is any express law for it; and nothing should ever be implied as law, which leads to unjust, or absurd consequences.

• • • • •

Our popular government has often been called an ex-

periment. Two points in it, our people have already settled
—the successful *establishing,* and the successful *administer-
ing* of it. One still remains—its successful *maintenance*
against a formidable [internal] attempt to overthrow it. It
is now for them to demonstrate to the world, that those
who can fairly carry an election, can also suppress a rebellion—that ballots are the rightful, and peaceful, successors of bullets; and that when ballots have fairly, and
constitutionally, decided, there can be no successful appeal, back to bullets; that there can be no successful appeal, except to ballots themselves, at succeeding elections.
Such will be a great lesson of peace; teaching men that
what they cannot take by an election, neither can they
take it by a war—teaching all, the folly of being the be-
ginners of a war.

Lest there be some uneasiness in the minds of candid
men, as to what is to be the course of the government, towards the Southern States, *after* the rebellion shall have
been suppressed, the Executive deems it proper to say, it
will be his purpose then, as ever, to be guided by the Constitution, and the laws; and that he probably will have no
different understanding of the powers, and duties of the
Federal government, relatively to the rights of the States,
and the people, under the Constitution, than that expressed in the inaugural address.

He desires to preserve the government, that it may be
administered for all, as it was administered by the men
who made it. Loyal citizens everywhere, have the right
to claim this of their government; and the government has
no right to withhold, or neglect it. It is not perceived that,
in giving it, there is any coercion, any conquest, or any
subjugation, in any just sense of those terms.

The Constitution provides, and all the States have accepted the provision, that "The United States shall guarantee to every State in this Union a republican form of
government." But, if a State may lawfully go out of the
Union, having done so, it may also discard the republican
form of government; so that to prevent its going out, is an
indispensable *means,* to the *end,* of maintaining the guaranty mentioned; and when an end is lawful and obligatory,
the indispensable means to it, are also lawful, and obligatory.

It was with the deepest regret that the Executive found the duty of employing the war-power, in defence of the government, forced upon him. He could but perform this duty, or surrender the existence of the government. No compromise, by public servants, could, in this case, be a cure; not that compromises are not often proper, but that no popular government can long survive a marked precedent, that those who carry an election, can only save the government from immediate destruction, by giving up the main point, upon which the people gave the election. The people themselves, and not their servants, can safely reverse their own deliberate decisions. As a private citizen, the Executive could not have consented that these institutions shall perish; much less could he, in betrayal of so vast, and so sacred a trust, as these free people had confided to him. He felt that he had no moral right to shrink; nor even to count the chances of his own life, in what might follow. In full view of his great responsibility, he has, so far, done what he has deemed his duty. You will now, according to your own judgment, perform yours. He sincerely hopes that your views, and your action, may so accord with his, as to assure all faithful citizens, who have been disturbed in their rights, of a certain, and speedy restoration to them, under the Constitution, and the laws.

And having thus chosen our course, without guile, and with pure purpose, let us renew our trust in God, and go forward without fear, and with manly hearts.

48. Becoming a Strategist:
MEMORANDA WRITTEN AFTER THE DEFEAT AT
BULL RUN, JULY, 1861

FOUR more states seceded after hostilities had begun at Fort Sumter, and Richmond, Virginia, became the capital of the enlarged Confederacy. On July 21, 1861, Union forces suffered a humiliating defeat in the first major engagement of the war at Bull Run, southwest of Washington. These notes jotted down a few days later reveal Lincoln's growing inclination to assume a share of the responsibility for military strategy.

July 23, 1861

1 Let the plan for making the Blockade effective be pushed forward with all possible despatch.

2 Let the volunteer forces at Fort-Monroe & vicinity—under Genl. Butler—be constantly drilled, disciplined, and instructed without more for the present.

3. Let Baltimore be held, as now, with a gentle, but firm, and certain hand.

4 Let the force now under Patterson, or Banks, be strengthened, and made secure in it's possition.

5. Let the forces in Western Virginia act, till further orders, according to instructions, or orders from Gen. McClellan.

6. [Let] Gen. Fremont push forward his organization, and opperations in the West as rapidly as possible, giving rather special attention to Missouri.

7 Let the forces late before Manassas, except the three months men, be reorganized as rapidly as possible, in their camps here and about Arlington

8. Let the three months forces, who decline to enter the longer service, be discharged as rapidly as circumstances will permit.

9. Let the new volunteer forces be brought forward as fast as possible; and especially into the camps on the two sides of the river here.

July 27, 1861

When the foregoing shall have been substantially attended to—

1. Let Manassas junction, (or some point on one or other of the railroads near it;); and Strasburg, be seized, and permanently held, with an open line from Washington to Manassas; and open line from Harper's Ferry to Strasburg—the military men to find the way of doing these.

2. This done, a joint movement from Cairo on Memphis; and from Cincinnati on East Tennessee.

49. *A Troublesome General:*
LETTER TO JOHN C. FRÉMONT, SEPTEMBER 2, 1861

JOHN C. FRÉMONT, celebrated explorer and Republican presidential nominee in 1856, was appointed to command the Department of the West, with headquarters at Fort Leavenworth. On August 30, 1861, he issued a rash proclamation placing Missouri under martial law, ordering wholesale executions, and confiscating the property and freeing the slaves of all persons supporting the Confederate cause. Lincoln responded immediately with a letter that was partly an order and partly a request. He pointed out that Congress had authorized the liberation of slaves only if they were actually used in hostile military activities.

Private and confidential.

Washington D. C. Sept. 2, 1861.

Major General Fremont:

My dear Sir: Two points in your proclamation of August 30th give me some anxiety. First, should you shoot a man, according to the proclamation, the Confederates would very certainly shoot our best man in their hands in retaliation; and so, man for man, indefinitely. It is therefore my order that you allow no man to be shot, under the proclamation, without first having my approbation or consent.

Secondly, I think there is great danger that the closing paragraph, in relation to the confiscation of property, and the liberating slaves of traiterous owners, will alarm our Southern Union friends, and turn them against us—perhaps ruin our rather fair prospect for Kentucky. Allow me therefore to ask, that you will as of your own motion, modify that paragraph so as to conform to the *first* and *fourth* sections of the act of Congress, entitled, "An act to confiscate property used for insurrectionary purposes," approved August 6th, 1861, and a copy of which act I herewith send you. This letter is written in a spirit of caution and not of censure.

I send it by a special messenger, in order that it may certainly and speedily reach you. Yours very truly,

A. Lincoln

50. *The Frémont Episode Continued:*
LETTER TO ORVILLE H. BROWNING, SEPTEMBER 22, 1861

FRÉMONT stubbornly refused to countermand his emancipation order until explicitly directed to do so in a second letter from Lincoln, dated September 11 and released for publication. The revocation drew many indignant protests from militant anti-slavery men. More surprising to Lincoln, however, were the objections of his friend Orville H. Browning, a conservative Republican who had been appointed to replace Douglas in the Senate after the latter's untimely death. Despite the hope expressed in this letter to Browning, the President soon found it necessary to remove Frémont from his command. The final sentence refers to another problem general, Stephen A. Hurlbut of Illinois, whose habitual drunkenness was common gossip.

Private & confidential.

Executive Mansion
Washington Sept 22d 1861.

Hon. O. H. Browning
My dear Sir:

Yours of the 17th is just received; and coming from you, I confess it astonishes me. That you should object to my adhering to a law, which you had assisted in making, and presenting to me, less than a month before, is odd enough. But this is a very small part. Genl. Fremont's proclamation, as to confiscation of property, and the liberation of slaves, is *purely political,* and not within the range of *military* law, or necessity. If a commanding General finds a necessity to seize the farm of a private owner, for a pasture, an encampment, or a fortification, he has the right to do so, and to so hold it, as long as the necessity lasts; and this is within military law, because within military necessity. But to say the farm shall no longer belong to the owner, or his heirs forever; and this as well when the farm is not needed for military purposes as when it is, is purely political, without the savor of military law about it. And the same is true of slaves. If the General needs them, he can seize them, and use them; but when the need is past, it is not for him to fix their permanent future condition. That must be settled according to laws made by law-makers, and not by military proclamations. The proclamation in the point in question, is simply "dictatorship." It assumes that the general may do *anything* he pleases—confiscate the lands and free the slaves of *loyal* people, as well as of disloyal ones. And going the whole figure I have no doubt would be more popular with some thoughtless people, than that which has been done! But I cannot assume this reckless position; nor allow others to assume it on my responsibility. You speak of it as being the only means of *saving* the government. On the contrary it is itself the surrender of the government. Can it be pretended that it is any longer the government of the U.S.—any government of Constitution and laws,—wherein a General, or a President, may make permanent rules of property by proclamation?

I do not say Congress might not with propriety pass a law, on the point, just such as General Fremont proclaimed. I do not say I might not, as a member of Congress, vote for it. What I object to, is, that I as President, shall expressly or impliedly seize and exercise the permanent legislative functions of the government.

So much as to principle. Now as to policy. No doubt the thing was popular in some quarters, and would have been more so if it had been a general declaration of emancipation. The Kentucky Legislature would not budge till that proclamation was modified; and Gen. Anderson telegraphed me that on the news of Gen. Fremont having actually issued deeds of manumission, a whole company of our Volunteers threw down their arms and disbanded.

I was so assured, as to think it probable, that the very arms we had furnished Kentucky would be turned against us. I think to lose Kentucky is nearly the same as to lose the whole game. Kentucky gone, we can not hold Missouri, nor, as I think, Maryland. These all against us, and the job on our hands is too large for us. We would as well consent to separation at once, including the surrender of this capitol. On the contrary, if you will give up your restlessness for new positions, and back me manfully on the grounds upon which you and other kind friends gave me the election, and have approved in my public documents, we shall go through triumphantly.

You must not understand I took my course on the proclamation *because* of Kentucky. I took the same ground in a private letter to General Fremont before I heard from Kentucky.

You think I am inconsistent because I did not also forbid Gen. Fremont to shoot men under the proclamation. I understand that part to be within military law; but I also think, and so privately wrote Gen. Fremont, that it is impolitic in this, that our adversaries have the power, and will certainly exercise it, to shoot as many of our men as we shoot of theirs. I did not say this in the public letter, because it is a subject I prefer not to discuss in the hearing of our enemies.

There has been no thought of removing Gen. Fremont on any ground connected with his proclamation; and if there has been any wish for his removal on any ground, our mutual friend Sam. Glover can probably tell you what it was. I hope no real necessity for it exists on any ground.

Suppose you write to Hurlbut and get him to resign. Your friend as ever,

A. Lincoln

51. Ends and Means:

ANNUAL MESSAGE TO CONGRESS, DECEMBER 3, 1861

AFTER Bull Run, there was much maneuvering and preparation, but no more major battles were fought during 1861. General George B. McClellan, the new Union commander, was drilling his troops in preparation for a spring offensive against Richmond, and General Ulysses S. Grant had not yet begun his invasion of Tennessee. On December 3, after nine months in office, Lincoln submitted his first annual message to Congress. The closing section, in which he turned from specific reports and recommendations to a broader discussion of the war, is reproduced here.

. . . . The war continues. In considering the policy to be adopted for suppressing the insurrection, I have been anxious and careful that the inevitable conflict for this purpose shall not degenerate into a violent and remorseless revolutionary struggle. I have, therefore, in every case, thought it proper to keep the integrity of the Union prominent as the primary object of the contest on our part, leaving all questions which are not of vital military importance to the more deliberate action of the legislature.

In the exercise of my best discretion I have adhered to the blockade of the ports held by the insurgents, instead of putting in force, by proclamation, the law of Congress enacted at the late session, for closing those ports.

So, also, obeying the dictates of prudence, as well as the obligations of law, instead of transcending, I have adhered to the act of Congress to confiscate property used for insurrectionary purposes. If a new law upon the same subject shall be proposed, its propriety will be duly considered.

The Union must be preserved, and hence, all indispensable means must be employed. We should not be in haste to determine that radical and extreme measures, which may reach the loyal as well as the disloyal, are indispensable.

The inaugural address at the beginning of the Administration, and the message to Congress at the late special session, were both mainly devoted to the domestic controversy out of which the insurrection and consequent war have sprung. Nothing now occurs to add or subtract, to or from, the principles or general purposes stated and expressed in those documents.

The last ray of hope for preserving the Union peaceably, expired at the assault upon Fort Sumter; and a general review of what has occurred since may not be unprofitable. What was painfully uncertain then, is much better defined and more distinct now; and the progress of events is plainly in the right direction. The insurgents confidently claimed a strong support from north of Mason and Dixon's line; and the friends of the Union were not free from apprehension on the point. This, however, was soon settled definitely and on the right side. South of the line, noble little Delaware led off right from the first. Maryland was made to *seem* against the Union. Our soldiers were assaulted, bridges were burned, and railroads torn up, within her limits; and we were many days, at one time, without the ability to bring a single regiment over her soil to the capital. Now, her bridges and railroads are repaired and open to the government; she already gives seven regiments to the cause of the Union and none to the enemy; and her people, at a regular election, have sustained the Union, by a larger majority, and a larger aggregate vote than they ever before gave to any candidate, or any question. Kentucky, too, for some time in doubt, is now decidedly, and, I think, unchangeably, ranged on the side of the Union. Missouri is comparatively quiet; and I believe cannot again be overrun by the insurrectionists. These three States of Maryland, Kentucky, and Missouri, neither of which would promise a single soldier at first, have now an aggregate of not less than forty thousand in the field, for the Union; while, of their citizens, certainly not more than a third of that number, and they of doubtful whereabouts, and doubtful existence, are in arms against it. After a somewhat bloody struggle of months, winter closes on the Union people of western Virginia, leaving them masters of their own country.

An insurgent force of about fifteen hundred, for months dominating the narrow peninsular region, constituting the counties of Accomac and Northampton, and known as eastern shore of Virginia, together with some contiguous parts of Maryland, have laid down their arms; and the people there have renewed their allegiance to, and accepted the protection of, the old flag. This leaves no armed insurrectionist north of the Potomac, or east of the Chesapeake.

Also we have obtained a footing at each of the isolated points, on the southern coast, of Hatteras, Port Royal, Tybee Island, near Savannah, and Ship Island; and we likewise have some general accounts of popular movements, in behalf of the Union, in North Carolina and Tennessee.

These things demonstrate that the cause of the Union is advancing steadily and certainly southward.

Since your last adjournment, Lieutenant General Scott has retired from the head of the army. During his long life, the nation has not been unmindful of his merit; yet, on calling to mind how faithfully, ably and brilliantly he has served the country, from a time far back in our history, when few of the now living had been born, and thenceforward continually, I cannot but think we are still his debtors. I submit, therefore, for your consideration, what further mark of recognition is due to him, and to ourselves, as a grateful people.

With the retirement of General Scott came the executive duty of appointing, in his stead, a general-in-chief of the army. It is a fortunate circumstance that neither in council nor country was there, so far as I know, any difference of opinion as to the proper person to be selected. The retiring chief repeatedly expressed his judgment in favor of General McClellan for the position; and in this the nation seemed to give a unanimous concurrence. The designation of General McClellan is therefore in considerable degree, the selection of the Country as well as of the Executive; and hence there is better reason to hope there will be given him, the confidence, and cordial support thus, by fair implication, promised, and without which, he cannot, with so full efficiency, serve the country.

It has been said that one bad general is better than two good ones; and the saying is true, if taken to mean no more than that an army is better directed by a single mind, though inferior, than by two superior ones, at variance, and cross-purposes with each other.

And the same is true, in all joint operations wherein those engaged, *can* have none but a common end in view, and *can* differ only as to the choice of means. In a storm at sea, no one on board *can* wish the ship to sink; and yet, not unfrequently, all go down together, because too many will direct, and no single mind can be allowed to control.

It continues to develop that the insurrection is largely, if not exclusively, a war upon the first principle of popular government—the rights of the people. Conclusive evidence of this is found in the most grave and maturely considered public documents, as well as in the general tone of the insurgents. In those documents we find the abridgement of the existing right of suffrage and the denial to the people of all right to participate in the selection of public offers, except the legislative boldly advocated, with labored arguments to prove that large control of the people in government, is the source of all political evil. Monarchy itself is sometimes hinted at as a possible refuge from the power of the people.

In my present position, I could scarcely be justified were I to omit raising a warning voice against this approach of returning despotism.

It is not needed, nor fitting here, that a general argument should be made in favor of popular institutions; but there is one point, with its connexions, not so hackneyed as most others, to which I ask a brief attention. It is the effort to place *capital* on an equal footing with, if not above *labor,* in the structure of government. It is assumed that labor is available only in connexion with capital; that nobody labors unless somebody else, owning capital, somehow by the use of it, induces him to labor. This assumed, it is next considered whether it is best that capital shall *hire* laborers, and thus induce them to work by their own consent, or *buy* them, and drive them to it without their consent. Having proceeded so far, it is naturally concluded that all laborers are either *hired* laborers, or what we call slaves. And further it is assumed that whoever is once a hired laborer, is fixed in that condition for life.

Now, there is no such relation between capital and labor as assumed; nor is there any such thing as a free man being fixed for life in the condition of a hired laborer. Both these assumptions are false, and all inferences from them are groundless.

Labor is prior to, and independent of, capital. Capital is only the fruit of labor, and could never have existed if labor had not first existed. Labor is the superior of capital, and deserves much the higher consideration. Capital has its rights, which are as worthy of protection as any other rights. Nor is it denied that there is, and probably always will be, a relation between labor and capital, producing mutual benefits. The error is in assuming that the whole labor of community exists within that relation. A few men own capital, and that few avoid labor themselves, and, with their capital, hire or buy another few to labor for them. A large majority belong to neither class—neither work for others, nor have others working for them. In most of the southern States, a majority of the whole people of all colors are neither slaves nor masters; while in the northern a large majority are neither hirers nor hired. Men with their families—wives, sons, and daughters—work for themselves, on their farms, in their houses, and in their shops, taking the whole product to themselves, and asking no favors of capital on the one hand, nor of hired laborers or slaves on the other. It is not forgotten that a considerable number of persons mingle their own labor with capital—that is, they labor with their own hands, and also buy or hire others to labor for them; but this is only a mixed, and not a distinct class. No principle stated is disturbed by the existence of this mixed class.

Again: as has already been said, there is not, of necessity, any such thing as the free hired laborer being fixed to that condition for life. Many independent men everywhere in these States, a few years back in their lives, were hired laborers. The prudent, penniless beginner in the world, labors for wages awhile, saves a surplus with which to buy tools or land for himself; then labors on his own account another while, and at length hires another new beginner to help him. This is the just, and generous, and prosperous system, which opens the way to all—gives hope to all, and consequent energy, and progress, and improvement of condition to all. No men living are more worthy to be trusted than those who toil up from poverty—none less inclined to take, or touch, aught which they have not honestly earned. Let them beware of surrendering a political power which they already possess, and which, if surrendered, will surely be used to close the door of advancement against such as they, and to fix new disabilities and burdens upon them, till all of liberty shall be lost.

From the first taking of our national census to the last are seventy years; and we find our population at the end of the period eight times as great as it was at the beginning. The increase of those other things which men deem desirable has been even greater. We thus have at one view, what the popular principle applied to government, through the machinery of the States and the Union, has produced in a given time; and also what, if firmly maintained, it promises for the future. There are already among us those, who, if the Union be preserved, will live to see it contain two hundred and fifty millions. The struggle of today, is not altogether for to-day—it is for a vast future also. With a reliance on Providence, all the more firm and earnest, let us proceed in the great task which events have devolved upon us.

52. *Blunt Words for a Malcontent:*
LETTER TO DAVID HUNTER, DECEMBER 31, 1861

GENERAL David Hunter, who had replaced Frémont in the West, was dissatisfied with his small command and complained that it amounted to "banishment." Lincoln did not mince words in his reply.

Executive Mansion, Washington,
Dec. 31, 1861.

Major General Hunter.

Dear Sir: Yours of the 23rd. is received; and I am constrained to say it is difficult to answer so ugly a letter in good temper. I am, as you intimate, losing much of the great confidence I placed in you, not from any act or omission of yours touching the public service, up to the time you were sent to Leavenworth, but from the flood of grumbling despatches and letters I have seen from you since. I knew you were being ordered to Leavenworth at the time it was done; and I aver that with as tender a regard for your honor and your sensibilities as I had for my own, it never occurred to me that you were being "humiliated, insulted and disgraced"; nor have I, up to this day, heard an intimation that you have been wronged, coming from any one but yourself. No one has blamed you for the retrograde movement from Springfield, nor for the information you gave Gen. Cameron; and this you could readily understand, if it were not for your unwarranted assumption that the ordering you to Leavenworth must necessarily have been done as a *punishment* for some *fault*. I thought then, and think yet, the position assigned to you is as respo[n]sible, and as honorable, as that assigned to Buell. I know that Gen. McClellan expected more important results from it. My impression is that at the time you were assigned to the new Western Department, it had not been determined to re-place Gen. Sherman in Kentucky; but of this I am not certain, because the idea that a command in Kentucky was very desireable, and one in the farther West, very undesireable, had never occurred to me. You constantly speak of being placed in command of only 3000. Now tell me, is not this mere impatience? Have you not known all the while that you are to command four or five times that many?

I have been, and am sincerely your friend; and if, as such, I dare to make a suggestion, I would say you are adopting the best possible way to ruin yourself. "Act well your part, there all the honor lies." He who does *something* at the head of one Regiment, will eclipse him who does *nothing* at the head of a hundred. Your friend as ever,
A. Lincoln

53. Eastern Tennessee:
LETTER TO DON C. BUELL, JANUARY 6, 1862

LINCOLN wanted Confederate forces cleared out of eastern Tennessee because the region was a stronghold of Unionist sympathies. He explained his concern to General Don C. Buell, who commanded the Army of the Ohio. Senator Andrew Johnson, mentioned in this letter, was soon to be appointed military governor of Tennessee.

Executive Mansion,
Washington, January 6th, 1862.

Brig. Gen. Buell

My dear Sir: Your despatch of yesterday has been received, and it disappoints and distresses me. I have shown it to Gen. McClellan, who says he will write you to-day. I am not competent to criticise your views; and therefore what I offer is merely in justification of myself. Of the two, I would rather have a point on the Railroad south of Cumberland Gap, than Nashville, first, because it cuts a great artery of the enemies' communication, which Nashville does not, and secondly because it is in the midst of loyal people, who would rally around it, while Nashville is not. Again, I cannot see why the movement on East Tennessee would not be a diversion in your favor, rather than a disadvantage, assuming that a movement towards Nashville is the main object.

But my distress is that our friends in East Tennessee are being hanged and driven to despair, and even now I fear, are thinking of taking rebel arms for the sake of personal protection. In this we lose the most valuable stake we have in the South. My despatch, to which yours is an answer, was sent with the knowledge of Senator Johnson and Representative Maynard of East Tennessee, and they will be upon me to know the answer, which I cannot safely show them. They would despair—possibly resign to go and save their families somehow, or die with them.

I do not intend this to be an order in any sense, but merely, as intimated before, to show you the grounds of my anxiety. Yours very Truly,

A. Lincoln

54. The Fundamental Problem:
LETTER TO DON C. BUELL, JANUARY 13, 1862

A subsequent letter to Buell contains this pithy exposition of overall military strategy.

I state my general idea of this war to be that we have the *greater* numbers, and the enemy has the *greater* facility of concentrating forces upon points of collision; that we must fail, unless we can find some way of making *our* advantage an over-match for *his;* and that this can only be done by menacing him with superior forces at *different* points, at the *same* time; so that we can safely attack one, or both, if he makes no change; and if he *weakens* one to *strengthen* the other, forbear to attack the strengthened one, but seize, and hold the weakened one, gaining so much.

55. The Way to Richmond:
LETTER TO GECRGE B. McCLELLAN, FEBRUARY 3, 1862

IN the East, General McClellan decided to move his army by water to a likely place on the Virginia coast and then strike in-land toward Richmond. Lincoln, who feared that the plan would leave Washington without adequate protection, preferred an advance straight southward.

Executive Mansion,
Washington, Feb. 3, 1862.

Major General McClellan

My dear Sir: You and I have distinct, and different plans for a movement of the Army of the Potomac—yours to be down the Chesapeake, up the Rappahannock to Urbana, and across land to the terminus of the Railroad on the York River—, mine to move directly to a point on the Railroad South West of Manassas.

If you will give me satisfactory answers to the following questions, I shall gladly yield my plan to yours.

1st. Does not your plan involve a greatly larger expenditure of *time,* and *money* than mine?

2nd. Wherein is a victory *more certain* by your plan than mine?

3rd. Wherein is a victory *more valuable* by your plan than mine?

4th. In fact, would it not be *less* valuable, in this, that it would break no great line of the enemie's communications, while mine would?

5th. In case of disaster, would not a safe retreat be more difficult by your plan than by mine? Yours truly,

A. Lincoln

56. The Peninsular Campaign:
LETTER TO GEORGE B. McCLELLAN, APRIL 9, 1862

DESPITE the President's doubts, McClellan insisted upon executing his plan. With characteristic skill he transported about 100,-000 troops down Chesapeake Bay to the tip of the York peninsula. But there his lack of aggressiveness as a field commander began to manifest itself. Choosing to reduce Yorktown by formal siege instead of taking it by assault, he was delayed for a month, and the Confederates were thus given time to organize their defenses. Throughout the campaign, McClellan repeatedly demanded more troops and complained that he was not adequately supported. The principal bone of contention was the corps commanded by General Irvin McDowell. Scheduled to move overland toward Richmond, it was withheld by Lincoln for the protection of Washington.

Washington,
April 9, 1862

Major General McClellan.
My dear Sir:

Your despatches complaining that you are not properly sustained, while they do not offend me, do pain me very much.

Blencker's Division was withdrawn from you before you left here; and you knew the pressure under which I did it, and, as I thought, acquiesced in it—certainly not without reluctance.

After you left, I ascertained that less than twenty thousand unorganized men, without a single field battery, were all you designed to be left for the defence of Washington, and Manassas Junction; and part of this even, was to go to Gen. Hooker's old position. Gen. Banks' corps, once designed for Manassas Junction, was diverted, and tied up on the line of Winchester and Strausburg, and could not leave it without again exposing the upper Potomac, and the Baltimore and Ohio Railroad. This presented, (or would present, when McDowell and Sumner should be gone) a great temptation to the enemy to turn back from the Rappahanock, and sack Washington. My explicit order that Washington should, by the judgment of *all* the commanders of Army corps, be left entirely secure, had been neglected. It was precisely this that drove me to detain McDowell.

I do not forget that I was satisfied with your arrangement to leave Banks at Mannassas Junction; but when that arrangement was broken up, and *nothing* was substituted for it, of course I was not satisfied. I was constrained to substitute something for it myself. And now allow me to ask "Do you really think I should permit the line from

Richmond, *via* Mannassas Junction, to this city to be entirely open, except what resistance could be presented by less than twenty thousand unorganized troops?" This is a question which the country will not allow me to evade.

There is a curious mystery about the *number* of troops now with you. When I telegraphed you on the 6th. saying you had over a hundred thousand with you, I had just obtained from the Secretary of War, a statement, taken as he said, from your own returns, making 108,000 then with you, and *en route* to you. You now say you will have but 85,000, when all *en route* to you shall have reached you. How can the discrepancy of 23,000 be accounted for?

As to Gen. Wool's command, I understand it is doing for you precisely what a like number of your own would have to do, if that command was away.

I suppose the whole force which has gone forward for you, is with you by this time; and if so, I think it is the precise time for you to strike a blow. By delay the enemy will relatively gain upon you—that is, he will gain faster, by *fortifications* and *re-inforcements,* than you can by *re-inforcements* alone.

And, once more let me tell you, it is indispensable to *you* that you strike a blow. *I* am powerless to help this. You will do me the justice to remember I always insisted, that going down the Bay in search of a field, instead of fighting at or near Mannassas, was only shifting, and not surmounting, a difficulty—that we would find the same enemy, and the same, or equal, intrenchments, at either place. The country will not fail to note—is now noting—that the present hesitation to move upon an intrenched enemy, is but the story of Manassas repeated.

I beg to assure you that I have never written you, or spoken to you, in greater kindness of feeling than now, nor with a fuller purpose to sustain you, so far as in my most anxious judgment, I consistently can. *But you must act.* Yours very truly,

A. Lincoln

57. *Emancipation Again:*
PRESIDENTIAL PROCLAMATION, MAY 19, 1862

GENERAL David Hunter, transferred from the West to command the Union forces holding certain points along the Southern coast, issued an order on May 9, 1862, freeing all slaves in South Carolina, Georgia, and Florida. Lincoln revoked the order, but seized the opportunity to renew his plea for gradual emancipation. He had already secured passage of a resolution in Congress promising financial assistance to any slave state that inaugurated such a program.

I, Abraham Lincoln, president of the United States, proclaim and declare, that the government of the United States, had no knowledge, information, or belief, of an intention on the part of General Hunter to issue such a proclamation; nor has it yet, any authentic information that the document is genuine. And further, that neither General Hunter, nor any other commander, or person, has been authorized by the Government of the United States, to make proclamations declaring the slaves of any State free; and that the supposed proclamation, now in question, whether genuine or false, is altogether void, so far as respects such declaration.

I further make known that whether it be competent for me, as Commander-in-Chief of the Army and Navy, to declare the Slaves of any state or states, free, and whether at any time, in any case, it shall have become a necessity indispensable to the maintenance of the government, to exercise such supposed power, are questions which, under my responsibility, I reserve to myself, and which I can not feel justified in leaving to the decision of commanders in the field. These are totally different questions from those of police regulations in armies and camps.

On the sixth day of March last, by a special message,

I recommended to Congress the adoption of a joint resolution to be substantially as follows:

> *Resolved,* That the United States ought to co-operate with any State which may adopt a gradual abolishment of slavery, giving to such State pecuniary aid, to be used by such State in its discretion to compensate for the inconveniences, public and private, produced by such change of system.

The resolution, in the language above quoted, was adopted by large majorities in both branches of Congress, and now stands an authentic, definite, and solemn proposal of the nation to the States and people most immediately interested in the subject matter. To the people of those states I now earnestly appeal. I do not argue. I beseech you to make the arguments for yourselves. You can not if you would, be blind to the signs of the times. I beg of you a calm and enlarged consideration of them, ranging, if it may be, far above personal and partizan politics. This proposal makes common cause for a common object, casting no reproaches upon any. It acts not the pharisee. The change it contemplates would come gently as the dews of heaven, not rending or wrecking anything. Will you not embrace it? So much good has not been done, by one effort, in all past time, as, in the providence of God, it is now your high privilege to do. May the vast future not have to lament that you have neglected it.

58. *The Seven Days:*

LETTER TO GEORGE B. McCLELLAN, JUNE 28, 1862

BY late June, McClellan had advanced to within a few miles of Richmond. In the fierce fighting of the "Seven Days' Battles," he was forced to draw back, but ably repulsed Confederate efforts to destroy his army. He had entered this critical phase of the campaign without much hope of success, protesting bitterly that his force was too small. Lincoln, realizing that Richmond could not be taken, urged his querulous commander to hold on and wait for reinforcements.

Washington City, D.C.
June 28, 1862

Major Gen. McClellan:

Save your Army at all events. Will send re-inforcements as fast as we can. Of course they can not reach you to-day, to-morrow, or next day. I have not said you were ungenerous for saying you needed re-inforcement. I thought you were ungenerous in assuming that I did not send them as fast as I could. I feel any misfortune to you and your Army quite as keenly as you feel it yourself. If you have had a drawn battle, or a repulse, it is the price we pay for the enemy not being in Washington. We protected Washington, and the enemy concentrated on you; had we stripped Washington, he would have been upon us before the troops sent could have got to you. Less than a week ago you notified us that re-inforcements were leaving Richmond to come in front of us. It is the nature of the case, and neither you or the government that is to blame. Please tell at once the present condition and aspect of things.

A. Lincoln

59. New Orleans Under Occupation:
LETTER TO REVERDY JOHNSON, JULY 26, 1862

IN the spring of 1862, a Union expedition captured New Orleans and occupied the neighboring territory. The local populace soon came to detest the commanding general, Benjamin F. Butler, and one of his brigadiers, John W. Phelps. Lincoln was informed of the growing resentment by Reverdy Johnson, a leading Maryland Unionist, who had been sent to investigate the situation. Johnson subsequently protested that Lincoln was entirely mistaken in what he said about their conversation in April 1861.

Executive Mansion,
Washington, July 26, 1862.

Hon Reverdy Johnson

My Dear Sir: Yours of the 16th. by the hand of Governor Shepley is received. It seems the Union feeling in Louisiana is being crushed out by the course of General Phelps. Please pardon me for believing that is a false pretense. The people of Louisiana—all intelligent people every where—know full well, that I never had a wish to touch the foundations of their society, or any right of theirs. With perfect knowledge of this, they forced a necessity upon me to send armies among them, and it is their own fault, not mine, that they are annoyed by the presence of General Phelps. They also know the remedy—know how to be cured of General Phelps. Remove the necessity of his presence. And might it not be well for them to consider whether they have not already had *time* enough to do this? If they can conceive of anything worse than General Phelps, within my power, would they not better be looking out for it? They very well know the way to avert all this is simply to take their place in the Union upon the old terms. If they will not do this, should they not receive harder blows rather than lighter ones?

You are ready to say I apply to *friends* what is due only to *enemies*. I distrust the *wisdom* if not the *sincerity* of friends, who would hold my hands while my enemies stab me. This appeal of professed friends has paralyzed me more in this struggle than any other one thing. You remember telling me the day after the Baltimore mob in April 1861, that it would crush all Union feeling in Maryland for me to attempt bringing troops over Maryland soil to Washington. I brought the troops notwithstanding, and yet there was Union feeling enough left to elect a Legislature the next autumn which in turn elected a very excellent Union U. S. Senator!

I am a patient man—always willing to forgive on the Christian terms of repentance; and also to give ample *time* for repentance. Still I must save this government if possible. What I *cannot* do, of course I *will* not do; but it may as well be understood, once for all, that I shall not surrender this game leaving any available card unplayed. Yours truly,

A. Lincoln

60. *The Paramount Object:*
LETTER TO HORACE GREELEY, AUGUST 22, 1862

IN the New York *Tribune* of August 20, 1862, Horace Greeley published a censorious open letter to the President entitled "The Prayer of Twenty Millions." His chief complaint was that Lincoln had shown far too much deference to the institution of slavery. Lincoln's prompt reply trenchantly defined the purpose of the war.

Executive Mansion,
Washington, August 22, 1862.

Hon. Horace Greely:
Dear Sir

I have just read yours of the 19th. addressed to myself through the New-York Tribune. If there be in it any statements, or assumptions of fact, which I may know to be erroneous, I do not, now and here, controvert them. If there be in it any inferences which I may believe to be falsely drawn, I do not now and here, argue against them. If there be perceptable in it an impatient and dictatorial tone, I waive it in deference to an old friend, whose heart I have always supposed to be right.

As to the policy I "seem to be pursuing" as you say, I have not meant to leave any one in doubt.

I would save the Union. I would save it the shortest way under the Constitution. The sooner the national authority can be restored; the nearer the Union will be "the Union as it was." If there be those who would not save the Union, unless they could at the same time *save* slavery, I do not agree with them. If there be those who would not save the Union unless they could at the same time *destroy* slavery, I do not agree with them. My paramount object in this struggle *is* to save the Union, and is *not* either to save or to destroy slavery. If I could save the Union without freeing *any* slave I would do it, and if I could save it by freeing *all* the slaves I would do it; and if I could save it by freeing some and leaving others alone I would also do that. What I do about slavery, and the colored race, I do because I believe it helps to save the Union; and what I forbear, I forbear because I do *not* believe it would help to save the Union. I shall do *less* whenever I shall believe what I am doing hurts the cause, and I shall do *more* whenever I shall believe doing more will help the cause. I shall try to correct errors when shown to be errors; and I shall adopt new views so fast as they shall appear to be true views.

I have here stated my purpose according to my view of *official* duty; and I intend no modification of my oft-expressed *personal* wish that all men every where could be free.   Yours,   A. Lincoln

61. *After Another Defeat:*

MEDITATION ON THE DIVINE WILL, SEPTEMBER, 1862

HAVING failed to take Richmond, McClellan was ordered to abandon the peninsular campaign and found himself reduced to a subordinate role in support of a new commander, General John Pope. At the second battle of Bull Run, August 29–30, 1862, Pope blundered his way to a severe defeat. Some time after receiving the bitter news, Lincoln wrote down these private thoughts about God and the war.

The will of God prevails. In great contests each party claims to act in accordance with the will of God. Both *may* be, and one *must* be wrong. God can not be *for,* and *against* the same thing at the same time. In the present civil war it is quite possible that God's purpose is something different from the purpose of either party—and yet the human instrumentalities, working just as they do, are of the best adaptation to effect His purpose. I am almost ready to say this is probably true—that God wills this contest, and wills that it shall not end yet. By his mere quiet power, on the minds of the now contestants, He could have either *saved* or *destroyed* the Union without a human contest. Yet the contest began. And having begun He could give the final victory to either side any day. Yet the contest proceeds.

62. *An Historic Step:*

THE PRELIMINARY EMANCIPATION PROCLAMATION, SEPTEMBER 22, 1862

DESPITE his letter to Greeley, Lincoln was already contemplating emancipation during the summer of 1862. He broached the subject at a cabinet meeting on July 22, but Seward persuaded him to wait until the military situation improved. Then came the severe setback at Bull Run, after which General Robert E. Lee thrust his victorious Confederate army northward into Maryland. Lincoln, reinstating McClellan to resist the invasion, still withheld his blow against slavery. To an abolition memorial from Chicago, he replied on September 13: "What *good* would a proclamation of emancipation from me do, especially as we are now situated? I do not want to issue a document that the whole world will see must necessarily be inoperative, like the Pope's bull against the comet!" Just four days later, however, Lee's advance was checked at the bloody battle of Antietam, and Lincoln responded with what is called the "preliminary" Emancipation Proclamation. In it, he promised to declare slavery abolished in all areas that were still in rebellion on January 1, 1863. The significant parts of the document are presented here.

I, Abraham Lincoln, President of the United States of America, and Commander-in-chief of the Army and Navy thereof, do hereby proclaim and declare that hereafter, as heretofore, the war will be prossecuted for the object of practically restoring the constitutional relation between the United States, and each of the states, and the people thereof, in which states that relation is, or may be suspended, or disturbed.

That it is my purpose, upon the next meeting of Congress to again recommend the adoption of a practical measure tendering pecuniary aid to the free acceptance or rejection of all slave-states, so called, the people whereof may not then be in rebellion against the United States, and which states, may then have voluntarily adopted, or thereafter may voluntarily adopt, immediate, or gradual abolishment of slavery within their respective limits; and that the effort to colonize persons of African descent, with their consent, upon this continent, or elsewhere, with the previously obtained consent of the Governments existing there, will be continued.

That on the first day of January in the year of our Lord, one thousand eight hundred and sixty-three, all persons held as slaves within any state, or designated part of a state, the people whereof shall then be in rebellion against the United States shall be then, thenceforward, and forever free; and the executive government of the United States, including the military and naval authority thereof, will recognize and maintain the freedom of such persons, and will do no act or acts to repress such persons, or any of them, in any efforts they may make for their actual freedom.

That the executive will, on the first day of January aforesaid, by proclamation, designate the States, and parts of states, if any, in which the people thereof respectively, shall then be in rebellion against the United States; and the fact that any state, or the people thereof shall, on that day be, in good faith represented in the Congress of the United States, by members chosen thereto, at elections wherein a majority of the qualified voters of such state shall have participated, shall, in the absence of strong countervailing testimony, be deemed conclusive evidence that such state and the people thereof, are not then in rebellion against the United States.

. . . . .

And the executive will in due time recommend that all citizens of the United States who shall have remained loyal thereto throughout the rebellion, shall (upon restoration of the constitutional relation between the United States, and their respective states, and people, if that relation shall have been suspended or disturbed) be compensated for all losses by acts of the United States, including the loss of slaves.

63. *Anxious Afterthoughts:*
LETTER TO HANNIBAL HAMLIN, SEPTEMBER 28, 1862

THE preliminary Emancipation Proclamation had a profound effect upon public opinion at home and abroad. Yet Lincoln, as he revealed in this letter to Vice-President Hannibal Hamlin, could not entirely repress some nagging doubts.

(*Strictly private.*)
Executive Mansion,
Washington, September 28, 1862.
My Dear Sir: Your kind letter of the 25th is just received. It is known to some that while I hope something from the proclamation, my expectations are not as sanguine as are those of some friends. The time for its effect southward has not come; but northward the effect should be instantaneous.

It is six days old, and while commendation in newspapers and by distinguished individuals is all that a vain man could wish, the stocks have declined, and troops come forward more slowly than ever. This, looked soberly in the face, is not very satisfactory. We have fewer troops in

the field at the end of six days than we had at the beginning—the attrition among the old outnumbering the addition by the new. The North responds to the proclamation
sufficiently in breath; but breath alone kills no rebels.

I wish I could write more cheerfully; nor do I thank
you the less for the kindness of your letter. Yours very
truly,   A. Lincoln

64. *Inertia Again:*

LETTER TO GEORGE B. McCLELLAN, OCTOBER 13,
1862

MCCLELLAN did not follow up his advantage after Antietam,
and Lee's army slipped back into Virginia. Lincoln, now under
heavy pressure from Republican leaders to dismiss his reluctant
commander, tried over and over to prod him into action.

Executive Mansion,
Washington, Oct. 13, 1862.

Major General McClellan
My dear Sir:

You remember my speaking to you of what I called your
over-cautiousness. Are you not over-cautious when you
assume that you can not do what the enemy is constantly
doing? Should you not claim to be at least his equal in
prowess, and act upon the claim?

As I understand, you telegraph Gen. Halleck that you
can not subsist your army at Winchester unless the Railroad from Harper's Ferry to that point be put in working
order. But the enemy does now subsist his army at Winchester at a distance nearly twice as great from railroad
transportation as you would have to do without the railroad last named. He now wagons from Culpepper C. H.
which is just about twice as far as you would have to do
from Harper's Ferry. He is certainly not more than half as
well provided with wagons as you are. I certainly should be
pleased for you to have the advantage of the Railroad from

Harper's Ferry to Winchester, but it wastes all the remainder of autumn to give it to you; and, in fact ignores the question of *time,* which can not, and must not be ignored.

Again, one of the standard maxims of war, as you know, is "to operate upon the enemy's communications as much as possible without exposing your own." You seem to act as if this applies *against* you, but can not apply in your *favor.* Change positions with the enemy, and think you not he would break your communication with Richmond within the next twentyfour hours? You dread his going into Pennsylvania. But if he does so in full force, he gives up his communications to you absolutely, and you have nothing to do but to follow, and ruin him; if he does so with less than full force, fall upon, and beat what is left behind all the easier.

Exclusive of the water line, you are now nearer Richmond than the enemy is by the route that you *can,* and he *must* take. Why can you not reach there before him, unless you admit that he is more than your equal on a march. His route is the arc of a circle, while yours is the chord. The roads are as good on yours as on his.

You know I desired, but did not order, you to cross the Potomac below, instead of above the Shenandoah and Blue Ridge. My idea was that this would at once menace the enemies' communications, which I would seize if he would permit. If he should move Northward I would follow him closely, holding his communications. If he should prevent our seizing his communications, and move towards Richmond, I would press closely to him, fight him if a favorable opportunity should present, and, at least, try to beat him to Richmond on the inside track. I say "try"; if we never try, we shall never succeed. If he make a stand at Winchester, moving neither North or South, I would fight him there, on the idea that if we can not beat him when he bears the wastage of coming to us, we never can when we bear the wastage of going to him. This proposition is a simple truth, and is too important to be lost sight of for a moment. In coming to us, he tenders us an advantage which we should not waive. We should not so operate as to merely drive him away. As we must beat him somewhere, or fail finally, we can do it, if at all, easier near to us, than far away. If we can not beat the enemy where he now is, we never can, he again being within the entrenchments of Richmond.

Recurring to the idea of going to Richmond on the inside track, the facility of supplying from the side away from the enemy is remarkable—as it were, by the different spokes of a wheel extending from the hub towards the rim —and this whether you move directly by the chord, or on the inside arc, hugging the Blue Ridge more closely. The chord-line, as you see, carries you by Aldie, Hay-Market, and Fredericksburg; and you see how turn-pikes, railroads, and finally, the Potomac by Acquia Creek, meet you at all points from Washington. The same, only the lines lengthened a little, if you press closer to the Blue Ridge part of the way. The gaps through the Blue Ridge I understand to be about the following distances from Harper's Ferry, towit: Vestal's five miles; Gregorie's, thirteen, Snicker's eighteen, Ashby's, twenty-eight, Mannassas, thirty-eight, Chester fortyfive, and Thornton's fifty-three. I should think it preferable to take the route nearest the enemy, disabling him to make an important move without your knowledge, and compelling him to keep his forces together, for dread of you. The gaps would enable you to attack if you should wish. For a great part of the way, you would be practically between the enemy and both Washington and Richmond, enabling us to spare you the greatest number of troops from here. When at length, running for Richmond ahead of him enables him to move this way; if he does so, turn and attack him in rear. But I think he should be engaged long before such point is reached. It is all easy if our troops march as well as the enemy; and it is unmanly to say they can not do it.

This letter is in no sense an order. Yours truly,

A. Lincoln

65. Defeat at the Polls:

LETTER TO CARL SCHURZ, NOVEMBER 10, 1862

THE autumn elections of 1862 resulted in many Democratic victories and constituted a sharp rebuke to Lincoln's administration. Military failure was obviously the predominant cause of popular discontent. Carl Schurz, leader of the German Republicans and now a brigadier general, insisted that the President had invited defeat by giving too much consideration and authority to Democrats like McClellan. Lincoln's reply closed with a gentle reminder that the partisan zeal of Republican commanders had not made them any more successful in the field.

"Private & Confidential"

Executive Mansion,
Washington, Nov. 10, 1862.

Gen. Schurz.

My dear Sir:

Yours of the 8th. was, to-day, read to me by Mrs. S[churz]. We have lost the elections; and it is natural that each of us will believe, and say, it has been because his peculiar views was not made sufficiently prominent. I think I know what it was, but I may be mistaken. Three main causes told the whole story. 1. The democrats were left in a majority by our friends going to the war. 2. The democrats observed this & determined to re-instate themselves in power, and 3. Our newspaper's, by vilifying and disparaging the administration, furnished them all the weapons to do it with. Certainly, the ill-success of the war had much to do with this.

You give a different set of reasons. If you had not made the following statements, I should not have suspected them to be true. "The defeat of the administration is the administrations own fault." (opinion) "It admitted its professed opponents to its counsels" (Asserted as a fact) "It placed the Army, now a great power in this Republic, into the hands of its' enemys" (Asserted as a fact) "In all personal questions, to be hostile to the party of the Government, seemed, to be a title to consideration." (Asserted as a fact) "If to forget the great rule, that if you are true to your friends, your friends will be true to you, and that you make your enemies stronger by placing them upon an equality with your friends." "Is it surprising that the opponents of the administration should have got into their hands the government of the principal states, after they have had for a long time the principal management of the war, the great business of the national government."

I can not dispute about the matter of opinion. On the the [*sic*] three matters (stated as facts) I shall be glad to have your evidence upon them when I shall meet you. The plain facts, as they appear to me, are these. The administration came into power, very largely in a minority of the popular vote. Notwithstanding this, it distributed to it's party friends as nearly all the civil patronage as any administration ever did. The war came. The administration could not even start in this, without assistance outside of it's party. It was mere nonsense to suppose a minority could put down a majority in rebellion. Mr. Schurz (now Gen. Schurz) was about here then & I do not recollect that he then considered all who were not republicans, were enemies of the government, and that none of them must be appointed to to [*sic*] military positions. He will correct me if I am mistaken. It so happened that very few of our friends had a military education or were of the profession of arms. It would have been a question whether the war should be conducted on military knowledge, or on political affinity, only that our own friends (I think Mr. Schurz included) seemed to think that such a question was inadmissable. Accordingly I have scarcely appointed a democrat to a command, who was not urged by many republicans and opposed by none. It was so as to McClellan. He was first brought forward by the Republican Governor of Ohio, & claimed, and contended for at the same time by the Republican Governor of Pennsylvania. I received recommendations from the republican delegations in congress, and I believe every one of them recommended a majority of democrats. But, after all many Republicans were appointed; and I mean no disparagement to them when I say I do not see that their superiority of success has been so marked as to throw great suspicion on the good faith of those who are not Republicans. Yours truly,

A. Lincoln

66. *Last Best Hope of Earth:*
ANNUAL MESSAGE TO CONGRESS, DECEMBER 1, 1862

DURING 1862, Congress abolished slavery in the territories and in the District of Columbia, but to go much further would require amendment of the Constitution. As for the President's program of military emancipation, due to be inaugurated on January 1, 1863, it was of doubtful legality and would apply only to those regions under Confederate control. Lincoln therefore decided to propose a more comprehensive and permanent solution for the slavery problem. In his Annual Message to Congress, he presented an eloquent argument for reunion on the grounds of geographical necessity, and then he recommended three constitutional amendments. The first authorized compensation to every state that abolished slavery before the year 1900. The second provided that all slaves liberated by "the chances of war" should retain their freedom, but with compensation to loyal owners. The third empowered Congress to appropriate money "for colonizing free colored persons, with their own consent, at any place or places without the United States." Such action, he believed, would shorten the war and remove the sole cause of domestic conflict. In general, Lincoln's finest literary efforts were prepared for oral delivery. These passages from his second Annual Message probably constitute the most notable exception.

A nation may be said to consist of its territory, its people, and its laws. The territory is the only part which is of certain durability. "One generation passeth away, and another generation cometh, but the earth abideth forever." It is of the first importance to duly consider, and estimate, this ever-enduring part. That portion of the earth's surface which is owned and inhabited by the people of the United States, is well adapted to be the home of one national family; and it is not well adapted for two, or more. Its vast extent, and its variety of climate and productions, are of advantage, in this age, for one people, whatever they might have been in former ages. Steam, telegraphs, and intelligence, have brought these, to be an advantageous combination, for one united people.

. . . . .

There is no line, straight or crooked, suitable for a national boundary, upon which to divide. Trace through, from east to west, upon the line between the free and slave country, and we shall find a little more than one-third of its length are rivers, easy to be crossed, and populated, or soon to be populated, thickly upon both sides; while nearly all its remaining length, are merely surveyor's lines, over which people may walk back and forth without any consciousness of their presence. No part of this line can be made any more difficult to pass, by writing it down on paper, or parchment, as a national boundary. The fact of separation, if it comes, gives up, on the part of the seceding section, the fugitive slave clause, along with all other constitutional obligations upon the section seceded from, while I should expect no treaty stipulation would ever be made to take its place.

But there is another difficulty. The great interior region, bounded east by the Alleghanies, north by the British dominions, west by the Rocky mountains, and south by the line along which the culture of corn and cotton meets, and which includes part of Virginia, part of Tennessee, all of Kentucky, Ohio, Indiana, Michigan, Wisconsin, Illinois, Missouri, Kansas, Iowa, Minnesota and the Territories of Dakota, Nebraska, and part of Colorado, already has above ten millions of people, and will have fifty millions within fifty years, if not prevented by any political folly or mistake. It contains more than one-third of the country owned by the United States—certainly more than one million of square miles. Once half as populous as Massachusetts already is, it would have more than seventy-five millions of people. A glance at the map shows that, territorially speaking, it is the great body of the republic. The other parts are but marginal borders to it, the magnificent region sloping west from the rocky mountains to the Pacific, being the deepest, and also the richest, in undeveloped resources. In the production of provisions, grains, grasses, and all which proceed from them, this great interior region is naturally one of the most important in the world. Ascertain from the statistics the small proportion of the region which has, as yet, been brought into cultivation, and also the large and rapidly increasing amount of its products, and we shall be overwhelmed with the magnitude of the prospect presented. An[d] yet this region has no sea-coast, touches no ocean anywhere. As part of one nation, its people now find, and may forever find, their way to Europe by New York, to South America and Africa by New Orleans, and to Asia by San Francisco. But separate our common country into two nations, as designed by the present rebellion, and every man of this great interior region is thereby cut off from some one or more of these outlets, not, perhaps, by a physical barrier, but by embarrassing and onerous trade regulations.

And this is true, *wherever* a dividing, or boundary line, may be fixed. Place it between the now free and slave country, or place it south of Kentucky, or north of Ohio, and still the truth remains, that none south of it, can trade to any port or place north of it, and none north of it, can trade to any port or place south of it, except upon terms dictated by a government foreign to them. These outlets, east, west, and south, are indispensable to the well-being of the people inhabiting, and to inhabit, this vast interior region. *Which* of the three may be the best, is no proper question. All, are better than either, and all, of right, belong to that people, and to their successors forever. True to themselves, they will not ask *where* a line of separation shall be, but will vow, rather, that there shall be no such line. Nor are the marginal regions less interested in these communications to, and through them, to the great outside world. They too, and each of them, must have access to this Egypt of the West, without paying toll at the crossing of any national boundary.

Our national strife springs not from our permanent part; not from the land we inhabit; not from our national homestead. There is no possible severing of this, but would multiply, and not mitigate, evils among us. In all its adaptations and aptitudes, it demands union, and abhors separation. In fact, it would, ere long, force reunion, however much of blood and treasure the separation might have cost.

Our strife pertains to ourselves—to the passing generations of men; and it can, without convulsion, be hushed forever with the passing of one generation.

. . . . .

The proposed emancipation would shorten the war, perpetuate peace, insure this increase of population, and proportionately the wealth of the country. With these, we should pay all the emancipation would cost, together with our other debt, easier than we should pay our other debt, without it. If we had allowed our old national debt to run at six per cent. per annum, simple interest, from the end of our revolutionary struggle until to day, without paying anything on either principal or interest, each man of us would owe less upon that debt now, than each man owed upon it then; and this because our increase of men, through the whole period, has been greater than six per cent.; has run faster than the interest upon the debt. Thus, time alone relieves a debtor nation, so long as its population increases faster than unpaid interest accumulates on its debt.

This fact would be no excuse for delaying payment of what is justly due; but it shows the great importance of time in this connexion—the great advantage of a policy by which we shall not have to pay until we number a hundred millions, what, by a different policy, we would have to pay now, when we number but thirty one millions. In a word, it shows that a dollar will be much harder to pay for the war, than will be a dollar for emancipation on the proposed plan. And then the latter will cost no blood, no precious life. It will be a saving of both.

. . . . .

I cannot make it better known than it already is, that I strongly favor colonization. And yet I wish to say there is an objection urged against free colored persons remaining in the country, which is largely imaginary, if not sometimes malicious.

It is insisted that their presence would injure, and displace white labor and white laborers. If there ever could be a proper time for mere catch arguments, that time surely is not now. In times like the present, men should utter nothing for which they would not willingly be responsible through time and in eternity. Is it true, then, that colored people can displace any more white labor, by being free, than by remaining slaves? If they stay in their old places, they jostle no white laborers; if they leave their old places, they leave them open to white laborers. Logically, there is neither more nor less of it. Emancipation, even without deportation, would probably enhance the wages of white labor, and, very surely, would not reduce them. Thus, the customary amount of labor would still have to be performed; the freed people would surely not do more than their old proportion of it, and very probably, for a time, would do less, leaving an increased part to white laborers, bringing their labor into greater demand, and, consequently, enhancing the wages of it. With deportation, even to a limited extent, enhanced wages to white labor is mathematically certain. Labor is like any other commodity in the market—increase the demand for it, and you increase the price of it. Reduce the supply of black labor, by colonizing the black laborer out of the country, and, by precisely so much, you increase the demand for, and wages of, white labor.

But it is dreaded that the freed people will swarm forth, and cover the whole land? Are they not already in the land? Will liberation make them any more numerous? Equally distributed among the whites of the whole country, and there would be but one colored to seven whites. Could the one, in any way, greatly disturb the seven? There are many communities now, having more than one free colored person, to seven whites; and this, without any apparent consciousness of evil from it. The District of Columbia, and the States of Maryland and Delaware, are all in this condition. The District has more than one free colored to six whites; and yet, in its frequent petitions to Congress, I believe it has never presented the presence of free colored persons as one of its grievances. But why should emancipation south, send the free people north? People, of any color, seldom run, unless there be something to run from. *Heretofore* colored people, to some extent, have fled north from bondage; and *now,* perhaps, from both bondage and destitution. But if gradual emancipation and deportation be adopted, they will have neither to flee from. Their old masters will give them wages at least until new laborers can be procured; and the freed men, in turn, will gladly give their labor for the wages, till new homes can be found for them, in congenial climes, and with people of their own blood and race. This proposition can be trusted on the mutual interests involved. And, in any event, cannot the north decide for itself, whether to receive them?

Again, as practice proves more than theory, in any case, has there been any irruption of colored people northward, because of the abolishment of slavery in this District last spring?

What I have said of the proportion of free colored persons to the whites, in the District, is from the census of 1860, having no reference to persons called contrabands, nor to those made free by the act of Congress abolishing slavery here.

The plan consisting of these articles is recommended, not but that a restoration of the national authority would be accepted without its adoption.

Nor will the war, nor proceedings under the proclamation of September 22, 1862, be stayed because of the *recommendation* of this plan. Its timely *adoption,* I doubt not, would bring restoration and thereby stay both.

And, notwithstanding this plan, the recommendation that Congress provide by law for compensating any State which may adopt emancipation, before this plan shall have been acted upon, is hereby earnestly renewed. Such would be only an advance part of the plan, and the same arguments apply to both.

This plan is recommended as a means, not in exclusion of, but additional to, all others for restoring and preserving the national authority throughout the Union. The subject is presented exclusively in its economical aspect. The plan would, I am confident, secure peace more speedily, and maintain it more permanently, than can be done by force alone; while all it would cost, considering amounts, and manner of payment, and times of payment, would be easier paid than will be the additional cost of the war if we rely solely upon force. It is much—very much—that it would cost no blood at all.

The plan is proposed as permanent constitutional law. It cannot become such without the concurrence of, first, two-thirds of Congress, and, afterwards, three-fourths of the States. The requisite three-fourths of the States will necessarily include seven of the Slave states. Their concurrence, if obtained, will give assurance of their severally adopting emancipation, at no very distant day, upon the new constitutional terms. This assurance would end the struggle now, and save the Union forever.

I do not forget the gravity which should characterize a paper addressed to the Congress of the nation by the Chief Magistrate of the nation. Nor do I forget that some of you are my seniors, nor that many of you have more experience than I, in the conduct of public affairs. Yet I trust that in view of the great responsibility resting upon me, you will perceive no want of respect to yourselves, in any undue earnestness I may seem to display.

Is it doubted, then, that the plan I propose, if adopted, would shorten the war, and thus lessen its expenditure of money and of blood? Is it doubted that it would restore the national authority and national prosperity, and perpetuate both indefinitely? Is it doubted that we here—Congress and Executive—can secure its adoption? Will not the good people respond to a united, and earnest appeal from us? Can we, can they, by any other means, so certainly, or so speedily, assure these vital objects? We can succeed only by concert. It is not "can *any* of us *imagine* better?" but "can we *all* do better?" Object whatsoever is possible, still the question recurs "can we do better?" The dogmas of the quiet past, are inadequate to the stormy present. The occasion is piled high with difficulty, and we must rise with the occasion. As our case is new, so we must think anew, and act anew. We must disenthrall ourselves, and then we shall save our country.

Fellow-citizens, *we* cannot escape history. We of this Congress and this administration, will be remembered in spite of ourselves. No personal significance, or insignificance, can spare one or another of us. The fiery trial through which we pass, will light us down, in honor or dishonor, to the latest generation. We *say* we are for the

Union. The world will not forget that we say this. We know how to save the Union. The world knows we do know how to save it. We—even *we here*—hold the power, and bear the responsibility. In *giving* freedom to the *slave,* we *assure* freedom to the *free*—honorable alike in what we give, and what we preserve. We shall nobly save, or meanly lose, the last best, hope of earth. Other means may succeed; this could not fail. The way is plain, peaceful, generous, just—a way which, if followed, the world will forever applaud, and God must forever bless.

67. *This Sad World of Ours:*

LETTER TO FANNY McCULLOUGH, DECEMBER 23, 1862

LINCOLN removed McClellan in November 1862 and appointed General Ambrose E. Burnside to command the Army of the Potomac. But at Fredericksburg on December 13, Lee administered another terrible beating to the Union forces. So ended a dark year, which had also been one of personal tragedy for the President and his wife. William Wallace ("Willie") Lincoln, a bright lad of eleven years, died on February 20. Now, with Robert away at Harvard, only nine-year-old Thomas ("Tad") remained in the family circle. For Mary Lincoln, sick with grief, there were other heavy blows in 1862. Two of her half-brothers in Confederate service were killed, and a third would give his life at Vicksburg the following year. Thus Lincoln was drawing upon his own experience with sorrow when he wrote these words of comfort to the daughter of an old friend, Lieutenant Colonel William McCullough, who had been killed in action on December 5.

Executive Mansion,
Washington, December 23, 1862

Dear Fanny:

It is with deep grief that I learn of the death of your kind and brave Father; and, especially, that it is affecting your young heart beyond what is common in such cases. In this sad world of ours, sorrow comes to all; and, to the young, it comes with bitterest agony, because it takes them unawares. The older have learned to ever expect it. I am anxious to afford some alleviation of your present distress. Perfect relief is not possible, except with time. You can not now realize that you will ever feel better. Is not this so? And yet it is a mistake. You are sure to be happy again. To know this, which is certainly true, will make you some less miserable now. I have had experience enough to know what I say; and you need only to believe it, to feel better at once. The memory of your dear Father, instead of an agony, will yet be a sad sweet feeling in your heart, of a purer, and holier sort than you have known before.

Please present my kind regards to your afflicted mother.

Your sincere friend,   A. Lincoln.

Miss. Fanny McCullough.

68. The Day of Liberation:
EMANCIPATION PROCLAMATION, JANUARY 1, 1863

THE most famous public document from Lincoln's hand was issued, as he had promised, on New Year's Day, 1863. Designated a military measure taken by the President in his role as Commander-in-Chief, the Emancipation Proclamation did not apply to the border slave states, to Tennessee, or to those parts of Virginia and Louisiana that were occupied by Union forces. Hence it bestowed freedom only upon slaves beyond the immediate reach of Federal power. Yet as a commitment for the future, it transformed the character of the war. Two paragraphs that Lincoln quoted from his preliminary Proclamation of September 22, 1862, are omitted here.

January 1, 1863

By the President of the United States of America:
A Proclamation.

Whereas, on the twentysecond day of September, in the year of our Lord one thousand eight hundred and sixty two, a proclamation was issued by the President of the United States. . . .

Now, therefore I, Abraham Lincoln, President of the United States, by virtue of the power in me vested as Commander-in-Chief, of the Army and Navy of the United States in time of actual armed rebellion against authority and government of the United States, and as a fit and necessary war measure for suppressing said rebellion, do, on this first day of January, in the year of our Lord one thousand eight hundred and sixty three, and in accordance with my purpose so to do publicly proclaimed for the full period of one hundred days, from the day first above mentioned, order and designate as the States and parts of States wherein the people thereof respectively, are this day in rebellion against the United States, the following, towit:

Arkansas, Texas, Louisiana, (except the Parishes of St. Bernard, Plaquemines, Jefferson, St. Johns, St. Charles, St. James [,] Ascension, Assumption, Terrebonne, Lafourche, St. Mary, St. Martin, and Orleans, including the City of New-Orleans) Mississippi, Alabama, Florida, Georgia, South-Carolina, North-Carolina, and Virginia, (except the fortyeight counties designated as West Virginia, and also the counties of Berkeley, Accomac, Northampton, Elizabeth-City, York, Princess Ann, and Norfolk, including the cities of Norfolk & Portsmouth [)]; and which excepted parts are, for the present, left precisely as if this proclamation were not issued.

And by virtue of the power, and for the purpose aforesaid, I do order and declare that all persons held as slaves within said designated States, and parts of States, are, and henceforward shall be free; and that the Executive government of the United States, including the military and naval authorities thereof, will recognize and maintain the freedom of said persons.

And I hereby enjoin upon the people so declared to be free to abstain from all violence, unless in necessary self-defence; and I recommend to them that, in all cases when allowed, they labor faithfully for reasonable wages.

And I further declare and make known, that such persons of suitable condition, will be received into the armed service of the United States to garrison forts, positions, stations, and other places, and to man vessels of all sorts in said service.

And upon this act, sincerely believed to be an act of justice, warranted by the Constitution, upon military necessity, I invoke the considerate judgment of mankind, and the gracious favor of Almighty God.

In witness whereof, I have hereunto set my hand and caused the seal of the United States to be affixed.

[Seal]   Done at the City of Washington, this first day of January, in the year of our Lord one thousand eight hundred and sixty three, and of the Independence of the United States of America the eighty-seventh.

By the President: Abraham Lincoln
William H. Seward, Secretary of State

69. Emancipation Defended:

LETTER TO JOHN A. McCLERNAND, JANUARY 8, 1863

LINCOLN explained and justified the Emancipation Proclamation in a letter to General John A. McClernand, an Illinois Democrat. He also commented on McClernand's report that certain "officers of high rank in the rebel service" were ready for peace.

Executive Mansion,
Washington, January 8, 1863.

Major General McClernand

My dear Sir: Your interesting communication by the hand of Major Scates is received. I never did ask more, nor ever was willing to accept less, than for all the States, and the people thereof, to take and hold their places, and their rights, in the Union, under the Constitution of the United States. For this alone have I felt authorized to struggle; and I seek neither more nor less now. Still, to use a coarse, but an expressive figure, broken eggs can not be mended. I have issued the emancipation proclamation, and I can not retract it.

After the commencement of hostilities I struggled nearly a year and a half to get along without touching the "institution"; and when finally I conditionally determined to touch it, I gave a hundred days fair notice of my purpose, to all the States and people, within which time they could have turned it wholly aside, by simply again becoming good citizens of the United States. They chose to disregard it, and I made the peremptory proclamation on what appeared to me to be a military necessity. And being made, it must stand. As to the States not included in it, of course they can have their rights in the Union as of old. Even the people of the states included, if they choose, need not to be hurt by it. Let them adopt systems of apprenticeship for the colored people, conforming substantially to the most approved plans of gradual emancipation; and, with the aid they can have from the general government, they may be nearly as well off, in this respect, as if the present trouble had not occurred, and much better off than they can possibly be if the contest continues persistently.

As to any dread of my having a "purpose to enslave, or exterminate, the whites of the South," I can scarcely believe that such dread exists. It is too absurd. I believe you can be my personal witness that no man is less to be dreaded for undue severity, in any case.

If the friends you mention really wish to have peace upon the old terms, they should act at once. Every day makes the case more difficult. They can so act, with entire safety, so far as I am concerned.

I think you would better not make this letter public; but you may rely confidently on my standing by whatever I have said in it. Please write me if any thing more comes to light. Yours very truly,

A. Lincoln.

70. Encouragement From Abroad:

REPLY TO THE WORKINGMEN OF MANCHESTER,
JANUARY 19, 1863

DURING the early years of the Civil War, there was some danger
that European powers might intervene in such a way as to aid
the Confederacy. Many Southern leaders believed that the English need for cotton would eventually compel open resistance
to the Federal blockade. Yet Britain remained officially neutral,
and the North received warm support from the very workers
who suffered most when cotton mills were forced to shut down.
Lincoln expressed his gratitude in response to resolutions forwarded from a public meeting in Manchester, center of the
English textile industry.

Executive Mansion, Washington,
January 19, 1863.

To the workingmen of Manchester:

I have the honor to acknowledge the receipt of the address and resolutions which you sent to me on the eve
of the new year.

When I came, on the fourth day of March, 1861,
through a free and constitutional election, to preside in
the government of the United States, the country was
found at the verge of civil war. Whatever might have been
the cause, or whosoever the fault, one duty paramount
to all others was before me, namely, to maintain and preserve at once the Constitution and the integrity of the
federal republic. A conscientious purpose to perform this
duty is a key to all the measures of administration which
have been, and to all which will hereafter be pursued.
Under our form of government, and my official oath, I
could not depart from this purpose if I would. It is not
always in the power of governments to enlarge or restrict
the scope of moral results which follow the policies that

they may deem it necessary for the public safety, from time to time, to adopt.

I have understood well that the duty of self-preservation rests solely with the American people. But I have at the same time been aware that favor or disfavor of foreign nations might have a material influence in enlarging and prolonging the struggle with disloyal men in which the country is engaged. A fair examination of history has seemed to authorize a belief that the past action and influences of the United States were generally regarded as having been beneficent towards mankind. I have therefore reckoned upon the forbearance of nations. Circumstances, to some of which you kindly allude, induced me especially to expect that if justice and good faith should be practiced by the United States, they would encounter no hostile influence on the part of Great Britain. It is now a pleasant duty to acknowledge the demonstration you have given of your desire that a spirit of peace and amity towards this country may prevail in the councils of your Queen, who is respected and esteemed in your own country only more than she is by the kindred nation which has its home on this side of the Atlantic.

I know and deeply deplore the sufferings which the workingmen at Manchester and in all Europe are called to endure in this crisis. It has been often and studiously represented that the attempt to overthrow this government, which was built upon the foundation of human rights, and to substitute for it one which should rest exclusively on the basis of human slavery, was likely to obtain the favor of Europe. Through the actions of our disloyal citizens the workingmen of Europe have been subjected to a severe trial, for the purpose of forcing their sanction to that attempt. Under these circumstances, I cannot but regard your decisive utterance upon the question as an instance of sublime Christian heroism which has not been surpassed in any age or in any country. It is, indeed, an energetic and reinspiring assurance of the inherent power of truth and of the ultimate and universal triumph of justice, humanity, and freedom. I do not doubt that the sentiments you have expressed will be sustained by your great nation, and, on the other hand, I have no hesitation in assuring you that they will excite admiration, esteem, and the most reciprocal feelings of friendship among the American people. I hail this interchange of sentiment, therefore, as an augury that, whatever else may happen, whatever misfortune may befall your country or my own, the peace and friendship which now exist between the two nations will be, as it shall be my desire to make them, perpetual.

Abraham Lincoln

71. *Portrait of a New Commander:*
LETTER TO JOSEPH HOOKER, JANUARY 26, 1863

STILL seeking a winner, Lincoln replaced Burnside with "Fighting Joe" Hooker, a corps commander whose virtues and shortcomings were catalogued in this remarkably blunt letter.

Executive Mansion,
Washington, January 26, 1863.

Major General Hooker:
General:

I have placed you at the head of the Army of the Potomac. Of course I have done this upon what appear to me to be sufficient reasons. And yet I think it best for you to know that there are some things in regard to which, I am not quite satisfied with you. I believe you to be a brave and skilful soldier, which, of course, I like. I also believe you do not mix politics with your profession, in which you are right. You have confidence in yourself, which is a valuable, if not an indispensable quality. You are ambitious, which, within reasonable bounds, does good rather than harm. But I think that during Gen. Burnside's command of the Army, you have taken counsel of your ambition, and thwarted him as much as you could, in which you did a great wrong to the country, and to a most meritorious and honorable brother officer. I have heard, in such way as to believe it, of your recently saying that both the Army and the Government needed a Dictator. Of course it was not *for* this, but in spite of it, that I have given you the command. Only those generals who gain successes, can set up dictators. What I now ask of you is military success, and I will risk the dictatorship. The government will support you to the utmost of it's ability, which is neither more nor less than it has done and will do for all commanders. I much fear that the spirit which you have aided to infuse into the Army, of criticising their Commander, and withholding confidence from him, will now turn upon you. I shall assist you as far as I can, to put it down. Neither you, nor Napoleon, if he were alive again, could get any good out of an army, while such a spirit prevails in it.

And now, beware of rashness. Beware of rashness, but with energy, and sleepless vigilance, go forward, and give us victories.

Yours very truly,

A. Lincoln

72. *Strategy for Hooker:*
MEMORANDUM, APRIL, 1863

LINCOLN probably wrote this memorandum during a visit to General Hooker's headquarters in early April 1863. With the lesson of Fredericksburg still fresh in his mind, he advised a policy of constant pressure, instead of frontal assault, upon Lee's army.

My opinion is, that just now, with the enemy directly ahead of us, there is *no* eligible route for us into Richmond; and consequently a question of preference between the Rappahannock route, and the James River route is a contest about nothing. Hence our prime object is the enemies' army in front of us, and is not with, or about, Richmond—at all, unless it be incidental to the main object.

What then? The two armies are face to face with a narrow river between them. Our communications are shorter and safer than are those of the enemy. For this reason, we can, with equal powers fret him more than he can us. I do not think that by raids towards Washington he can derange the Army of the Potomac at all. He has no distant opperations which can call any of the Army of the Potomac away; we have such operations which may call him away, at least in part. While he remains in tact, I do not think we should take the disadvantage of attacking him in his entrenchments; but we should continually harrass and menace him, so that he shall have no leisure, nor safety in sending away detachments. If he weakens himself, then pitch into him.

73. *Failure of a Weather Prophet:*

ENDORSEMENT, APRIL 28, 1863, ON LETTER FROM FRANCIS L. CAPEN

HOOKER devised a plan for a turning movement against the Confederate army, but his progress was slowed by heavy rains. Lincoln, always eager to enlist science and technology in the war effort, gave serious attention to the self-advertised qualifications of one Francis L. Capen as a meteorologist. He was quickly disillusioned, however.

April 28, 1863

It seems to me Mr. Capen knows nothing about the weather, in advance. He told me three days ago that it would not rain again till the 30th. of April or 1st. of May. It is raining now & has been for ten hours. I can not spare any more time to Mr. Capen.

A. Lincoln

74. Another Critic Answered:

LETTER TO ISAAC N. ARNOLD, MAY 26, 1863

DESPITE his sound strategy and superior force, Hooker was out-maneuvered and defeated by Lee at Chancellorsville in the first week of May 1863. Meanwhile, the war proceeded much more favorably in the West. There Grant, after a brilliant and daring campaign, was beginning his siege of Vicksburg, virtually the last important Confederate stronghold on the Mississippi. Yet the failures in Virginia caused mounting dissatisfaction. Congressman Isaac N. Arnold of Chicago recommended dismissal of Henry W. Halleck, a competent administrator who in 1862 had succeeded McClellan as General-in-Chief. Arnold blamed Halleck for the eclipse of popular generals like Benjamin F. Butler, John C. Frémont, and Franz Sigel.

Private & confidential

Executive Mansion,
Washington, May 26, 1863.

Hon. I. N. Arnold.

My dear Sir:

Your letter advising me to dismiss Gen. Halleck is received. If the public believe, as you say, that he has driven Fremont, Butler, and Sigel from the service, they believe what I know to be false; so that if I were to yield to it, it would only be to be instantly beset by some other demand based on another falsehood equally gross. You know yourself that Fremont was relieved at his own request, before Halleck could have had any thing to do with it—went out near the end of June, while Halleck only came in near the end of July. I know equally well that no wish of Halleck's had any thing to do with the removal of Butler or Sigel. Sigel, like Fremont, was relieved at his own request, pressed upon me almost constantly for six months, and upon complaints that could have been made as justly by almost any corps commander in the army, and more justly by some. So much for the way they got out. Now a word as to their not getting back. In the early Spring, Gen. Fremont sought active service again; and, as it seemed to me, sought it in a very good, and reasonable spirit. But he holds the highest rank in the Army, except McClellan, so that I could not well offer him a subordinate command. Was I to displace Hooker, or Hunter, or Rosecrans, or Grant, or Banks? If not, what was I to do? And similar to this, is the case of both the others. One month after Gen. Butler's return, I offered him a position in which I thought and still think, he could have done himself the highest credit, and the country the greatest service, but he declined it. When Gen. Sigel was relieved, at his own request as I have said, of course I had to put another in command of his corps. Can I instantly thrust that other out to put him in again?

And now my good friend, let me turn your eyes upon another point. Whether Gen. Grant shall or shall not consummate the capture of Vicksburg, his campaign from the beginning of this month up to the twenty second day of it, is one of the most brilliant in the world. His corps commanders, & Division commanders, in part, are McClernand, McPherson, Sherman, Steele, Hovey, Blair, & Logan. And yet taking Gen. Grant & these seven of his generals, and you can scarcely name one of them that has not been constantly denounced and opposed by the same men who are now so anxious to get Halleck out, and Fremont & Butler & Sigel in. I believe no one of them went through the Senate easily, and certainly one failed to get through at all. I am compelled to take a more impartial and unprejudiced view of things. Without claiming to be your superior, which I do not, my position enables me to understand my duty in all these matters better than you possibly can, and I hope you do not yet doubt my integrity. Your friend, as ever

A. Lincoln

75. The Missouri Nuisance:
LETTER TO JOHN M. SCHOFIELD, MAY 27, 1863

ONE of Lincoln's most vexing problems was the situation in Missouri, where factional quarrels and conflicts of authority kept the state in an uproar. "I have been tormented with it beyond endurance," he complained. Appointing a new army commander for the region, he volunteered this explanation and counsel.

Executive Mansion,
Washington, May 27. 1863.

Gen. J. M. Schofield

My dear Sir: Having relieved Gen. Curtis and assigned you to the command of the Department of the Missouri— I think it may be of some advantage for me to state to you why I did it. I did not relieve Gen. Curtis because of any full conviction that he had done wrong by commission or omission. I did it because of a conviction in my mind that the Union men of Missouri, constituting, when united, a vast majority of the whole people, have entered into a pestilent factional quarrel among themselves, Gen. Curtis, perhaps not of choice, being the head of one faction, and Gov. Gamble that of the other. After months of labor to reconcile the difficulty, it seemed to grow worse and worse until I felt it my duty to break it up some how; and as I could not remove Gov. Gamble, I had to remove Gen. Curtis. Now that you are in the position, I wish you to undo nothing merely because Gen. Curtis or Gov. Gamble did it; but to exercise your own judgment, and do *right* for the public interest. Let your military measures be strong enough to repel the invader and keep the peace, and not so strong as to unnecessarily harrass and persecute the people. It is a difficult *role,* and so much greater will be the honor if you perform it well. If both factions, or neither, shall abuse you, you will probably be about

right. Beware of being assailed by one, and praised by
the other. Yours truly,

A. Lincoln

76. On the Defensive:
TELEGRAM TO JOSEPH HOOKER, JUNE 10, 1863

AFTER his victory at Chancellorsville, Lee began an invasion of
the North on a route that circled west of Washington. Hooker
proposed, as a bold countermove, to strike directly at Richmond,
but Lincoln disapproved.

"Cypher"

United States Military Telegraph
War Department, Washington DC.
June 10, 1863

Major General Hooker

Your long despatch of to-day is just received. If left
to me, I would not go South of the Rappahannock, upon
Lee's moving North of it. If you had Richmond invested
to-day, you would not be able to take it in twenty days;
meanwhile, your communications, and with them, your
army would be ruined. I think *Lee's* Army, and not *Richmond,* is your true objective point. If he comes towards
the Upper Potomac, follow on his flank, and on the inside
track, shortening your lines, whilst he lengthens his. Fight
him when opportunity offers. If he stays where he is, fret
him, and fret him.

A. Lincoln

77. *Arbitrary Arrests and Constitutional Rights:*
LETTER TO ERASTUS CORNING AND OTHERS,
JUNE 12, 1863

THE military arrest in May 1863 of Clement L. Vallandigham, a notorious Ohio "copperhead," drew violent protests from many Democrats. A public meeting at Albany, New York, accused Lincoln of exceeding his constitutional powers and suppressing civil liberties. In a lengthy reply, the President argued that the Constitution authorized extraordinary measures to meet the extraordinary problem of domestic rebellion. Substantial excerpts from the letter are reproduced here.

Prior to my installation here, it had been inculcated that any State had a lawful right to secede from the national Union, and that it would be expedient to exercise the right whenever the devotees of the doctrine should fail to elect a President to their own liking. I was elected contrary to their liking; and, accordingly, so far as it was legally possible, they had taken seven States out of the Union, had seized many of the United States forts, and had fired upon the United States flag, all before I was inaugurated, and, of course, before I had done any official act whatever. The Rebellion thus begun soon ran into the present Civil War; and, in certain respects, it began on very unequal terms between the parties. The insurgents had been preparing for it more than thirty years, while the Government had taken no steps to resist them. The former had carefully considered all the means which could be turned to their account. It undoubtedly was a well-pondered reliance with them that, in their own unrestricted efforts to destroy Union, Constitution, and law, all together, the Government would, in great degree, be restrained by the same Constitution and law from arresting their progress. Their sympathizers pervaded all departments of the Government and nearly all communities of the people. From this material under cover of "liberty of speech," "liberty of the press," and "habeas corpus," they hoped to keep on foot among us a most efficient corps of spies, informers, suppliers, and aiders and abettors of their cause in a thousand ways. They knew that in times such as they were inaugurating, by the Constitution itself, the "habeas corpus" might be suspended; but they also knew they had friends who would make a question as to *who* was to suspend it; meanwhile, their spies and others might remain at large to help on their cause. Or, if, as has happened, the Executive should suspend the writ, without ruinous waste of time, instances of arresting innocent persons might occur, as are always likely to occur in such cases; and then a clamor could be raised in regard to this, which might be, at least, of some service to the insurgent cause. It needed no very keen perception to discover this part of the enemy's programme, so soon as, by open hostilities, their machinery was fairly put in motion. Yet, thoroughly imbued with a reverence for the guaranteed rights of individuals, I was slow to adopt the strong measures which by degrees I have been forced to regard as being within the exceptions of the Constitution, and as indispensable to the public safety. Nothing is better known to history than that courts of justice are utterly incompetent to such cases. Civil courts are organized chiefly for trials of individuals, or, at most, of few individuals acting in concert; and this in quiet times, and on charges of crimes well defined in the law. Even in times of peace, bands of horse-thieves and robbers frequently grow too numerous and powerful for the ordinary courts of justice. But what comparison, in numbers, have such bands ever borne to the insurgent sympathizers even in many of the loyal states? Again: a jury too frequently has at least one member more ready to hang the panel than to hang the traitor. And yet, again, he who dissuades one man from volunteering, or induces one soldier to desert, weakens the Union cause as much as he who kills a Union soldier in battle. Yet this dissuasion or inducement may be so conducted as to be no defined crime of which any civil court could take cognizance.

Ours is a case of rebellion—so called by the resolutions before me—in fact, a clear, flagrant, and gigantic case of rebellion; and a provision of the Constitution that "the privilege of the writ of habeas corpus shall not be suspended, unless when, in cases of rebellion or invasion, the public safety may require it," is *the* provision which specially applies to our present case. This provision plainly attests the understanding of those who made the Constitution, that ordinary courts of justice are inadequate to "cases of rebellion"—attests their purpose that, in such cases, men may be held in custody whom the courts, acting on ordinary rules, would discharge. Habeas corpus does not discharge men who are proved to be guilty of defined crime; and its suspension is allowed by the Constitution on purpose that men may be arrested and held who cannot be proved to be guilty of defined crime, "when, in cases of rebellion or invasion, the public safety may require it." This is precisely our present case—a case of rebellion, wherein the public safety *does* require the suspension. Indeed, arrests by process of courts, and arrests in cases of rebellion, do not proceed altogether upon the same basis. The former is directed at the small percentage of ordinary and continuous perpetration of crime; while the latter is directed at sudden and extensive uprisings against the Government, which at most, will succeed or fail in no great length of time. In the latter case, arrests are made, not so much for what has been done, as for what probably would be done. The latter is more for the preventive and less for the vindictive than the former. In such cases, the purposes of men are much more easily understood than in cases of ordinary crime.

· · · · ·

By the third resolution, the meeting indicated their opinion that military arrests may be constitutional in localities where rebellion actually exists, but that such arrests are unconstitutional in localities where rebellion or insurrection does *not* actually exist. They insist that such arrests shall not be made "outside of the lines of necessary military occupation, and the scenes of insurrection." Inasmuch, however, as the Constitution itself makes no such distinction, I am unable to believe that there *is* any such constitutional distinction. I concede that the class of arrests complained of can be constitutional only when, in cases of rebellion or invasion, the public safety may require them; and I insist that in such cases they are constitutional *wherever* the public safety does require them; as well in places to which they may prevent the Rebellion extending as in those where it may be already prevailing; as well where they may restrain mischievous interference with the raising and supplying of armies to suppress the Rebellion, as where the Rebellion may actually be; as well where they may restrain the enticing of men out of the army, as where they would prevent mutiny in the army; equally constitutional at all places where they will conduce to the public safety, as against the dangers of rebellion or invasion. Take the particular case mentioned by the meeting. It is asserted, in substance, that Mr. Vallandigham was, by a military commander, seized and tried "for no other reason than words addressed to a public meeting, in criticism of the course of the Administration, and in condemnation of the Military orders of the General." Now, if there be no mistake about this; if this assertion is the truth and the whole truth; if there was no other reason for the arrest, then I concede that the arrest was wrong. But the arrest, as I understand, was made for a very different reason. Mr. Vallandigham avows his hostility to the War on the part of the Union; and his arrest was made because he was laboring, with some effect, to prevent the raising of troops; to encourage desertions from the army; and to leave the Rebellion without an adequate military force to suppress it. He was not arrested because he was damaging the political prospects of the Administration, or the personal interests of the Commanding General, but because he was damaging the Army, upon the existence and vigor of which the life of the Nation depends. He was warring upon the Military, and this gave the Military constitutional jurisdiction to lay hands upon him. If Mr. Vallandigham was not damaging the military power of the country, then his arrest was made on mistake of fact, which I would be glad to correct on reasonably satisfactory evidence.

I understand the meeting, whose resolutions I am considering, to be in favor of suppressing the Rebellion by military force—by armies. Long experience has shown that armies cannot be maintained unless desertions shall be punished by the severe penalty of death. The case requires, and the law and the Constitution sanction, this punishment. Must I shoot a simple-minded soldier boy who deserts, while I must not touch a hair of a wily agitator who induces him to desert? This is none the less injurious when effected by getting a father, or brother, or friend, into a public meeting, and there working upon his feelings till he is persuaded to write the soldier boy that he is fighting in a bad cause, for a wicked Administration of a contemptible Government, too weak to arrest and punish him if he shall desert. I think that in such a case to silence the agitator and save the boy is not only constitutional, but withal a great mercy.

If I be wrong on this question of constitutional power, my error lies in believing that certain proceedings are constitutional when, in cases of rebellion or invasion, the public safety requires them, which would not be constitutional when, in the absence of rebellion or invasion, the public safety does *not* require them; in other words, that the Constitution is not, in its application, in all respects the same, in cases of rebellion or invasion involving the public safety, as it is in time of profound peace and public security. The Constitution itself makes the distinction; and I can no more be persuaded that the Government can constitutionally take no strong measures in time of rebellion, because it can be shown that the same could not be lawfully taken in time of peace, than I can be persuaded that a particular drug is not good medicine for a sick man, because it can be shown not to be good food for a well one. Nor am I able to appreciate the danger apprehended by the meeting that the American people will, by means of military arrests during the Rebellion, lose the right of Public Discussion, the Liberty of Speech and the Press, the Law of Evidence, Trial by Jury, and Habeas Corpus, throughout the indefinite peaceful future, which I trust lies before them, any more than I am able to believe that a man could contract so strong an appetite for emetics during temporary illness as to persist in feeding upon them during the remainder of his healthful life.

.   .   .   .   .

One of the resolutions expresses the opinion of the meeting that arbitrary arrests will have the effect to divide and distract those who should be united in suppressing the Rebellion, and I am specifically called on to discharge Mr. Vallandigham. I regard this as, at least, a fair appeal to me on the expediency of exercising a Constitutional power which I think exists. In response to such appeal, I have to say, it gave me pain when I learned that Mr. Vallandigham had been arrested—that is, I was pained that there should have seemed to be a necessity for arresting him—and that it will afford me great pleasure to discharge him so soon as I can, by any means, believe the public safety will not suffer by it. I further say that, as the war progresses, it appears to me, opinion and action, which were in great confusion at first, take shape and fall into more regular channels, so that the necessity for strong dealing with them gradually decreases. I have every reason to desire that it should cease altogether; and far from the least is my regard for the opinions and wishes of those who, like the meeting at Albany, declare their purpose to sustain the Government in every Constitutional and lawful measure to suppress the Rebellion. Still, I must continue to do so much as may seem to be required by the public safety.

78. An Untimely Feud:
LETTER TO JOSEPH HOOKER, JUNE 16, 1863

WHILE Lee pushed his army northward, Hooker was becoming restive under the authority of Halleck. Lincoln tried to patch up their difference, but without success. On June 28, Hooker asked to be relieved and was replaced by General George G. Meade.

(*Private.*)

Executive Mansion, Washington, D. C., June 16, 1863.

My dear General: I send you this by the hand of Captain Dahlgren. Your despatch of 11:30 A.M. to-day is just received. When you say I have long been aware that you do not enjoy the confidence of the major-general commanding, you state the case much too strongly.

You do not lack his confidence in any degree to do you any harm. On seeing him, after telegraphing you this morning, I found him more nearly agreeing with you than I was myself. Surely you do not mean to understand that I am withholding my confidence from you when I happen to express an opinion (certainly never discourteously) differing from one of your own.

I believe Halleck is dissatisfied with you to this extent only, that he knows that you write and telegraph ("report," as he calls it) to me. I think he is wrong to find fault with this; but I do not think he withholds any support from you on account of it. If you and he would use the same frankness to one another, and to me, that I use to both of you, there would be no difficulty. I need and must have the professional skill of both, and yet these suspicions tend to deprive me of both.

I believe you are aware that since you took command of the army I have not believed you had any chance to effect anything till now. As it looks to me, Lee's now returning toward Harper's Ferry gives you back the chance that I thought McClellan lost last fall. Quite possibly I was wrong both then and now; but, in the great responsibility resting upon me, I cannot be entirely silent. Now, all I ask is that you will be in such mood that we can get into our action the best cordial judgment of yourself and General Halleck, with my poor mite added, if indeed he and you shall think it entitled to any consideration at all. Yours as ever,

A. Lincoln.

79. War Profiteering:

LETTER TO WILLIAM P. KELLOGG, JUNE 29, 1863

AS Union forces gained control of the lower Mississippi, trading in cotton became a lucrative business. Lincoln described the vicious consequences in this letter to a former Illinois congressman who had requested a special trading permit.

Executive Mansion,
Washington, June 29, 1863.

Hon. Wm. Kellogg.
My dear Sir:

I have received, and read, your pencil note. I think you do not know how embarrassing your request is. Few things are so troublesome to the government as the fierceness with which the profits of trading in cotten are sought. The temptation is so great that nearly every body wishes to be in it; and when in, the question of profit controls all, regardless of whether the cotten seller is loyal or rebel, or whether he is paid in corn-meal or gun-powder. The officers of the army, in numerous instances, are believed to connive and share the profits, and thus the army itself is diverted from fighting the rebels to speculating in cotten; and steam-boats and wagons in the pay of the government, are set to gathering and carrying cotten, and the soldiers to loading cotten-trains and guarding them.

The matter deeply affects the Treasury and War Departments, and has been discussed again and again in the cabinet. What can, and what can not be done, has, for the time been settled, and it seems to me I can not safely break over it. I know it is thought that one case is not much, but how can I favor one and deny another. One case can not be kept a secret. The authority given would be utterly ineffectual until it is shown; and when shown, every body knows of it. The administration would do for you as much as for any other man; and I personally would do some more than for most others; but really I can not involve myself and the Government as this would do. Yours as ever,

A. Lincoln

80. *Victory in the West:*
LETTER TO ULYSSES S. GRANT, JULY 13, 1863

ON July 4, 1863, after more than a month of siege, the Confederate commander in Vicksburg surrendered. Lincoln, gratefully aware that a first-rate Union general at last emerged, sent this delightfully informal note of congratulation to the victorious Grant.

Executive Mansion,
Washington, July 13, 1863.

Major General Grant
My dear General:

I do not remember that you and I ever met personally. I write this now as a grateful acknowledgment for the almost inestimable service you have done the country. I wish to say a word further. When you first reached the vicinity of Vicksburg, I thought you should do, what you finally did—march the troops across the neck, run the batteries with the transports, and thus go below; and I never had any faith, except a general hope that you knew better than I, that the Yazoo Pass expedition, and the like, could succeed. When you got below, and took Port-Gibson, Grand Gulf, and vicinity, I thought you should go down the river and join Gen. Banks; and when you turned Northward East of the Big Black, I feared it was a mistake. I now wish to make the personal acknowledgment that you were right, and I was wrong. Yours very truly,

A. Lincoln

81. Gettysburg and After:
LETTER TO GEORGE G. MEADE, JULY 14, 1863

AT the decisive battle of Gettysburg, July 1–3, 1863, Lee was defeated and forced to withdraw from Pennsylvania. Lincoln's joy changed to disappointment, however, when Meade allowed the Confederate army to escape across the Potomac. Meade, sensitive to criticism, asked in vain to be relieved from command. Lincoln promptly drafted, but did not sign or send, this reproachful letter.

Executive Mansion,
Washington, July 14, 1863.

Major General Meade:

I have just seen your despatch to Gen. Halleck, asking to be relieved of your command, because of a supposed censure of mine. I am very—*very*—grateful to you for the magnificient success you gave the cause of the country at Gettysburg; and I am sorry now to be the author of the slightest pain to you. But I was in such deep distress myself that I could not restrain some expression of it. I had been oppressed nearly ever since the battles at Gettysburg, by what appeared to be evidences that yourself, and Gen. Couch, and Gen. Smith, were not seeking a collision with the enemy, but were trying to get him across the river without another battle. What these evidences were, if you please, I hope to tell you at some time, when we shall both feel better. The case, summarily stated is this. You fought and beat the enemy at Gettysburg; and, of course, to say the least, his loss was as great as yours. He retreated; and you did not, as it seemed to me, pressingly pursue him; but a flood in the river detained him, till, by slow degrees, you were again upon him. You had at least twenty thousand veteran troops directly with you, and as many more raw ones within supporting distance, all in addition to those who fought with you at

Gettysburg; while it was not possible that he had received a single recruit; and yet you stood and let the flood run down, bridges be built, and the enemy move away at his leisure, without attacking him. And Couch and Smith! The latter left Carlisle in time, upon all ordinary calculation, to have aided you in the last battle at Gettysburg; but he did not arrive. At the end of more than ten days, I believe twelve, under constant urging, he reached Hagerstown from Carlisle, which is not an inch over fiftyfive miles, if so much. And Couch's movement was very little different.

Again, my dear general, I do not believe you appreciate the magnitude of the misfortune involved in Lee's escape. He was within your easy grasp, and to have closed upon him would, in connection with our other late successes, have ended the war. As it is, the war will be prolonged indefinitely. If you could not safely attack Lee last monday, how can you possibly do so South of the river, when you can take with you very few more than two thirds of the force you then had in hand? It would be unreasonable to expect, and I do not expect you can now effect much. Your golden opportunity is gone, and I am distressed immeasurably because of it.

I beg you will not consider this a prossecution, or persecution of yourself. As you had learned that I was dissatisfied, I have thought it best to kindly tell you why.

82. *Threats and Counterthreats:*
PRESIDENTIAL ORDER, JULY 30, 1863

THE enlistment of Negroes in the Union army provoked Confederate decrees authorizing enslavement of such troops when captured and execution of their white officers. In retaliation, Lincoln signed this severe order drafted by the War Department. Although some atrocities were apparently committed against Negro soldiers, neither side carried out its threats in any systematic way.

Executive Mansion, Washington D.C July 30, 1863

It is the duty of every government to give protection to its citizens, of whatever class, color, or condition, and especially to those who are duly organized as soldiers in the public service. The law of nations and the usages and customs of war as carried on by civilized powers, permit no distinction as to color in the treatment of prisoners of war as public enemies. To sell or enslave any captured person, on account of his color, and for no offence against the laws of war, is a relapse into barbarism and a crime against the civilization of the age.

The government of the United States will give the same protection to all its soldiers, and if the enemy shall sell or enslave anyone because of his color, the offense shall be punished by retaliation upon the enemy's prisoners in our possession.

It is therefore ordered that for every soldier of the United States killed in violation of the laws of war, a rebel solider shall be executed; and for every one enslaved by the enemy or sold into slavery, a rebel soldier shall be placed at hard labor on the public works and continued at such labor until the other shall be released and receive the treatment due to a prisoner of war.

Abraham Lincoln

83. *Thoughts on Reconstruction:*

LETTER TO NATHANIEL P. BANKS, AUGUST 5, 1863

AS the fortunes of the Confederacy declined, Lincoln gave more and more thought to the problem of reconstructing the Union. Louisiana, occupied since 1862, offered an opportunity for experiment. A movement to establish a loyal state government was under way, encouraged by General George F. Shepley, the military governor, and by General Nathaniel P. Banks, who commanded the Department of the Gulf. Lincoln, having received word from Banks through George S. Boutwell, a Massachusetts

Republican, wrote to describe what he would like to see happen in Louisiana. His concern about Mexico was inspired by the French intervention which culminated later in the short-lived reign of Emperor Maximilian I.

> Executive Mansion, Washington,
> August 5, 1863.

My dear General Banks:

Being a poor correspondent is the only apology I offer for not having sooner tendered my thanks for your very successful, and very valuable military operations this year. The final stroke in opening the Mississippi never should, and I think never will, be forgotten.

Recent events in Mexico, I think, render early action in Texas more important than ever. I expect, however, the General-in-Chief, will address you more fully upon this subject.

Governor Boutwell read me to-day that part of your letter to him, which relates to Louisiana affairs. While I very well know what I would be glad for Louisiana to do, it is quite a different thing for me to assume direction of the matter. I would be glad for her to make a new Constitution recognizing the emancipation proclamation, and adopting emancipation in those parts of the state to which the proclamation does not apply. And while she is at it, I think it would not be objectionable for her to adopt some practical system by which the two races could gradually live themselves out of their old relation to each other, and both come out better prepared for the new. Education for young blacks should be included in the plan. After all, the power, or element, of "contract" may be sufficient for this probationary period; and, by it's simplicity, and flexibility, may be the better.

As an anti-slavery man I have a motive to desire emancipation, which pro-slavery men do not have; but even they have strong enough reason to thus place themselves again under the shield of the Union; and to thus perpetually hedge against the recurrence of the scenes through which we are now passing.

Gov. Shepley has informed me that Mr. Durant is now taking a registry, with a view to the election of a Constitutional convention in Louisiana. This, to me, appears proper. If such convention were to ask my views, I could present little else than what I now say to you. I think the thing should be pushed forward, so that if possible, it's mature work may reach here by the meeting of Congress.

For my own part I think I shall not, in any event, retract the emancipation proclamation; nor, as executive, ever return to slavery any person who is free by the terms of that proclamation, or by any of the acts of Congress.

If Louisiana shall send members to Congress, their admission to seats will depend, as you know, upon the respective Houses, and not upon the President.

If these views can be of any advantage in giving shape, and impetus, to action there, I shall be glad for you to use them prudently for that object. Of course you will confer with intelligent and trusty citizens of the State, among whom I would suggest Messrs. Flanders, Hahn, and Durant; and to each of whom I now think I may send copies of this letter. Still it is perhaps better to not make the letter generally public. Yours very truly,

A. Lincoln

84. Lincoln on Shakespeare:
LETTERS TO JAMES H. HACKETT, AUGUST 17, NOVEMBER 2, 1863

ATTENDING the theater was one of Lincoln's favorite forms of relaxation. In March 1863, he saw a performance of *Henry IV*, with James H. Hackett playing Falstaff. Hackett had just published a book about Shakespeare's plays, and he sent a copy to the President. Lincoln acknowledged the gift on August 17, adding a few sentences about his own reading of Shakespeare. Hackett printed a broadside of this letter "for private distribution only," but it soon appeared in the press, with many derisive comments on the President's new role as literary critic. Writing October 22, Hackett apologized for what had happened. Lincoln's good-humored reply of November 2 was carefully marked "private."

Executive Mansion,
Washington, August 17, 1863.

My dear Sir:

Months ago I should have acknowledged the receipt of your book, and accompanying kind note; and I now have to beg your pardon for not having done so.

For one of my age, I have seen very little of the drama. The first presentation of Falstaff I ever saw was yours here, last winter or spring. Perhaps the best compliment I can pay is to say, as I truly can, I am very anxious to see it again. Some of Shakespeare's plays I have never read; while others I have gone over perhaps as frequently as any unprofessional reader. Among the latter are Lear, Richard Third, Henry Eighth, Hamlet, and especially Macbeth. I think nothing equals Macbeth. It is wonderful. Unlike you gentlemen of the profession, I think the soliloquy in Hamlet commencing "O, my offence is rank" surpasses that commencing "To be, or not to be." But pardon this small attempt at criticism. I should like to hear you pronounce the opening speech of Richard the Third. Will you not soon visit Washington again? If you do, please call and let me make your personal acquaintance. Yours truly,

James H. Hackett, Esq.   A. Lincoln.

———————

Private

Executive Mansion,
Washington, Nov. 2, 1863.

James H. Hackett
My dear Sir:

Yours of Oct. 22nd. is received, as also was, in due course, that of Oct. 3rd. I look forward with pleasure to the fulfilment of the promise made in the former.

Give yourself no uneasiness on the subject mentioned in that of the 22nd.

My note to you I certainly did not expect to see in print; yet I have not been much shocked by the newspaper comments upon it. Those comments constitute a fair specimen of what has occurred to me through life. I have endured a great deal of ridicule without much malice; and have received a great deal of kindness, not quite free from ridicule. I am used to it. Yours truly,

A. Lincoln

85. *Pleading His Own Case:*

LETTER TO JAMES C. CONKLING, AUGUST 26, 1863

SPRINGFIELD, Illinois, had been the scene of a mass demonstration by "Peace" Democrats in June 1863. Local Republican leaders resolved to counter with a big meeting of their own and invited Lincoln to attend. He declined, but sent this letter for public reading. Addressed to an old friend, it was a stalwart defense of his major policies and purposes.

Executive Mansion,
Washington, August 26, 1863.

Hon. James C. Conkling
My Dear Sir:

Your letter inviting me to attend a mass-meeting of unconditional Union-men, to be held at the Capital of Illinois, on the 3d day of September, has been received.

It would be very agreeable to me, to thus meet my old friends, at my own home; but I can not, just now, be absent from here, so long as a visit there, would require.

The meeting is to be of all those who maintain unconditional devotion to the Union; and I am sure my old political friends will thank me for tendering, as I do, the nation's gratitude to those other noble men, whom no partizan malice, or partizan hope, can make false to the nation's life.

There are those who are dissatisfied with me. To such I would say: You desire peace; and you blame me that we do not have it. But how can we attain it? There are but three conceivable ways. First, to suppress the rebellion by force of arms. This, I am trying to do. Are you for it?

If you are, so far we are agreed. If you are not for it, a second way is, to give up the Union. I am against this. Are you for it? If you are, you should say so plainly. If you are not for *force*, nor yet for *dissolution*, there only remains some imaginable *compromise*. I do not believe any compromise, embracing the maintenance of the Union, is now possible. All I learn, leads to a directly opposite belief. The strength of the rebellion, is its military—its army. That army dominates all the country, and all the people, within its range. Any offer of terms made by any man or men within that range, in opposition to that army, is simply nothing for the present; because such man or men, have no power whatever to enforce their side of a compromise, if one were made with them. To illustrate— Suppose refugees from the South, and peace men of the North, get together in convention, and frame and proclaim a compromise embracing a restoration of the Union; in what way can that compromise be used to keep Lee's army out of Pennsylvania? Meade's army can keep Lee's army out of Pennsylvania; and, I think, can ultimately drive it out of existence. But no paper compromise, to which the controllers of Lee's army are not agreed, can, at all, affect that army. In an effort at such compromise we should waste time, which the enemy would improve to our disadvantage; and that would be all. A compromise, to be effective, must be made either with those who control the rebel army, or with the people first liberated from the domination of that army, by the success of our own army. Now allow me to assure you, that no word or intimation, from that rebel army, or from any of the men controlling it, in relation to any peace compromise, has ever come to my knowledge or belief. All charges and insinuations to the contrary, are deceptive and groundless. And I promise you, that if any such proposition shall hereafter come, it shall not be rejected, and kept a secret from you. I freely acknowledge myself the servant of the people, according to the bond of service—the United States constitution; and that, as such, I am responsible to them.

But, to be plain, you are dissatisfied with me about the negro. Quite likely there is a difference of opinion between you and myself upon that subject. I certainly wish that all men could be free, while I suppose you do not.

Yet I have neither adopted, nor proposed any measure, which is not consistent with even your view, provided you are for the Union. I suggested compensated emancipation; to which you replied you wished not to be taxed to buy negroes. But I had not asked you to be taxed to buy negroes, except in such way, as to save you from greater taxation to save the Union exclusively by other means.

You dislike the emancipation proclamation; and, perhaps, would have it retracted. You say it is unconstitutional—I think differently. I think the constitution invests its commander-in-chief, with the law of war, in time of war. The most that can be said, if so much, is, that slaves are property. Is there—has there ever been—any question that by the law of war, property, both of enemies and friends, may be taken when needed? And is it not needed whenever taking it, helps us, or hurts the enemy? Armies, the world over, destroy enemies' property when they can not use it; and even destroy their own to keep it from the enemy. Civilized belligerents do all in their power to help themselves, or hurt the enemy, except a few things regarded as barbarous or cruel. Among the exceptions are the massacre of vanquished foes, and non-combatants, male and female.

But the proclamation, as law, either is valid, or is not valid. If it is not valid, it needs no retraction. If it is valid, it can not be retracted, any more than the dead can be brought to life. Some of you profess to think its retraction would operate favorably for the Union. Why better *after* the retraction, than *before* the issue? There was more than a year and a half of trial to suppress the rebellion before the proclamation issued, the last one hundred days of which passed under an explicit notice that it was coming, unless averted by those in revolt, returning to their allegiance. The war has certainly progressed as favorably for us, since the issue of the proclamation as before. I know as fully as one can know the opinions of others, that some of the commanders of our armies in the field who have given us our most important successes, believe the emancipation policy, and the use of colored troops, constitute the heaviest blow yet dealt to the rebellion; and that, at least one of those important successes, could not have been achieved when it was, but for the aid of black soldiers. Among the commanders holding these views are some who have never had any affinity with what is called abolitionism, or with republican party politics; but who hold them purely as military opinions. I submit these opinions as being entitled to some weight against the objections, often urged, that emancipation, and arming the blacks, are unwise as military measures, and were not adopted, as such, in good faith.

You say you will not fight to free negroes. Some of them seem willing to fight for you; but, no matter. Fight you, then, exclusively to save the Union. I issued the proclamation on purpose to aid you in saving the Union. Whenever you shall have conquered all resistance to the Union, if I shall urge you to continue fighting, it will be an apt time, then, for you to declare you will not fight to free negroes.

I thought that in your struggle for the Union, to whatever extent the negroes should cease helping the enemy, to that extent it weakened the enemy in his resistance to you. Do you think differently? I thought that whatever negroes can be got to do as soldiers, leaves just so much less for white soldiers to do, in saving the Union. Does it appear otherwise to you? But negroes, like other people, act upon motives. Why should they do any thing for us, if we will do nothing for them? If they stake their lives for us, they must be prompted by the strongest motive— even the promise of freedom. And the promise being made, must be kept.

The signs look better. The Father of Waters again goes unvexed to the sea. Thanks to the great North-West for it. Nor yet wholly to them. Three hundred miles up, they met New-England, Empire, Key-Stone, and Jersey, hewing their way right and left. The Sunny South too, in more colors than one, also lent a hand. On the spot, their part of the history was jotted down in black and white. The job was a great national one; and let none be banned who bore an honorable part in it. And while those who have cleared the great river may well be proud, even that is not all. It is hard to say that anything has been more bravely, and well done, than at Antietam, Murfreesboro, Gettysburg, and on many fields of lesser note. Nor must

Uncle Sam's Web-feet be forgotten. At all the watery margins they have been present. Not only on the deep sea, the broad bay, and the rapid river, but also up the narrow muddy bayou, and wherever the ground was a little damp, they have been, and made their tracks. Thanks to all. For the great republic—for the principle it lives by, and keeps alive—for man's vast future,—thanks to all.

Peace does not appear so distant as it did. I hope it will come soon, and come to stay; and so come as to be worth the keeping in all future time. It will then have been proved that, among free men, there can be no successful appeal from the ballot to the bullet; and that they who take such appeal are sure to lose their case, and pay the cost. And then, there will be some black men who can remember that, with silent tongue, and clenched teeth, and steady eye, and well-poised bayonet, they have helped mankind on to this great consummation; while, I fear, there will be some white ones, unable to forget that, with malignant heart, and deceitful speech, they have strove to hinder it.

Still let us not be over-sanguine of a speedy final triumph. Let us be quite sober. Let us diligently apply the means, never doubting that a just God, in his own good time, will give us the rightful result. Yours very truly,

A. Lincoln

86. Stalemate on the Rapidan:

LETTER TO HENRY W. HALLECK, SEPTEMBER 19, 1863

MEADE had followed Lee southward until the two armies faced each other across the Rapidan River, a tributary of the Rappahannock. The Union commander, reluctant to attempt a crossing against an enemy well situated for defense, asked what he should do next. In commenting upon the query, Lincoln again emphasized two fundamentals of strategy: that the numerical superiority of Northern troops should somehow be made to yield an advantage, and that the primary objective should be to destroy Lee's army as a fighting force, rather than to take Richmond.

Executive Mansion
Washington, Sept. 19, 1863.

Major General Halleck:

By Gen. Meade's despatch to you of yesterday it appears that he desires your views and those of the government, as to whether he shall advance upon the enemy. I am not prepared to order, or even advise an advance in this case, wherein I know so little of particulars, and wherein he, in the field, thinks the risk is so great, and the promise of advantage so small. And yet the case presents matter for very serious consideration in another aspect. These two armies confront each other across a small river, substantially midway between the two Capitals, each defending it's own Capital, and menacing the other. Gen. Meade estimates the enemies infantry in front of him at not less than forty thousand. Suppose we add fifty per cent to this, for cavalry, artillery, and extra duty men stretching as far as Richmond, making the whole force of the enemy sixty thousand. Gen. Meade, as shown by the returns, has with him, and between him and Washington, of the same classes of well men, over ninety thousand. Neither can bring the whole of his men into a battle; but each can bring as large a per centage in as the other. For a battle, then, Gen. Meade has three men to Gen. Lee's two. Yet, it having been determined that choosing ground, and standing on the defensive, gives so great advantage that the three can not safely attack the two, the three are left simply standing on the defensive also. If the enemies sixty thousand are sufficient to keep our ninety thousand away from Richmond, why, by the same rule, may not forty thousand of ours keep their sixty thousand away from Washington, leaving us fifty thousand to put to some other use? Having practically come to the mere defensive, it seems to be no economy at all to employ twice as many men for that object as are needed. With no object, certainly, to mislead myself, I can perceive no fault in this statement, unless we admit we are not the equal of the enemy man for man. I hope you will consider it.

To avoid misunderstanding, let me say that to attempt to fight the enemy slowly back into his intrenchments at Richmond, and there to capture him, is an idea I have been trying to repudiate for quite a year. My judgment is so clear against it, that I would scarcely allow the attempt to be made, if the general in command should desire to make it. My last attempt upon Richmond was to get McClellan, when he was nearer there than the enemy was, to run in ahead of him. Since then I have constantly desired the Army of the Potomac, to make Lee's army, and not Richmond, it's objective point. If our army can not fall upon the enemy and hurt him where he is, it is plain to me it can gain nothing by attempting to follow him over a succession of intrenched lines into a fortified city. Yours truly,

A. Lincoln

87. *Immortal Words:*
THE GETTYSBURG ADDRESS, NOVEMBER 19, 1863

THE dedication of a national cemetery at Gettysburg was scheduled for November 19, 1863. Lincoln accepted an invitation to attend the ceremony and make a few appropriate remarks after the principal speaker, Edward Everett, had finished his address. The next day, Everett wrote to the President: "I should be glad, if I could flatter myself that I came as near to the central idea of the occasion, in two hours, as you did in two minutes." There are several versions of what Lincoln said at Gettysburg, including his own handwritten draft and the transcriptions of newspaper reporters. In addition, he prepared three subsequent copies, each time making one or more changes. This is the final text—his most polished version for posterity, rather than the most accurate reproduction of the words actually uttered at Gettysburg.

Four score and seven years ago our fathers brought forth on this continent, a new nation, conceived in Liberty, and dedicated to the proposition that all men are created equal.

Now we are engaged in a great civil war, testing whether that nation, or any nation so conceived and so dedicated, can long endure. We are met on a great battle-field of that war. We have come to dedicate a portion of that field, as a final resting place for those who here gave their lives that that nation might live. It is altogether fitting and proper that we should do this.

But, in a larger sense, we can not dedicate—we can not consecrate—we can not hallow—this ground. The brave men, living and dead, who struggled here, have consecrated it, far above our poor power to add or detract. The world will little note, nor long remember what we say here, but it can never forget what they did here. It is for us the living, rather, to be dedicated here to the unfinished work which they who fought here have thus far so nobly advanced. It is rather for us to be here dedicated to the great task remaining before us—that from these honored dead we take increased devotion to that cause for which they gave the last full measure of devotion—that we here highly resolve that these dead shall not have died in vain—that this nation, under God, shall have a new birth of freedom—and that government of the people, by the people, for the people, shall not perish from the earth.

88. *A Plan of Reconstruction:*

PRESIDENTIAL PROCLAMATION, DECEMBER 8, 1863

THE Eastern battlefront was relatively quiet during the later months of 1863, but in the West, both Knoxville and Chattanooga, Tennessee, were seized by Union forces and held against counterattacks. With renewed confidence of ultimate victory, Lincoln turned his attention to the problems of peace and restoration. By proclamation, he offered amnesty, with certain conditions and exceptions, to those persons who had participated in the rebellion, and he set forth his famous "ten-per-cent plan" for reconstruction of the Southern states.

December 8, 1863

By the President of the United States of America:
A Proclamation.

Whereas, in and by the Constitution of the United States, it is provided that the President "shall have power to grant reprieves and pardons for offences against the United States, except in cases of impeachment;" and

Whereas a rebellion now exists whereby the loyal State governments of several States have for a long time been subverted, and many persons have committed and are now guilty of treason against the United States; and

Whereas, with reference to said rebellion and treason, laws have been enacted by Congress declaring forfeitures and confiscation of property and liberation of slaves, all upon terms and conditions therein stated, and also declaring that the President was thereby authorized at any time thereafter, by proclamation, to extend to persons who may have participated in the existing rebellion, in any State or part thereof, pardon and amnesty, with such exceptions and at such times and on such conditions as he may deem expedient for the public welfare; and

Whereas the congressional declaration for limited and conditional pardon accords with well-established judicial exposition of the pardoning power; and

Whereas, with reference to said rebellion, the President of the United States has issued several proclamations, with provisions in regard to the liberation of slaves; and

Whereas it is now desired by some persons heretofore engaged in said rebellion to resume their allegiance to the United States, and to reinaugurate loyal State governments within and for their respective States; therefore,

I, Abraham Lincoln, President of the United States, do proclaim, declare, and make known to all persons who have, directly or by implication, participated in the existing rebellion, except as hereinafter excepted, that a full pardon is hereby granted to them and each of them, with restoration of all rights of property, except as to slaves, and in property cases where rights of third parties shall have intervened, and upon the condition that every such person shall take and subscribe an oath, and thenceforward keep and maintain said oath inviolate; and which oath shall be registered for permanent preservation, and shall be of the tenor and effect following, to wit:

"I, _____, do solemnly swear, in presence of Almighty God, that I will henceforth faithfully support, protect and defend the Constitution of the United States, and the union of the States thereunder; and that I will, in like manner, abide by and faithfully support all acts of Congress passed during the existing rebellion with reference to slaves, so long and so far as not repealed, modified or held void by Congress, or by decision of the Supreme Court; and that I will, in like manner, abide by and faithfully support all proclamations of the President made during the existing rebellion having reference to slaves, so long and so far as not modified or declared void by decision of the Supreme Court. So help me God."

The persons excepted from the benefits of the foregoing provisions are all who are, or shall have been, civil or diplomatic officers or agents of the so-called confederate government; all who have left judicial stations under the United States to aid the rebellion; all who are, or shall have been, military or naval officers of said so-called confederate government above the rank of colonel in the army, or of lieutenant in the navy; all who left seats in the United States Congress to aid the rebellion; all who resigned commissions in the army or navy of the United States, and afterwards aided the rebellion; and all who have engaged in any way in treating colored persons or white persons, in charge of such, otherwise than lawfully as prisoners of war, and which persons may have been found in the United States service, as soldiers, seamen, or in any other capacity.

And I do further proclaim, declare, and make known, that whenever, in any of the States of Arkansas, Texas, Louisiana, Mississippi, Tennessee, Alabama, Georgia, Florida, South Carolina, and North Carolina, a number of persons, not less than one-tenth in number of the votes cast in such State at the Presidential election of the year of our Lord one thousand eight hundred and sixty, each having taken the oath aforesaid and not having since violated it, and being a qualified voter by the election law of the State existing immediately before the so-called act of secession, and excluding all others, shall re-establish a State government which shall be republican, and in no wise contravening said oath, such shall be recognized as the true government of the State, and the State shall receive thereunder the benefits of the constitutional provision which declares that "The United States shall guaranty to every State in this union a republican form of government, and shall protect each of them against invasion; and, on application of the legislature, or the executive, (when the legislature cannot be convened,) against domestic violence."

And I do further proclaim, declare, and make known that any provision which may be adopted by such State government in relation to the freed people of such State, which shall recognize and declare their permanent freedom, provide for their education, and which may yet be consistent, as a temporary arrangement, with their present condition as a laboring, landless and homeless class, will not be objected to by the national Executive. And it is suggested as not improper, that, in constructing a loyal State government in any State, the name of the State, the boundary, the subdivisions, the constitution, and the general code of laws, as before the rebellion, be maintained, subject only to the modifications made necessary by the conditions hereinbefore stated, and such others, if any, not contravening said conditions, and which may be deemed expedient by those framing the new State government.

To avoid misunderstanding, it may be proper to say that this proclamation, so far as it relates to State governments, has no reference to States wherein loyal State governments have all the while been maintained. And for the same reason, it may be proper to further say that whether members sent to Congress from any State shall be admitted to seats, constitutionally rests exclusively with the respective Houses, and not to any extent with the Executive. And still further, that this proclamation is intended to present the people of the States wherein the national authority has been suspended, and loyal State governments have been subverted, a mode in and by which the national authority and loyal State governments may be re-established within said States, or in any of them; and, while the mode presented is the best the Executive can suggest, with his present impressions, it must not be understood that no other possible mode would be acceptable.

89. *The Reconstruction Program Explained:*
ANNUAL MESSAGE TO CONGRESS, DECEMBER 8, 1863

MOST of Lincoln's third Annual Message was no doubt prepared by department heads, but he drafted this closing section himself. It is a survey of the year's events and an explanation of his plans for reconstruction, as enunciated in the proclamation just issued.

When Congress assembled a year ago the war had already lasted nearly twenty months, and there had been many conflicts on both land and sea, with varying results.

The rebellion had been pressed back into reduced limits; yet the tone of public feeling and opinion, at home and abroad, was not satisfactory. With other signs, the popular elections, then just past, indicated uneasiness among ourselves, while amid much that was cold and menacing the kindest words coming from Europe were uttered in accents of pity, that we were too blind to surrender a hopeless cause. Our commerce was suffering greatly by a few armed vessels built upon and furnished from foreign shores, and we were threatened with such additions from the same quarter as would sweep our trade from the sea and raise our blockade. We had failed to elicit from European governments anything hopeful upon this subject. The preliminary emancipation proclamation, issued in September, was running its assigned period to the beginning of the new year. A month later the final proclamation came, including the announcement that colored men of suitable condition would be received into the war service. The policy of emancipation, and of employing black soldiers, gave to the future a new aspect, about which hope, and fear, and doubt contended in uncertain conflict. According to our political system, as a matter of civil administration, the general government had no lawful power to effect emancipation in any State, and for a long time it had been hoped that the rebellion could be suppressed without resorting to it as a military measure. It was all the while deemed possible that the necessity for it might come, and that if it should, the crisis of the contest would then be presented. It came, and as was anticipated, it was followed by dark and doubtful days. Eleven months having now passed, we are permitted to take another review. The rebel borders are pressed still further back, and by the complete opening of the Mississippi the country dominated by the rebellion is divided into distinct parts, with no practical communication between them. Tennessee and Arkansas have been substantially cleared of insurgent control, and influential citizens in each, owners of slaves and advocates of slavery at the beginning of the rebellion, now declare openly for emancipation in their respective States. Of those States not included in the emancipation proclamation, Maryland, and Missouri, neither of which three years ago would tolerate any restraint upon the extension of slavery into new territories, only dispute now as to the best mode of removing it within their own limits.

Of those who were slaves at the beginning of the rebellion, full one hundred thousand are now in the United States military service, about one-half of which number actually bear arms in the ranks; thus giving the double advantage of taking so much labor from the insurgent cause, and supplying the places which otherwise must be filled with so many white men. So far as tested, it is difficult to say they are not as good soldiers as any. No servile insurrection, or tendency to violence or cruelty, has marked the measures of emancipation and arming the blacks. These measures have been much discussed in foreign countries, and contemporary with such discussion the tone of public sentiment there is much improved. At home the same measures have been fully discussed, supported, criticised, and denounced, and the annual elections following are highly encouraging to those whose official duty it is to bear the country through this great trial. Thus we have the new reckoning. The crisis which threatened to divide the friends of the Union is past.

Looking now to the present and future, and with reference to a resumption of the national authority within the States wherein that authority has been suspended, I have thought fit to issue a proclamation, a copy of which is herewith transmitted. On examination of this proclamation it will appear, as is believed, that nothing is attempted beyond what is amply justified by the Constitution. True, the form of an oath is given, but no man is coerced to take it. The man is only promised a pardon in case he voluntarily takes the oath. The Constitution authorizes the Executive to grant or withhold the pardon at his own absolute discretion; and this includes the power to grant on terms, as is fully established by judicial and other authorities.

It is also proffered that if, in any of the States named, a State government shall be, in the mode prescribed, set up, such government shall be recognized and guarantied by the United States, and that under it the State shall, on the constitutional conditions, be protected against invasion and domestic violence. The constitutional obligation of the United States to guaranty to every State in the Union a republican form of government, and to protect the State, in the cases stated, is explicit and full. But why tender the benefits of this provision only to a State government set up in this particular way? This section of the Constitution contemplates a case wherein the element within a State, favorable to republican government, in the Union, may be too feeble for an opposite and hostile element external to, or even within the State; and such are precisely the cases with which we are now dealing.

An attempt to guaranty and protect a revived State government, constructed in whole, or in preponderating part, from the very element against whose hostility and violence it is to be protected, is simply absurd. There must be a test by which to separate the opposing elements, so as to build only from the sound; and that test is a sufficiently liberal one, which accepts as sound whoever will make a sworn recantation of his former unsoundness.

But if it be proper to require, as a test of admission

to the political body, an oath of allegiance to the Constitution of the United States, and to the Union under it, why also to the laws and proclamations in regard to slavery? Those laws and proclamations were enacted and put forth for the purpose of aiding in the suppression of the rebellion. To give them their fullest effect, there had to be a pledge for their maintenance. In my judgment they have aided, and will further aid, the cause for which they were intended. To now abandon them would be not only to relinquish a lever of power, but would also be a cruel and an astounding breach of faith. I may add at this point, that while I remain in my present position I shall not attempt to retract or modify the emancipation proclamation; nor shall I return to slavery any person who is free by the terms of that proclamation, or by any of the acts of Congress. For these and other reasons it is thought best that support of these measures shall be included in the oath; and it is believed the Executive may lawfully claim it in return for pardon and restoration of forfeited rights, which he has clear constitutional power to withhold altogether, or grant upon the terms which he shall deem wisest for the public interest. It should be observed, also, that this part of the oath is subject to the modifying and abrogating power of legislation and supreme judicial decision.

The proposed acquiescence of the national Executive in any reasonable temporary State arrangement for the freed people is made with the view of possibly modifying the confusion and destitution which must, at best, attend all classes by a total revolution of labor throughout whole States. It is hoped that the already deeply afflicted people in those States may be somewhat more ready to give up the cause of their affliction, if, to this extent, this vital matter be left to themselves; while no power of the national Executive to prevent an abuse is abridged by the proposition.

The suggestion in the proclamation as to maintaining the political framework of the States on what is called reconstruction, is made in the hope that it may do good without danger of harm. It will save labor and avoid great confusion.

But why any proclamation now upon this subject? This

question is beset with the conflicting views that the step might be delayed too long or be taken too soon. In some States the elements for resumption seem ready for action, but remain inactive, apparently for want of a rallying point —a plan of action. Why shall A adopt the plan of B, rather than B that of A? And if A and B should agree, how can they know but that the general government here will reject their plan? By the proclamation a plan is presented which may be accepted by them as a rallying point, and which they are assured in advance will not be rejected here. This may bring them to act sooner than they otherwise would.

The objections to a premature presentation of a plan by the national Executive consists in the danger of committals on points which could be more safely left to further developments. Care has been taken to so shape the document as to avoid embarrassments from this source. Saying that, on certain terms, certain classes will be pardoned, with rights restored, it is not said that other classes, or other terms, will never be included. Saying that reconstruction will be accepted if presented in a specified way, it is not said it will never be accepted in any other way.

The movements, by State action, for emancipation in several of the States, not included in the emancipation proclamation, are matters of profound gratulation. And while I do not repeat in detail what I have heretofore so earnestly urged upon this subject, my general views and feelings remain unchanged; and I trust that Congress will omit no fair opportunity of aiding these important steps to a great consummation.

In the midst of other cares, however important, we must not lose sight of the fact that the war power is still our main reliance. To that power alone can we look, yet for a time, to give confidence to the people in the contested regions, that the insurgent power will not again overrun them. Until that confidence shall be established, little can be done anywhere for what is called reconstruction. Hence our chiefest care must still be directed to the army and navy, who have thus far borne their harder part so nobly and well. And it may be esteemed fortunate that in giving the greatest efficiency to these indispensable arms, we do also honorably recognize the gallant men, from commander to sentinel, who compose them, and to whom, more than to others, the world must stand indebted for the home of freedom disenthralled, regenerated, enlarged, and perpetuated.

90. *A Time for Real Patriots:*

LETTER TO THOMAS COTTMAN, DECEMBER 15, 1863

IN this communication to one of Louisiana's "reconstructed rebels," Lincoln emphasized his desire for a flexible program of restoration, with details adjusted to suit local conditions. He was also beginning to anticipate some of the evils that would plague the postwar era.

Executive Mansion,
Washington, December 15, 1863.

Dr. Thomas Cottman
My dear Sir:

You were so kind as to say this morning that you desire to return to Louisiana, and to be guided by my wishes, to some extent, in the part you may take in bringing that state to resume her rightful relation to the general government.

My wishes are in a general way expressed as well as I can express them, in the Proclamation issued on the 8th of the present month, and in that part of the annual message which relates to that proclamation. It there appears that I deem the sustaining of the emancipation proclamation, where it applies, as indispensable; and I add here that I would esteem it fortunate, if the people of Louisiana should themselves place the remainder of the state upon the same footing, and then, if in their discretion it should appear best, make some temporary provision for the whole of the freed people, substantially as suggested in the last proclamation. I have not put forth the plan in that proclamation, as a Procrustean bed, to which exact conformity is to be indispensable; and in Louisiana particularly, I wish that labor already done, which varies from that plan in no important particular, may not be thrown away.

The strongest wish I have, not already publicly expressed, is that in Louisiana and elsewhere, all sincere Union men would stoutly eschew cliqueism, and, each yielding something in minor matters, all work together. Nothing is likely to be so baleful in the great work before us, as stepping aside of the main object to consider who will get the offices if a small matter shall go thus, and who else will get them, if it shall go otherwise. It is a time now for real patriots to rise above all this. As to the particulars of what I may think best to be done in any state, I have publicly stated certain points, which I have thought indispensable to the reestablishment and maintenance of the national authority; and I go no further than this because I wish to avoid both the substance and the appearance of dictation.

91. *Negro Suffrage:*
LETTER TO MICHAEL HAHN, MARCH 13, 1864

DURING the debates with Douglas, Lincoln had stated flatly that he was not in favor of giving Negroes the right to vote. The war having altered his views, however, he ventured this suggestion to the newly elected Union Governor of Louisiana. His recommendation was not adopted.

Private

> Executive Mansion,
> Washington,
> March 13, 1864.

Hon. Michael Hahn
My dear Sir:
I congratulate you on having fixed your name in history as the first free-state Governor of Louisiana. Now you are about to have a Convention which, among other things,

will probably define the elective franchise. I barely suggest for your private consideration, whether some of the colored people may not be let in—as, for instance, the very intelligent, and especially those who have fought gallantly in our ranks. They would probably help, in some trying time to come, to keep the jewel of liberty within the family of freedom. But this is only a suggestion, not to the public, but to you alone. Yours truly,

A. Lincoln

92. On Emancipation and Negro Soldiers:
LETTER TO ALBERT G. HODGES, APRIL 4, 1864

ON March 26, 1864, Lincoln conferred with three prominent Kentuckians: Governor Thomas E. Bramlette, former Senator Archibald Dixon, and Albert G. Hodges, a newspaper editor. They told him that many people in their state were unhappy about the policy of enlisting freedmen. The President made a "little speech" explaining how he had been brought to the point of issuing the Emancipation Proclamation and employing Negroes as soldiers. They went away satisfied, and Lincoln, at Hodges' request, agreed to put the substance of what he had said in writing.

Executive Mansion,
Washington, April 4, 1864.

A. G. Hodges, Esq
Frankfort, Ky.

My dear Sir: You ask me to put in writing the substance of what I verbally said the other day, in your presence, to Governor Bramlette and Senator Dixon. It was about as follows:

"I am naturally anti-slavery. If slavery is not wrong, nothing is wrong. I can not remember when I did not so think, and feel. And yet I have never understood that the Presidency conferred upon me an unrestricted right to act officially upon this judgment and feeling. It was in the oath I took that I would, to the best of my ability, preserve, protect, and defend the Constitution of the United States. I could not take the office without taking the oath. Nor was it my view that I might take an oath to get power, and break the oath in using the power. I understood, too, that in ordinary civil administration this oath even forbade me to practically indulge my primary abstract judgment on the moral question of slavery. I had publicly declared this many times, and in many ways. And I aver that, to this day, I have done no official act in mere deference to my abstract judgment and feeling on slavery. I did understand however, that my oath to preserve the constitution to the best of my ability, imposed upon me the duty of preserving, by every indispensable means, that government—that nation—of which that constitution was the organic law. Was it possible to lose the nation, and yet preserve the constitution? By general law life *and* limb must be protected; yet often a limb must be amputated to save a life; but a life is never wisely given to save a limb. I felt that measures, otherwise unconstitutional, might become lawful, by becoming indispensable to the preservation of the constitution, through the preservation of the nation. Right or wrong, I assumed this ground, and now avow it. I could not feel that, to the best of my ability, I had even tried to preserve the constitution, if, to save slavery, or any minor matter, I should permit the wreck of government, country, and Constitution all together. When, early in the war, Gen. Fremont attempted military emancipation, I forbade it, because I did not then think it an indispensable necessity. When a little later, Gen. Cameron, then Secretary of War, suggested the arming of the blacks, I objected, because I did not yet think it an indispensable necessity. When, still later, Gen. Hunter attempted military emancipation, I again forbade it, because I did not yet think the indispensable necessity had come. When, in March, and May, and July 1862 I made earnest, and successive appeals to the border states to favor compensated emancipation, I believed the indispensable necessity for military emancipation, and arming the blacks would come, unless averted by that measure. They declined the proposition; and I was, in my best judgment, driven to the alternative of either surrendering the Union, and with it, the Constitution, or of laying strong hand upon the colored element. I chose the latter. In choosing it, I hoped for greater gain than loss; but of this, I was not enurely confident. More than a year of trial now shows no loss by it in our foreign relations, none in our home popular sentiment, none in our white military force,—no loss by it any how or any where. On the contrary, it shows a gain of quite a hundred and thirty thousand soldiers, seamen, and laborers. These are palpable facts, about which, as facts, there can be no cavilling. We have the men; and we could not have had them without the measure.

"And now let any Union man who complains of the measure, test himself by writing down in one line that he is for subduing the rebellion by force of arms; and in the next, that he is for taking these hundred and thirty thousand men from the Union side, and placing them where they would be but for the measure he condemns. If he can not face his case so stated, it is only because he can not face the truth."

I add a word which was not in the verbal conversation. In telling this tale I attempt no compliment to my own sagacity. I claim not to have controlled events, but confess plainly that events have controlled me. Now, at the end of three years struggle the nation's condition is not what either party, or any man devised, or expected. God alone can claim it. Whither it is tending seems plain. If God now wills the removal of a great wrong, and wills also that we of the North as well as you of the South, shall pay fairly for our complicity in that wrong, impartial history will find therein new cause to attest and revere the justice and goodness of God. Yours truly,

A. Lincoln

93. A Change of Command:
LETTER TO ULYSSES S. GRANT, APRIL 30, 1864

IN March 1864, Lincoln promoted Grant to general-in-chief of the Union armies, reducing Halleck to a subordinate role as chief of staff. Meade continued in command of the Army of the Potomac, but with Grant at his elbow, supervising operations. As preparations for a new campaign matured, Lincoln made it plain that he was giving Grant a free hand.

Executive Mansion Washington,
April 30, 1864

Lieutenant General Grant:

Not expecting to see you again before the Spring campaign opens, I wish to express, in this way, my entire satisfaction with what you have done up to this time, so far as I understand it. The particulars of your plans I neither know, or seek to know. You are vigilant and self-reliant; and, pleased with this, I wish not to obtrude any constraints or restraints upon you. While I am very anxious that any great disaster, or the capture of our men in great numbers, shall be avoided, I know these points are less likely to escape your attention than they would be mine. If there is anything wanting which is within my power to give, do not fail to let me know it.

And now with a brave Army, and a just cause, may God sustain you. Yours very truly,

A. Lincoln

94. Nominated for a Second Term:

REPLY TO A DELEGATION FROM THE NATIONAL UNION LEAGUE, JUNE 9, 1864

THE American people demonstrated the stability of their political institutions by holding a presidential election on schedule in the midst of civil war. There was more than a little dissatisfaction with Lincoln's leadership inside his own party, but some clumsy efforts to set him aside got nowhere. The Republicans, now calling themselves the Union party, renominated him at Baltimore in June 1864 and chose Andrew Johnson of Tennessee as his new running mate. Lincoln expressed his gratitude to a delegation from the Union League, which had been organized to rally support for the war.

Gentlemen: I can only say, in response to the kind remarks of your chairman, as I suppose, that I am very grateful for the renewed confidence which has been accorded to me, both by the convention and by the National League. I am not insensible at all to the personal compliment there is in this; yet I do not allow myself to believe that any but a small portion of it is to be appropriated as a personal compliment. The convention and the nation, I am assured, are alike animated by a higher view of the interests of the country for the present and the great future, and that part I am entitled to appropriate as a compliment is only that part which I may lay hold of as being the opinion of the convention and of the League, that I am not entirely unworthy to be intrusted with the place I have occupied for the last three years. I have not permitted myself, gentlemen, to conclude that I am the best man in the country; but I am reminded, in this connection, of a story of an old Dutch farmer, who remarked to a companion once that "it was not best to swap horses when crossing streams."

95. The Genesis of Radical Reconstruction:
PRESIDENTIAL PROCLAMATION, JULY 8, 1864

RADICAL Republicans like Senator Benjamin F. Wade of Ohio and Representative Henry W. Davis of Maryland objected to Lincoln's program of reconstruction, insisting that it was too lenient and that it usurped the authority of Congress. Incorporating their views in the Wade-Davis bill, a much harsher plan, they secured its passage on July 2, 1864. Lincoln killed the measure with a pocket veto and then issued a curious proclamation explaining his action. The proposal, he declared, would be quite acceptable as one of several alternatives offered to the South, but it should not be imposed uniformly upon every Southern state. The dissimulation here was almost impudent, for Lincoln knew very well that Southerners would never voluntarily adopt the congressional plan in preference to his own. Wade and Davis, infuriated by the veto, responded with a manifesto savagely denouncing the President.

July 8, 1864

By the President of the United States.

A Proclamation.

Whereas, at the late Session, Congress passed a Bill, "To guarantee to certain States, whose governments have been usurped or overthrown, a republican form of Government," a copy of which is hereunto annexed:

And whereas, the said Bill was presented to the President of the United States, for his approval, less than one hour before the *sine die* adjournment of said Session, and was not signed by him:

And whereas, the said Bill contains, among other things, a plan for restoring the States in rebellion to their proper practical relation in the Union, which plan expresses the sense of Congress upon that subject, and which plan it is now thought fit to lay before the people for their consideration:

Now, therefore, I, Abraham Lincoln, President of the United States, do proclaim, declare, and make known, that, while I am, (as I was in December last, when by proclamation I propounded a plan for restoration) unprepared, by a formal approval of this Bill, to be inflexibly committed to any single plan of restoration; and, while I am also unprepared to declare, that the free-state constitutions and governments, already adopted and installed in Arkansas and Louisiana, shall be set aside and held for nought, thereby repelling and discouraging the loyal citizens who have set up the same, as to further effort; or to declare a constitutional competency in Congress to abolish slavery in States, but am at the same time sincerely hoping and expecting that a constitutional amendment, abolishing slavery throughout the nation, may be adopted, nevertheless, I am fully satisfied with the system for restoration contained in the Bill, as one very proper plan for the loyal people of any State choosing to adopt it; and that I am, and at all times shall be, prepared to give the Executive aid and assistance to any such people, so soon as the military resistance to the United States shall have been suppressed in any such State, and the people thereof shall have sufficiently returned to their obedience to the Constitution and the laws of the United States,—in which cases, military Governors will be appointed, with directions to proceed according to the Bill.

96. *Peace Talk and Politics:*
DRAFT OF A LETTER TO ISAAC M. SCHERMER-HORN, SEPTEMBER 12, 1864

IN the spring of 1864, Grant launched his great offensive. By June he was crossing the James River and hurling troops against Petersburg, south of Richmond. These assaults failed, however, and the battlelines hardened, as the Union army settled down to a long siege. Grant's casualty lists had been frightful, and yet the result seemed to be only another stalemate. Many voices in the North cried out for a negotiated peace. Some demanded repudiation of emancipation as a war objective. The Democratic party, nominating a military celebrity, General McClellan, while adopting a peace platform, scented victory in the presidential contest. Lincoln's prospects appeared dubious, and certain Republican malcontents were scheming to force his withdrawal from the race. But then came the stirring news that on September 1, General William T. Sherman had captured Atlanta. Renewed hope inspirited the Republican campaign. This letter defending his record was drafted by Lincoln for reading at a Union mass meeting in Buffalo. He left it unfinished, however, having decided to avoid any semblance of electioneering.

Executive Mansion,
Washington, Sept. 12, 1864.

Isaac M. Schemerhorn
My dear Sir:

Yours inviting me to attend a Union Mass Meeting at Buffalo is received. Much is being said about peace; and no man desires peace more ardently than I. Still I am yet unprepared to give up the Union for a peace which, so achieved, could not be of much duration. The preservation of our Union was *not* the sole avowed object for which the war was commenced. It was commenced for precisely the reverse object—*to destroy our Union.* The insurgents commenced it by firing upon the Star of the West, and on Fort Sumpter, and by other similar acts. It is true, however, that the administration accepted the war thus commenced, for the sole avowed object of preserving our Union; and it is not true that it has since been, or will be, prossecuted by this administration, for any other object. In declaring this, I only declare what I can know, and do know to be true, and what no other man can know to be false.

In taking the various steps which have led to my present position in relation to the war, the public interest and my private interest, have been perfectly paralel, because in no other way could I serve myself so well, as by truly serving the Union. The whole field has been open to me, where to choose. No place-hunting necessity has been upon me urging me to seek a position of antagonism to some other man, irrespective of whether such position might be favorable or unfavorable to the Union.

Of course I may err in judgment, but my present position in reference to the rebellion is the result of my best judgment, and according to that best judgment, it is the only position upon which any Executive can or could save the Union. Any substantial departure from it insures the success of the rebellion. An armistice—a cessation of hostilities—is the end of the struggle, and the insurgents would be in peaceable possession of all that has been struggled for. Any different policy in regard to the colored man, deprives us of his help, and this is more than we can bear. We can not spare the hundred and forty or fifty thousand now serving us as soldiers, seamen, and laborers. This is not a question of sentiment or taste, but one of physical force which may be measured and estimated as horse-power and Steam-power are measured and estimated. Keep it and you can save the Union. Throw it away, and the Union goes with it. Nor is it possible for any Administration to retain the service of these people with the express or implied understanding that upon the first convenient occasion, they are to be re-inslaved. It *can* not be; and it *ought* not to be.

97. *The Soldiers' Vote:*

LETTER TO WILLIAM T. SHERMAN, SEPTEMBER 19, 1864

AGAIN certain state elections in October would serve as a preliminary test of strength between the presidential candidates. Indeed, by their effect upon party morale, they might even determine the outcome of a close contest. Lincoln was especially anxious about Indiana and wanted soldiers' votes to offset the unpopularity of the military draft.

Executive Mansion, Washington, D. C.
September 19th, 1864

Major General Sherman,
The State election of Indiana occurs on the 11th. of October, and the loss of it to the friends of the Govern-

ment would go far towards losing the whole Union cause.
The bad effect upon the November election, and especially
the giving the State Government to those who will oppose
the war in every possible way, are too much to risk, if it
can possibly be avoided. The draft proceeds, notwithstanding its strong tendency to lose us the State. Indiana
is the only important State, voting in October, whose soldiers cannot vote in the field. Any thing you can safely do
to let her soldiers, or any part of them, go home and vote
at the State election, will be greatly in point. They need
not remain for the Presidential election, but may return to
you at once. This is, in no sense, an order, but is merely
intended to impress you with the importance, to the army
itself, of your doing all you safely can, yourself being the
judge of what you can safely do. Yours truly,

A. Lincoln

98. *Calm Words in a Crisis:*
RESPONSE TO A SERENADE, OCTOBER 19, 1864

UNION candidates carried Indiana and Pennsylvania in October,
but by such narrow margins that the presidential election remained in doubt. Wild rumors were circulating about what
would happen if McClellan should win. Lincoln attempted to
dispel them when he was serenaded by Marylanders celebrating
the abolition of slavery in their state.

Friends and Fellow-citizens:

I am notified that this is a compliment paid me by the
loyal Marylanders, resident in this District. I infer that
the adoption of the new constitution for the State, furnishes
the occasion; and that, in your view, the extirpation of
slavery constitutes the chief merit of the new constitution.
Most heartily do I congratulate you, and Maryland, and
the nation, and the world, upon the event. I regret that it
did not occur two years sooner, which I am sure would

have saved to the nation more money than would have met all the private loss incident to the measure. But it has come at last, and I sincerely hope it's friends may fully realize all their anticipations of good from it; and that it's opponents may, by it's effects, be agreeably and profitably, disappointed.

A word upon another subject.

Something said by the Secretary of State in his recent speech at Auburn, has been construed by some into a threat that, if I shall be beaten at the election, I will, between then and the end of my constitutional term do what I may be able, to ruin the government.

Others regard the fact that the Chicago Convention adjourned, not *sine die,* but to meet again, if called to do so by a particular individual, as the intimation of a purpose that if their nominee shall be elected, he will at once seize control of the government. I hope the good people will permit themselves to suffer no uneasiness on either point. I am struggling to maintain government, not to overthrow it. I am struggling especially to prevent others from overthrowing it. I therefore say, that if I shall live, I shall remain President until the fourth of next March; and that whoever shall be constitutionally elected therefor in November, shall be duly installed as President on the fourth of March; and that in the interval I shall do my utmost that whoever is to hold the helm for the next voyage, shall start with the best possible chance to save the ship.

This is due to the people both on principle, and under the constitution. Their will, constitutionally expressed, is the ultimate law for all. If they should deliberately resolve to have immediate peace even at the loss of their country, and their liberty, I know not the power or the right to resist them. It is their own business, and they must do as they please with their own. I believe, however, they are still resolved to preserve their country and their liberty; and in this, in office or out of it, I am resolved to stand by them.

I may add that in this purpose to save the country and it's liberties, no classes of people seem so nearly unanamous as the soldiers in the field and the seamen afloat. Do they

not have the hardest of it? Who should quail while they
do not?

God bless the soldiers and seamen, with all their brave
commanders.

99. *Victory at the Polls:*
RESPONSE TO A SERENADE, NOVEMBER 10, 1864

ON November 8, 1864, Lincoln won reelection by an overwhelming majority in the electoral college, although the popular
vote was close in a number of states. Speaking to a crowd of
jubilant serenaders, he found something more important in the
contest than its outcome.

It has long been a grave question whether any government, not *too* strong for the liberties of its people, can be
strong *enough* to maintain its own existence, in great
emergencies.

On this point the present rebellion brought our republic
to a severe test; and a presidential election occurring in
regular course during the rebellion added not a little to the
strain. If the loyal people, *united,* were put to the utmost
of their strength by the rebellion, must they not fail when
divided, and partially paralized, by a political war among
themselves?

But the election was a necessity.

We can not have free government without elections; and
if the rebellion could force us to forego, or postpone a
national election, it might fairly claim to have already conquered and ruined us. The strife of the election is but
human-nature practically applied to the facts of the case.
What has occurred in this case, must ever recur in similar
cases. Human-nature will not change. In any future great
national trial, compared with the men of this, we shall have
as weak, and as strong; as silly and as wise; as bad and
good. Let us, therefore, study the incidents of this, as

philosophy to learn wisdom from, and none of them as wrongs to be revenged.

But the election, along with its incidental, and undesirable strife, has done good too. It has demonstrated that a people's government can sustain a national election, in the midst of a great civil war. Until now it has not been known to the world that this was a possibility. It shows also how *sound,* and how *strong* we still are. It shows that, even among candidates of the same party, he who is most devoted to the Union, and most opposed to treason, can receive most of the people's votes. It shows also, to the extent yet known, that we have more men now, than we had when the war began. Gold is good in its place; but living, brave, patriotic men, are better than gold.

But the rebellion continues; and now that the election is over, may not all, having a common interest, re-unite in a common effort, to save our common country? For my own part I have striven, and shall strive to avoid placing any obstacle in the way. So long as I have been here I have not willingly planted a thorn in any man's bosom.

While I am deeply sensible to the high compliment of a re-election; and duly grateful, as I trust, to Almighty God for having directed my countrymen to a right conclusion, as I think, for their own good, it adds nothing to my satisfaction that any other man may be disappointed or pained by the result.

May I ask those who have not differed with me, to join with me, in this same spirit towards those who have?

And now, let me close by asking three hearty cheers for our brave soldiers and seamen and their gallant and skilful commanders.

100. So Costly a Sacrifice:
LETTER TO LYDIA BIXBY, NOVEMBER 21, 1864

THIS famous letter of sympathy to Mrs. Bixby was published in contemporary newspapers, but the original document has never been found. Facsimiles widely circulated and displayed are forgeries. Efforts to establish Lincoln's secretary, John Hay, as the real author, have met with little success. The information which inspired the letter turned out to be erroneous. Mrs. Bixby did have five sons in military service, but only two were killed in action, and at least one of the other three was a deserter. Yet Lincoln, in a sense, was addressing his condolence to all the bereaved mothers of the Union.

Executive Mansion,
Washington, Nov. 21, 1864.

Dear Madam,—I have been shown in the files of the War Department a statement of the Adjutant General of Massachusetts, that you are the mother of five sons who have died gloriously on the field of battle.

I feel how weak and fruitless must be any words of mine which should attempt to beguile you from the grief of a loss so overwhelming. But I cannot refrain from tendering to you the consolation that may be found in the thanks of the Republic they died to save.

I pray that our Heavenly Father may assuage the anguish of your bereavement, and leave you only the cherished memory of the loved and lost, and the solemn pride that must be yours, to have laid so costly a sacrifice upon the altar of Freedom. Yours, very sincerely and respectfully,   A. Lincoln.

Mrs. Bixby.

101. The War Continues:

ANNUAL MESSAGE TO CONGRESS, DECEMBER 6, 1864

SHERMAN'S army had nearly completed its famous march from Atlanta to the sea when Lincoln submitted his fourth Annual Message to Congress. Now, with the end of the war in sight, he gave some attention to its effect upon the growth of the nation. The latter part of the document is presented here.

The war continues. Since the last annual message all the important lines and positions then occupied by our forces have been maintained, and our arms have steadily advanced; thus liberating the regions left in rear, so that Missouri, Kentucky, Tennessee and parts of other States have again produced reasonably fair crops.

The most remarkable feature in the military operations of the year is General Sherman's attempted march of three hundred miles directly through the insurgent region. It tends to show a great increase of our relative strength that our General-in-Chief should feel able to confront and hold in check every active force of the enemy, and yet to detach a well-appointed large army to move on such an expedition. The result not yet being known, conjecture in regard to it is not here indulged.

Important movements have also occurred during the year to the effect of moulding society for durability in the Union. Although short of complete success, it is much in the right direction, that twelve thousand citizens in each of the States of Arkansas and Louisiana have organized loyal State governments with free constitutions, and are earnestly struggling to maintain and administer them. The movements in the same direction, more extensive, though less definite in Missouri, Kentucky and Tennessee, should not be overlooked. But Maryland presents the example of complete success. Maryland is secure to Liberty and Union for all the future. The genius of rebellion will no more claim Maryland. Like another foul spirit, being driven out, it may seek to tear her, but it will woo her no more.

At the last session of Congress a proposed amendment of the Constitution abolishing slavery throughout the United States, passed the Senate, but failed for lack of the requisite two-thirds vote in the House of Representatives. Although the present is the same Congress, and nearly the same members, and without questioning the wisdom or patriotism of those who stood in opposition, I venture to recommend the reconsideration and passage of the measure at the present session. Of course the abstract question is not changed; but an intervening election shows, almost certainly, that the next Congress will pass the measure if this does not. Hence there is only a question of *time* as to when the proposed amendment will go to the States for their action. And as it is to so go, at all events, may we not agree that the sooner the better? It is not claimed that the election has imposed a duty on members to change their views or their votes, any further than, as an additional element to be considered, their judgment may be affected by it. It is the voice of the people now, for the first time, heard upon the question. In a great national crisis, like ours, unanimity of action among those seeking a common end is very desirable—almost indispensable. And yet no approach to such unanimity is attainable, unless some deference shall be paid to the will of the majority, simply because it is the will of the majority. In this case the common end is the maintenance of the Union; and, among the means to secure that end, such will, through the election, is most clearly declared in favor of such constitutional amendment.

The most reliable indication of public purpose in this country is derived through our popular elections. Judging by the recent canvass and its result, the purpose of the people, within the loyal States, to maintain the integrity of the Union, was never more firm, nor more nearly unanimous, than now. The extraordinary calmness and good order with which the millions of voters met and mingled at the polls, give strong assurance of this. Not only all those who supported the Union ticket, so called, but a great majority of the opposing party also, may be fairly claimed to entertain, and to be actuated by, the same purpose. It is an unanswerable argument to this effect, that no candidate for any office whatever, high or low, has ventured to seek votes on the avowal that he was for giving up the Union. There have been much impugning of motives, and much heated controversy as to the proper means and best mode of advancing the Union cause; but on the distinct issue of Union or no Union, the politicians have shown their instinctive knowledge that there is no diversity among the people. In affording the people the fair opportunity of showing, one to another and to the world, this firmness and unanimity of purpose, the election has been of vast value to the national cause.

The election has exhibited another fact not less valuable to be known—the fact that we do not approach exhaustion in the most important branch of national resources—that of living men. While it is melancholy to reflect that the war has filled so many graves, and carried mourning to so many hearts, it is some relief to know that, compared with the surviving, the fallen have been so few. While corps, and divisions, and brigades, and regiments have formed, and fought, and dwindled, and gone out of existence, a great majority of the men who composed them are still living. The same is true of the naval service. The election returns prove this. So many voters could not else be found. The States regularly holding elections, both now and four years ago, to wit, California, Connecticut, Delaware, Illinois, Indiana, Iowa, Kentucky, Maine, Maryland, Massachusetts, Michigan, Minnesota, Missouri, New Hampshire, New Jersey, New York, Ohio, Oregon, Pennsylvania, Rhode Island, Vermont, West Virginia, and Wisconsin cast 3,982,011 votes now, against 3,870.222 cast then, showing an aggregate now of 3,982,011. To this is to be added 33,762 cast now in the new States of Kansas and Nevada, which States did not vote in 1860, thus swelling the aggregate to 4,015.773 and the net increase during the three years and a half of war to 145,551. A table is appended showing particulars. To this again should be added the number of all soldiers in the field from Massachusetts, Rhode Island, New Jersey, Delaware, Indiana, Illinois, and California, who, by the laws of those States, could not vote away from their homes, and which number cannot be less than 90,000. Nor yet is this all. The number in organized Territories is triple now what it was four years ago, while thousands, white and black, join us as the national arms press back the insurgent lines. So much is shown, affirmatively and negatively, by the election. It is not material to inquire *how* the increase has been produced, or to show that it would have been *greater* but for the war, which is probably true. The important fact remains demonstrated, that we have *more* men *now* than we had when the war *began*; that we are not exhausted, nor in process of exhaustion; that we are *gaining* strength, and may, if need be, maintain the contest indefinitely. This as to men. Material resources are now more complete and abundant than ever.

The national resources, then, are unexhausted, and, as we believe, inexhaustible. The public purpose to re-establish and maintain the national authority is unchanged, and, as we believe, unchangeable. The manner of continuing the effort remains to choose. On careful consideration of all the evidence accessible it seems to me that no attempt at negotiation with the insurgent leader could result in any good. He would accept nothing short of severance of the Union—precisely what we will not and cannot give. His declarations to this effect are explicit and oft-repeated. He does not attempt to deceive us. He affords us no excuse to deceive ourselves. He cannot voluntarily reaccept the Union; we cannot voluntarily yield it. Between him and us the issue is distinct, simple, and inflexible. It is an issue which can only be tried by war, and decided by victory. If we yield, we are beaten; if the Southern people fail him, he is beaten. Either way, it would be the victory and defeat following war. What is true, however, of him who heads the insurgent cause, is not necessarily true of those who follow. Although he cannot reaccept the Union, they can. Some of them, we know, already desire peace and reunion. The number of such may increase. They can, at any moment, have peace simply by laying down their arms and submitting to the national authority under the Constitution. After so much, the government could not, if it would, maintain war against them. The loyal people would not sustain or allow it. If questions should remain, we would adjust them by the peaceful means of legislation, conference, courts, and votes, operating only in constitutional and lawful channels. Some certain, and other possible, questions are, and would be, beyond the Executive power to adjust; as, for instance, the admission of members into Congress, and whatever might require the appropriation of money. The Executive power itself would be greatly diminished by the cessation of actual war. Pardons and remissions of forfeitures, however, would still be within Executive control. In what spirit and temper this control would be exercised can be fairly judged of by the past.

A year ago general pardon and amnesty, upon specified terms, were offered to all, except certain designated classes; and, it was, at the same time, made known that the excepted classes were still within contemplation of special clemency. During the year many availed themselves of the general provision, and many more would, only that the signs of bad faith in some led to such precautionary measures as rendered the practical process less easy and certain. During the same time also special pardons have been granted to individuals of the excepted classes, and no voluntary application has been denied. Thus, practically, the door has been, for a full year, open to all, except such as were not in condition to make free choice—that is, such as were in custody or under constraint. It is still so open to all. But the time may come—probably will come—when public duty shall demand that it be closed; and that, in lieu, more rigorous measures than heretofore shall be adopted.

In presenting the abandonment of armed resistance to the national authority on the part of the insurgents, as the only indispensable condition to ending the war on the part of the government, I retract nothing heretofore said as to slavery. I repeat the declaration made a year ago, that "while I remain in my present position I shall not attempt to retract or modify the emancipation proclamation, nor shall I return to slavery any person who is free by the terms of that proclamation, or by any of the Acts of Congress." If the people should, by whatever mode or means, make it an Executive duty to re-enslave such persons, another, and not I, must be their instrument to perform it.

In stating a single condition of peace, I mean simply to say that the war will cease on the part of the government, whenever it shall have ceased on the part of those who began it.

102. Savannah Taken:

LETTER TO WILLIAM T. SHERMAN, DECEMBER 26, 1864

IN a vain effort to draw Sherman out of Georgia, Confederate General John B. Hood had begun an invasion of Tennessee. Near Nashville on December 15 and 16, 1864, his army was decisively beaten and put to rout by Union forces under General

George H. Thomas. A few days later, Sherman captured Savannah, Georgia, and presented it to Lincoln as a "Christmas gift."

Executive Mansion, Washington,
Dec. 26, 1864.

My dear General Sherman:

Many, many, thanks for your Christmas-gift—the capture of Savannah.

When you were about leaving Atlanta for the Atlantic coast, I was *anxious,* if not fearful; but feeling that you were the better judge, and remembering that "nothing risked, nothing gained" I did not interfere. Now, the undertaking being a success, the honor is all yours; for I believe none of us went farther than to acquiesce. And, taking the work of Gen. Thomas into the count, as it should be taken, it is indeed a great success. Not only does it afford the obvious and immediate military advantages; but, in showing to the world that your army could be divided, putting the stronger part to an important new service, and yet leaving enough to vanquish the old opposing force of the whole—Hood's army—it brings those who sat in darkness, to see a great light. But what next? I suppose it will be safer if I leave Gen. Grant and yourself to decide.

Please make my grateful acknowledgments to your whole army, officers and men. Yours very truly,

A. Lincoln.

103. *A Family Problem:*

LETTER TO ULYSSES S. GRANT, JANUARY 19, 1865

ROBERT LINCOLN graduated from Harvard in 1864. There were murmurs of public disapproval when he entered law school instead of military service, but Mary Lincoln, with two sons already in the grave, did not want him to enlist. At last the President sent this somewhat embarrassed request to General

Grant, who readily consented. On February 11, 1865, Robert became an assistant adjutant general with the rank of captain.

> Executive Mansion, Washington,
> Jan. 19, 1865.

Lieut. General Grant:

Please read and answer this letter as though I was not President, but only a friend. My son, now in his twenty second year, having graduated at Harvard, wishes to see something of the war before it ends. I do not wish to put him in the ranks, nor yet to give him a commission, to which those who have already served long, are better entitled, and better qualified to hold. Could he, without embarrassment to you, or detriment to the service, go into your Military family with some nominal rank, I, and not the public, furnishing his necessary means? If no, say so without the least hesitation, because I am as anxious, and as deeply interested, that you shall not be encumbered as you can be yourself. Yours truly,

> A. Lincoln

104. The Second Term:

REPLY TO A NOTIFICATION COMMITTEE, MARCH 1, 1865

WHILE Grant tightened his grip upon Petersburg and Richmond, Sherman's army moved northward into the Carolinas. On March 1, 1865, a committee from Congress visited the President to notify him officially of his reelection. This is Lincoln's brief response.

Having served four years in the depths of a great and yet unended national peril, I can view this call to a second term, in nowise more flatteringly to myself, than as an expression of the public judgment, that I may better finish a difficult work, in which I have labored from the first, than could any one less severely schooled to the task.

In this view, and with assured reliance on that Almighty Ruler who has so graceously sustained us thus far; and with increased gratitude to the generous people for their continued confidence, I accept the renewed trust, with it's yet onerous and perplexing duties and responsibilities.

Please communicate this to the two Houses of Congress.

105. *With Malice Toward None:*
SECOND INAUGURAL ADDRESS, MARCH 4, 1865

LINCOLN'S second inaugural address, his crowning literary achievement, is remembered primarily for the magnanimous spirit and lyrical beauty of its close.

At this second appearing to take the oath of the presidential office, there is less occasion for an extended address than there was at the first. Then a statement, somewhat in detail, of a course to be pursued, seemed fitting and proper. Now, at the expiration of four years, during which public declarations have been constantly called forth on every point and phase of the great contest which still absorbs the attention, and engrosses the energies of the nation, little that is new could be presented. The progress of our arms, upon which all else chiefly depends, is as well known to the public as to myself; and it is, I trust, reasonably satisfactory and encouraging to all. With high hope for the future, no prediction in regard to it is ventured.

On the occasion corresponding to this four years ago, all thoughts were anxiously directed to an impending civil-war. All dreaded it—all sought to avert it. While the inaugural address was being delivered from this place, devoted altogether to *saving* the Union without war, insurgent agents were in the city seeking to *destroy* it without war—seeking to dissolve the Union, and divide effects, by negotiation. Both parties deprecated war; but one of them would *make* war rather than let the nation survive; and the other would *accept* war rather than let it perish. And the war came.

One eighth of the whole population were colored slaves, not distributed generally over the Union, but localized in the Southern part of it. These slaves constituted a peculiar and powerful interest. All knew that this interest was, somehow, the cause of the war. To strengthen, perpetuate, and extend this interest was the object for which the insurgents would rend the Union, even by war; while the government claimed no right to do more than to restrict the territorial enlargement of it. Neither party expected for the war, the magnitude, or the duration, which it has already attained. Neither anticipated that the *cause* of the conflict might cease with, or even before, the conflict itself should cease. Each looked for an easier triumph, and a result less fundamental and astounding. Both read the same Bible, and pray to the same God; and each invokes His aid against the other. It may seem strange that any men should dare to ask a just God's assistance in wringing their bread from the sweat of other men's faces; but let us judge not that we be not judged. The prayers of both could not be answered; that of neither has been answered fully. The Almighty has His own purposes. "Woe unto the world because of offences! for it must needs be that offences come; but woe to that man by whom the offence cometh!" If we shall suppose that American Slavery is one of those offences which, in the providence of God, must needs come, but which, having continued through His appointed time, He now wills to remove, and that He gives to both North and South, this terrible war, as the woe due to those by whom the offence came, shall we discern therein any departure from those divine attributes which the believers in a Living God always ascribe to Him? Fondly do we hope —fervently do we pray—that this mighty scourge of war may speedily pass away. Yet, if God wills that it continue, until all the wealth piled by the bond-man's two hundred and fifty years of unrequited toil shall be sunk, and until every drop of blood drawn with the lash, shall be paid by another drawn with the sword, as was said three thousand years ago, so still it must be said "the judgments of the Lord, are true and righteous altogether"

With malice toward none; with charity for all; with

firmness in the right, as God gives us to see the right, let us strive on to the finish the work we are in; to bind up the nation's wounds; to care for him who shall have borne the battle, and for his widow, and his orphan—to do all which may achieve and cherish a just, and a lasting peace, among ourselves, and with all nations.

106. *Evaluation:*
LETTER TO THURLOW WEED, MARCH 15, 1865

REPLYING to a laudatory note from Thurlow Weed, famous New York editor and politician, Lincoln calculated the immediate effect and eventual significance of his inaugural address.

> Executive Mansion,
> Washington, March 15, 1865

Thurlow Weed, Esq.
My dear Sir:
Every one likes a compliment. Thank you for yours on my little notification speech, and on the recent Inaugeral Address. I expect the latter to wear as well as—perhaps better than—any thing I have produced; but I believe it is not immediately popular. Men are not flattered by being shown that there has been a difference of purpose between the Almighty and them. To deny it, however, in this case, is to deny that there is a God governing the world. It is a truth which I thought needed to be told; and as whatever of humiliation there is in it, falls most directly on myself. I thought others might afford for me to tell it. Yours truly
> A. Lincoln

107. Celebrating Victory:
RESPONSE TO A SERENADE, APRIL 10, 1865

THEIR position no longer tenable, Confederate forces began to evacuate Richmond on April 2. One week later, Lee surrendered to Grant at Appomattox. Rejoicing throngs gathered outside the White House again and again on April 10. This is one of Lincoln's impromptu responses, as recorded by a newspaper reporter.

"FELLOW CITIZENS: I am very greatly rejoiced to find that an occasion has occurred so pleasurable that the people cannot restrain themselves. [Cheers.] I suppose that arrangements are being made for some sort of a formal demonstration, this, or perhaps, to-morrow night. [Cries of 'We can't wait,' 'We want it now,' &c.] If there should be such a demonstration, I, of course, will be called upon to respond, and I shall have nothing to say if you dribble it all out of me before. [Laughter and applause.] I see you have a band of music with you. [Voices, 'We have two or three.'] I propose closing up this interview by the band performing a particular tune which I will name. Before this is done, however, I wish to mention one or two little circumstances connected with it. I have always thought 'Dixie' one of the best tunes I have ever heard. Our adversaries over the way attempted to appropriate it, but I insisted yesterday that we fairly captured it. [Applause.] I presented the question to the Attorney General, and he gave it as his legal opinion that it is our lawful prize. [Laughter and applause.] I now request the band to favor me with its performance."

108. And Now Reconstruction:
LAST PUBLIC ADDRESS, APRIL 11, 1865

TO a celebrating crowd that assembled on the White House lawn during the evening of April 11, Lincoln spoke for the last time in public. Three nights later, he was murdered at Ford's Theater by John Wilkes Booth. The speech makes an imperfect conclusion to his writings because for Lincoln it marked a new beginning. With little effort at eloquence and only a brief acknowledgment of the military victory, he talked earnestly about the problems of reconstruction. It was the speech of a man going to work again after having finished one heavy task. It was a voice interrupted in the middle of a sentence.

We meet this evening, not in sorrow, but in gladness of heart. The evacuation of Petersburg and Richmond, and the surrender of the principal insurgent army, give hope of a righteous and speedy peace whose joyous expression can not be restrained. In the midst of this, however, He, from Whom all blessings flow, must not be forgotten. A call for a national thanksgiving is being prepared, and will be duly promulgated. Nor must those whose harder part gives us the cause of rejoicing, be overlooked. Their honors must not be parcelled out with others. I myself, was near the front, and had the high pleasure of transmitting much of the good news to you; but no part of the honor, for plan or execution, is mine. To Gen. Grant, his skilful officers, and brave men, all belongs. The gallant Navy stood ready, but was not in reach to take active part.

By these recent successes the re-inauguration of the national authority—reconstruction—which has had a large share of thought from the first, is pressed much more closely upon our attention. It is fraught with great difficulty. Unlike the case of a war between independent nations, there is no authorized organ for us to treat with. No one man has authority to give up the rebellion for any other man. We simply must begin with, and mould from, disorganized and discordant elements. Nor is it a small additional embarrassment that we, the loyal people, differ among ourselves as to the mode, manner, and means of reconstruction.

As a general rule, I abstain from reading the reports of attacks upon myself, wishing not to be provoked by that to which I can not properly offer an answer. In spite of this precaution, however, it comes to my knowledge that I am much censured for some supposed agency in setting up, and seeking to sustain, the new State Government of Louisiana. In this I have done just so much as, and no more than, the public knows. In the Annual Message of Dec. 1863 and accompanying Proclamation, I presented *a* plan of re-construction (as the phrase goes) which, I promised, if adopted by any State, should be acceptable to, and sustained by, the Executive government of the nation. I distinctly stated that this was not the only plan which might possibly be acceptable; and I also distinctly protested that the Executive claimed no right to say when, or whether members should be admitted to seats in Congress from such States. This plan was, in advance, submitted to the then Cabinet, and distinctly approved by every member of it. One of them suggested that I should then, and in that connection, apply the Emancipation Proclamation to the theretofore excepted parts of Virginia and Louisiana; that I should drop the suggestion about apprenticeship for freed-people, and that I should omit the protest against my own power, in regard to the admission of members to Congress; but even he approved every part and parcel of the plan which has since been employed or touched by the action of Louisiana. The new constitution of Louisiana, declaring emancipation for the whole State, practically applies the Proclamation to the part previously excepted. It does not adopt apprenticeship for freed-people; and it is silent, as it could not well be otherwise, about the admission of members to Congress. So that, as it applies to Louisiana, every member of the Cabinet fully approved the plan. The Message went to Congress, and I received many commendations of the plan, written and verbal; and not a single objection to it, from any professed emancipationist, came to my knowledge, until after the news reached Washington that the people of Louisiana had begun to move in accordance with it. From about July 1862, I had corresponded with different persons, supposed to be interested, seeking a reconstruction of a State government for Louisiana. When the Message of 1863, with the plan before mentioned, reached New-Orleans, Gen. Banks wrote me that he was confident the people, with his military co-operation, would reconstruct, substantially on that plan. I wrote him, and some of them to try it; they tried it, and the result is known. Such only has been my agency in getting up the Louisiana government. As to sustaining it, my promise is out, as before stated. But, as bad promises are better broken than kept, I shall treat this as a bad promise, and break it, whenever I shall be convinced that keeping it is adverse to the public interest. But I have not yet been so convinced.

I have been shown a letter on this subject, supposed to be an able one, in which the writer expresses regret that my mind has not seemed to be definitely fixed on the question whether the seceded States, so called, are in the Union or out of it. It would perhaps, add astonishment to his regret, were he to learn that since I have found professed Union men endeavoring to make that question, I have *purposely* forborne any public expression upon it. As appears to me that question has not been, nor yet is, a practically material one, and that any discussion of it, while it thus remains practically immaterial, could have no effect other than the mischievous one of dividing our friends. As yet, whatever it may hereafter become, that question is bad, as the basis of a controversy, and good for nothing at all—a merely pernicious abstraction.

We all agree that the seceded States, so called, are out of their proper practical relation with the Union; and that the sole object of the government, civil and military, in regard to those States is to again get them into that proper practical relation. I believe it is not only possible, but in fact, easier, to do this, without deciding, or even considering, whether these states have even been out of the Union, than with it. Finding themselves safely at home, it would be utterly immaterial whether they had ever been abroad. Let us all join in doing the acts necessary to restoring the proper practical relations between these states and the

Union; and each forever after, innocently indulge his own opinion whether, in doing the acts, he brought the States from without, into the Union, or only gave them proper assistance, they never having been out of it.

The amount of constituency, so to speak, on which the new Louisiana government rests, would be more satisfactory to all, if it contained fifty, thirty, or even twenty thousand, instead of only about twelve thousand, as it does. It is also unsatisfactory to some that the elective franchise is not given to the colored man. I would myself prefer that it were now conferred on the very intelligent, and on those who serve our cause as soldiers. Still the question is not whether the Louisiana government, as it stands, is quite all that is desirable. The question is "Will it be wiser to take it as it is, and help to improve it; or to reject, and disperse it?" "Can Louisiana be brought into proper practical relation with the Union *sooner* by *sustaining,* or by *discarding* her new State Government?"

Some twelve thousand voters in the heretofore slave-state of Louisiana have sworn allegiance to the Union, assumed to be the rightful political power of the State, held elections, organized a State government, adopted a free-state constitution, giving the benefit of public schools equally to black and white, and empowering the Legislature to confer the elective franchise upon the colored man. Their Legislature has already voted to ratify the constitutional amendment recently passed by Congress, abolishing slavery throughout the nation. These twelve thousand persons are thus fully committed to the Union, and to perpetual freedom in the state—committed to the very things, and nearly all the things the nation wants—and they ask the nations recognition, and it's assistance to make good their committal. Now, if we reject, and spurn them, we do our utmost to disorganize and disperse them. We in effect say to the white men "You are worthless, or worse—we will neither help you, nor be helped by you." To the blacks we say "This cup of liberty which these, your old masters, hold to your lips, we will dash from you, and leave you to the chances of gathering the spilled and scattered contents in some vague and undefined when, where, and how." If this course, discouraging and paralyzing both white and black, has any tendency to bring Louisiana into proper practical relations with the Union, I have, so far, been unable to perceive it. If, on the contrary, we recognize, and sustain the new government of Louisiana the converse of all this is made true. We encourage the hearts, and nerve the arms of the twelve thousand to adhere to their work, and argue for it, and proselyte for it, and fight for it, and feed it, and grow it, and ripen it to a complete success. The colored man too, in seeing all united for him, is inspired with vigilance, and energy, and daring, to the same end. Grant that he desires the elective franchise, will he not attain it sooner by saving the already advanced steps toward it, than by running backward over them? Concede that the new government of Louisiana is only to what it should be as the egg is to the fowl, we shall sooner have the fowl by hatching the egg than by smashing it? Again, if we reject Louisiana, we also reject one vote in favor of the proposed amendment to the national constitution. To meet this proposition, it has been argued that no more than three fourths of those States which have not attempted secession are necessary to validly ratify the amendment. I do not commit myself against this, further than to say that such a ratification would be questionable, and sure to be persistently questioned; while a ratification by three fourths of all the States would be unquestioned and unquestionable.

I repeat the question. "Can Louisiana be brought into proper practical relation with the Union *sooner* by *sustaining* or by *discarding* her new State Government?

What has been said of Louisiana will apply generally to other States. And yet so great peculiarities pertain to each state; and such important and sudden changes occur in the same state; and, withal, so new and unprecedented is the whole case, that no exclusive, and inflexible plan can safely be prescribed as to details and colatterals. Such exclusive, and inflexible plan, would surely become a new entanglement. Important principles may, and must, be inflexible.

In the present *"situation"* as the phrase goes, it may be my duty to make some new announcement to the people of the South. I am considering, and shall not fail to act, when satisfied that action will be proper.

Selected Bibliography

WORKS OF LINCOLN

ROY P. BASLER, MARION DOLORES PRATT, AND LLOYD A. DUNLAP, eds., *The Collected Works of Abraham Lincoln.* 8 vols. plus Index. New Brunswick, N.J.: Rutgers University Press, 1953-55.

PAUL M. ANGLE, ed., *Created Equal? The Complete Lincoln-Douglas Debates of 1858.* Chicago: University of Chicago Press, 1958.

HARRY V. JAFFA, AND ROBERT W. JOHANNSEN, eds., *In the Name of the People: Speeches and Writings of Lincoln and Douglas in the Ohio Campaign of 1859.* Columbus: Ohio State University Press, 1959.

BIOGRAPHIES OF LINCOLN

BEVERIDGE, ALBERT J., *Abraham Lincoln, 1809–1858.* 2 vols. Boston: Houghton Mifflin Company, 1928.

CHARNWOOD, LORD (Godfrey Rathbone Benson), *Abraham Lincoln.* New York: Henry Holt & Company, 1917; New York: Pocket Books, 1939, 1952.

HERNDON, WILLIAM H., AND JESSE W. WEIK, *Herndon's Lincoln: The True Story of a Great Life.* 3 vols. Chicago: Belford, Clarke & Company, 1889. Paul M. Angle, ed., *Herndon's Life of Lincoln.* New York: Charles Boni, Inc., 1930; Cleveland: World Publishing Company, 1949; Greenwich, Conn.: Fawcett Publications, Inc., 1961.

LUTHIN, REINHARD H., *The Real Abraham Lincoln.* Englewood Cliffs, N.J.: Prentice-Hall, Inc., 1960.

RANDALL, JAMES G., *Lincoln the President.* 4 vols. (4th volume completed by Richard N. Current). New York: Dodd, Mead & Company, 1945-55.

SANDBURG, CARL, *Abraham Lincoln: The Prairie Years.* 2 vols. New York: Harcourt, Brace & Company, 1926. Sandburg, *Abraham Lincoln: The War Years.* 4 vols. New York: Harcourt, Brace & Company, 1939. Abridgments of the foregoing six volumes: New York: Harcourt, Brace & Company, 1954; 3 vols., New York: Dell Publishing Company, 1959.

THOMAS, BENJAMIN P., *Abraham Lincoln: a Biography.* New York: Alfred A. Knopf, Inc., 1952.

MONOGRAPHS, ESSAYS, AND OTHER STUDIES

ANDER, O. FRITIOF, ed., *Lincoln Images: Augustana College Centennial Essays.* Rock Island, Ill.: Augustana College Library, 1960.

BARINGER, WILLIAM, *Lincoln's Rise to Power.* Boston: Little, Brown & Company, 1937.

BASLER, ROY P., *The Lincoln Legend.* Boston: Houghton Mifflin Company, 1935.

CARMAN, HARRY J., AND REINHARD H. LUTHIN, *Lincoln and the Patronage.* New York: Columbia University Press, 1943.

CURRENT, RICHARD N., *Lincoln and the First Shot.* Philadelphia: J. B. Lippincott Company, 1963.

CURRENT, RICHARD N., *The Lincoln Nobody Knows.* New York: McGraw-Hill Book Company, 1958; New York: Hill and Wang, 1963.

DONALD, DAVID, *Lincoln Reconsidered; Essays on the Civil War Era.* New York: Alfred A. Knopf, Inc., 1956; Vintage edition, 1961.

DONALD, DAVID, *Lincoln's Herndon.* New York: Alfred A. Knopf, Inc., 1948.

FEHRENBACHER, DON E., *Prelude to Greatness: Lincoln in the 1850's.* Stanford, Calif.: Stanford University Press, 1962.

FRANK, JOHN P., *Lincoln as a Lawyer.* Urbana: University of Illinois Press, 1961.

GRAEBNER, NORMAN A., ed., *The Enduring Lincoln.* Urbana: University of Illinois Press, 1959.

HESSELTINE, WILLIAM B., *Lincoln and the War Governors.* New York: Alfred A. Knopf, Inc., 1948.

HESSELTINE, WILLIAM B., *Lincoln's Plan of Reconstruction.* Tuscaloosa, Ala.: Confederate Publishing Company, 1960.

JAFFA, HARRY V., *Crisis of the House Divided; an Interpretation of the Issues in the Lincoln-Douglas Debates.* New York: Doubleday and Company, 1959.

KING, WILLARD L., *Lincoln's Manager, David Davis.* Cambridge, Mass.: Harvard University Press, 1960.

LUTHIN, REINHARD H., *The First Lincoln Campaign.* Cambridge, Mass.: Harvard University Press, 1944.

POTTER, DAVID M., *Lincoln and His Party in the Secession Crisis.* New Haven: Yale University Press, 1942, 1962.

POTTER, DAVID M., *The Lincoln Theme and American National Historiography.* Oxford: Clarendon Press, 1948.

PRATT, HARRY E., *The Personal Finances of Abraham Lincoln.* Springfield, Ill.: Abraham Lincoln Association, 1943.

QUARLES, BENJAMIN, *Lincoln and the Negro.* New York: Oxford University Press, 1962.

RANDALL, JAMES G., *Lincoln the Liberal Statesman.* New York: Dodd, Mead & Company, 1947; New York: Apollo Editions, 1962.

RANDALL, RUTH PAINTER, *Mary Lincoln: Biography of a Marriage.* Boston: Little, Brown & Company, 1953.

STAMPP, KENNETH M., *And the War Came: The North and the Secession Crisis, 1860–1861.* Baton Rouge: Louisiana State University Press, 1950.

THOMAS, BENJAMIN P., *Portrait for Posterity; Lincoln and His Biographers.* New Brunswick, N. J.: Rutgers University Press, 1947.

WILLIAMS, THOMAS HARRY, *Lincoln and His Generals.* New York: Alfred A. Knopf, Inc., 1952.

WILLIAMS, THOMAS HARRY, *Lincoln and Radicals.* Madison: University of Wisconsin Press, 1941, 1960.

WILSON, EDMUND, *Patriotic Gore: Studies in the Literature of the American Civil War.* New York: Oxford University Press, 1962.

ZORNOW, WILLIAM F., *Lincoln and the Party Divided.* Norman: University of Oklahoma Press, 1954.